FRANCE

GOVERNMENT AN

FRANCE:
Government and Society

AN HISTORICAL SURVEY

Edited by

J. M. Wallace-Hadrill
Fellow of Merton College, Oxford

and

John McManners
Professor of History in the University of Leicester

METHUEN & CO LTD

11 NEW FETTER LANE LONDON EC4

First published in 1957
Second edition 1970
SBN 416 65700 1

First published as a University Paperback 1970
SBN 416 65710 9

© *1970 Methuen & Co*

Distributed in the U.S.A. by Barnes & Noble Inc.

Contents

━━━━━━━━━⊱⊙⊙⊙⊰⊱━━━━━

v

Maps

Introduction

—➤➤❈❈❈❈◀◀—

The lectures—they are no more—which have been
collected to form this volume were delivered in the
University of Oxford in the Hilary and Trinity Terms
of 1955. Their aim was to review, and to provoke thought
about, a particular aspect of the history of France, the inter-
action of government and society. To do this to good purpose it
seemed proper to us to start where the roots start, in France's
prehistory, and to continue until we reached the contemporary
scene, which the historian neglects at his peril. We have ex-
changed ideas and discussed overlapping themes, as is natural
among colleagues whose concern is the past and whose particular
delight is whatever touches France. Even so, each contribution
is highly individual and reflects the personal bent of the contri-
butor: it was never our intention to present, in the guise of
lectures, a formal historical survey. The reader, like those who
were kind enough to attend our lectures, must be supposed to
have an adequate grounding in French history as a whole.

Bibliographies are appended to each lecture. They are highly
compressed and selective, and seek merely to afford the first step
towards further specialized study. A secondary purpose is to
indicate where evidence for and discussion of controversial views
may be found. We have for the most part confined these bibliographies to writings in French and English, though much that
is relevant is of course to be found in other languages.

Note to 1970 edition

The text is unaltered, except for the correction of a few mis-
prints. The bibliographies have been throughly revised and
brought up to date.

BIBLIOGRAPHY

Except where otherwise indicated, the place of publication for
French books is Paris, and for works in English, London.

C. F. C. HAWKES

Prehistory and the Gaulish Peoples

These studies of Government and Society in France are to begin, by their promoters' wish, before what is properly French history. We are to start with the prehistory of Gaul—or, in the more exact French phrase, with its *préhistoire et protohistoire*. And I think this is more than just a compliment, though it is that indeed, to my subject as a prehistorian. It suggests a certain renewal of belief among historians —among some even if not all—that what we call prehistory can, if it is soundly reasoned, be important to them: not merely as a curtain-raiser, to amuse the audience settling down for their serious play, but as itself the play's first act.

That belief has been traditionally strong amongst the French. It is more deeply rooted in France than amongst us here, if only because there the coming of the Franks and of the other invading Germans, which led to the medieval renaming as 'Francia' of what had before been Gallia, the country of the Gauls, made historically less rupture of continuity, in life and institutions, than in our country did the coming of the English. Three long generations ago, Fustel de Coulanges was imperatively claiming France's place in the great spectacle of Government and Society in Antiquity, which he evoked as the indispensable first act for all who would attend to history thereafter. And since the ancient Gauls could be hailed as Celts, Celtic and Classical studies combined to make the show: beside the magisterial Fustel was the ardent D'Arbois de Jubainville, and as the nineteenth century passed into the twentieth, the mantles of both fell upon the willing shoulders of Camille Jullian. Moreover, Camille Jullian was able to fill out his historical work with the growing mass of French work in archaeology: the year 1908 saw published the first volumes both of his *Histoire de la Gaule* and of the *Manuel d'Archéologie* of Joseph Déchelette. When in 1914 Déchelette was killed in action, the *Manuel* had reached in four books the conquest of Gaul by Julius Caesar; when Jullian died in 1933, he had only just failed to carry his History into the fifth century A.D.—from the Roman Empire of the House of Theodosius to the Frankish kingdom of the Merovingian Clovis—and had written his last passionate vindication of his country as 'the eternal Gaul'. In 1907 he had told the Collège de France 'je crois de mon devoir de commencer par la préhistoire le récit de notre histoire nationale'; in 1931, when Déchelette's *Manuel* was resumed for Roman times by his friend Albert Grenier, he wrote in the preface that when the Roman Empire fell, Gaul yet survived: 'c'est elle qui, des débris romains, a fait notre France'.

Yes: the belief in the continuity of prehistory with history has indeed been strong in France. Theoretically at least, through the concept of *la protohistoire*, it is so still. Nevertheless, I shall not try to justify it simply by a *mystique* of 'la Gaule éternelle'. As will already appear from my quotations—and they could be extended likewise over the field of Roman Gaul—Jullian's patriotic exaggeration really did the doctrine harm. Yet the foundations from which he started, taken by themselves, were sound. Essentially, they were what Fustel's had been, and D'Arbois': to study people and their institutions, you must study them in their basic relation to their land. And here comes in again the contrast that I remarked upon just now between French historians and English. The Englishman—a Hodgkin, a Stenton, or a Myres—comparing his Anglo-Saxon England with prehistoric and Roman Britain, sees the evidences of continuity between them greatly exceeded by those of discontinuity. The Frenchman has only to look at the map, to hear positive exclamations of continuity from the great majority of his place-names. As the next lecture here will no doubt show more thoroughly, most of these have come down into French from a Gallo-Roman form: in the north Pouillé, in Burgundy Pouilly, in the centre Pauliat, in the south-west Paulhac, all mean *Pauliacum* or *Pauliacus fundus*, the domain of Paulus. But that form for an adjective is Gaulish, and sometimes the dominial family name is Gaulish too: Ivry, for example, stands for *Eburacum* from Gaulish Eburos. And it is notorious that towns and provinces in France, and not mountains and rivers only, most frequently bear names of Gaulish origin, as Paris from the tribal name Parisii, or Auvergne from the

Arverni. The hollow-topped hill of the Puy of Issolud (in the Dordogne) is the Uxellodunum—the high citadel: in Greek it would be Ὑψηλόπολις—where the Gauls made their last stand against Caesar in 51 B.C. Thus constantly reminded of his country's topographic continuity with the life of both Roman and pre-Roman Gaul, and rightly keeping his eyes fixed on the land, the Frenchman at once scents Gaulish antiquity in the institutions of the tenure of the land; and from the days of Fustel and D'Arbois onwards he has been steeped in ideas therefrom arising. Thus the fundamentals of my claim in this lecture are authentically French.

Now you may murmur here, perhaps, that names may survive while institutions change, and that French Ivry may have as little to do with Romano-Gaulish *Eburacum*, institutionally, as English York with Romano-British *Eburacum*, likewise its topographic forerunner, and the begetter, through Old English *Eoforwic* and Anglo-Danish *Jorvik*, of its modern name. If so, may I remind you of the position reached by a different branch of French historical studies from Camille Jullian's, though with a like descent from the thought and work of Fustel, and with a far closer appeal to modern students? What did Marc Bloch, summing up and crowning, for the *Cambridge Economic History of Europe*, his work in the *Caractères originaux de l'histoire rurale française*, say of the origins of the rural *seigneurie*, the manorial system that remained legally dominant in France till the Revolution? It grew, into the forms in which we know it from documents of the Carolingian ninth century and onwards, while slave-holding of the old Roman sort declined. But side by side with the 'servile' *manses*, which thus replaced former slave-estates, were 'free' *manses*, where former slavery will not explain the form that the tenants' dependence takes. The late-Roman rural system of the colonate, which lies broadly behind these forms, was maintained by Imperial legislation which stiffened and sharpened and aggravated the conditions of dependent land-tenure, but cannot be said to have created it outright; any more than the clientship, or commendation of small men to lords or patrons, was wholly new in late-Roman times. Behind those things again, and behind what institutions can be accepted for the Gaul of early Roman times, there are things that can be no other than pre-Roman, stretching back into prehistoric times, and for which prehistoric society alone can be held responsible. Though the personal names surviving for the French villages we noticed just now are most often Roman, we saw that they are usually of Gallo-Roman form and at least sometimes wholly Gaulish. And the institution they stand for cannot by any means be Roman purely: at most, the Romanization of something older, which can yet be dimly seen. That something can best be described as a social order comprising rural chiefs on the one hand, and on the other communities of peasants, living, either in villages or scattered, in dependence each upon its chief, while the chiefs' existence conversely depended upon theirs. The unit within the community is the family, in the large sense in which it consists roughly of the three generations expected to be living at one time; the chiefdom is a family unit likewise. 'Thus' concludes Bloch 'behind the classic *seigneurie* our inquiry reveals long and obscure beginnings. A very ancient structure of rural chiefdoms was the essential nucleus, and about it the centuries deposited their successive layers one by one'. Then, only then, came the Roman Empire, the invasions, the Merovingians, and the passage from Carolingian conditions to the fully feudal age that is most often studied.

Compared with the documentation at disposal for these later things, evidence for the early things is sparse. But it exists. In part, it can be reflected back on to them from among the later documents. In part, it can be drawn from philological studies, of which place-name study is not the only one—as those who know Professor L. R. Palmer's Oxford Inaugural lecture of 1954 will be aware. And in part, provided that the land can still be recognized, and made to yield knowledge of its past from surveys and findings of antiquities on and in it, evidence can be shown by archaeology. These things can be done in France; and the call to do them has been particularly voiced by Frenchmen. That those Frenchmen who have heard it have given a documentary or a philological response, hitherto, more often than an effective archaeological one, is a further truth; but at least it means that there is a vast deal in France for archaeology yet to do. And to do anything of that kind, however little, mindful of the great problem of historic continuity and historical change in Europe, and trying to make your little bit bear somehow upon it if you can, is to help put the theoretic unity of prehistory and history into practice. I therefore think it is a good thing—provided that it will really help; and certainly France, and the linkage of French history and Gaulish prehistory, can give plenty of opportunities for trying it. This is not to say that it is always easy—perhaps it is never that, though it is sometimes all too easy to do badly. But let me invite you to look at some few aspects of French or Gaulish prehistory more closely.

'Pour suivre ainsi' wrote Déchelette in introducing his *Manuel* 'dans tout son développement, la marche de la civilization depuis ses origines les plus reculées, la Gaule offre en Europe un champ d'observation vraiment privilégié'. Why is that? What is this Gaul? I turn to Mr C. E. Stevens, summarizing 'Gaul' in the *Oxford Classical Dictionary*. 'Geographically' he says 'the territory bounded by the Alps, the Rhine, the Ocean, the Pyrenees and the Mediterranean forms a unity, and most of its history has been a sequence of unifying cultural developments'. That is, if men will undertake to make a unified culture in that territory, its geographic unity will help them to succeed, and several times has done so. How much unified was the Gaul that the Romans conquered, is perhaps a question; in any case, they unified it. Mr Stevens goes on to observe that these unifications have been followed by catastrophes, producing disunity again, from which a fresh unification has had to be constructed. We are not to understand these catastrophes as ever so catastrophic as to destroy any previously formed unity completely and in all its elements. Some of these elements may persist, and be built again into the next unity to be formed, though probably not unaltered in the process. It is thus, in fact, that the prehistoric chiefdoms predicated by Marc Bloch will have survived the catastrophe of the conquest of Gaul by Caesar, to be built into the rural economy of the Gaulish Roman provinces, or that such a name as *Pauliacum* came through the Dark Ages to emerge as Pouilly or as Paulhac.

Yet there are elements in the Gaulish territory also which will assist catastrophes, and will prompt disunity. First, there is much physiographical diversity, on which French atlases and geography-books dilate with proper thoroughness, and of which one can quickly summon some recognition by just naming a few well-known and sharply contrasted features: the Alps from Mont Blanc to the Riviera, the plains of the Beauce, the forest of the Ardennes, the sand expanses of the Landes, the volcanic *massif central*, and so on. This diversity will facilitate and help to perpetuate a regionalism in France, which will always survive catastrophes that can destroy centrality. The regionalism, it is plain, has grown up in the pattern of the physiographic diversity; and having grown, it clings there. And though recent demographic studies have suggested that there has in modern times been considerably more coming and going, more *déplacement*, by individuals in rural France than one might expect, the tenacity of its regionalism is well known not only to demographers, but to students no less of the country's politics than of her *folklore*, or her gastronomy. Of the politics, the first student known to us is Caesar, and he has plenty to say of Gaul's regional diversity, and of the use to which he could so often turn it in his own politics of war. Behind his day, evidently, this regionalism has a long prehistory; not but what, perhaps more surprisingly, but as Mr Stevens' few lines rightly recognize, there is at least something of unity in the prehistory too.

Secondly, and sweeping the many particularities of *la Gaule régionale* into scarcely more than two broad zones, there is the division between the Mediterranean south, in climate and all things associated with climate a land unto itself, and the Oceanic or temperate remainder of the country. That division in the Early Middle Ages, as Mr R. W. Southern well points out in *The Making of the Middle Ages*, can be seen reflected in architecture, in law, and above all in language, where it becomes the distinction between the *Langue d'Oc* and the *Langue d'Oil* (*hoc* and *hoc ille* having been their distinguishing Low-Latin 'yes'-words). And the line from the Gironde to the Jura along which that distinction ran is but very little north of the frontier of the first Gallic province to be made by Rome, the *Gallia Transalpina* of 121 B.C. Directly, the medieval distinctions of south from north spring from the longer and stronger Romanization, which the next lecture will attest, of that first southern province; yet why had it had that? Because the world native to Rome as a Republic—before Caesar—was Mediterranean, and Rome here was taking purposely just what of Gaul was Mediterranean, because only round Mediterranean shores (in this case from Italy to Spain) did she wish to secure her power. The world beyond was alien.

In a sense, therefore, there are at least two Gauls. I say 'at least', because the Atlantic seaboard, at the corners of which the Celts of Brittany and the Biscayan Basques remain distinctive still, can

6

claim a distinctness of its own—or perhaps a claim each for north-west and south-west, those being the surviving two ends of an Atlantic zone long distinct within prehistory. Yet they are in fact only corner-pockets of the major non-Mediterranean zone of France which was in Caesar's day *Gallia Comata*, the Gaul 'of long hair' outside 'the Province'; and it is the distinctness of the Mediterranean south, the Midi, that is the strongest, because the most strongly climate-determined thing. In fact, as Mr Stevens has elsewhere noticed, 'to a geographer, there is no more remarkable aspect of Julius Caesar's career than his extension of the Roman Empire into a climatic area distinct from it, when he imposed conquest and annexation upon Gallia Comata'.

It is true that Caesar speaks of the whole territory thus conquered (*De Bello Gallico* I, 1, 1) as itself containing three divisions: 'Gallia est omnis' (taken as a whole) 'divisa in partis tris', inhabited by Belgae, Aquitanians, and Celtae, who, he says, differ each from the other in language, institutions and laws. But it is quite clear elsewhere that these peoples had much in common, which one could expect then to find throughout his 'Gallia omnis'. In speaking of Gaulish social structure, for example (*BG.*, VI, 13–15), Caesar plainly states that 'in omni Gallia' there were two sorts of upper class or *nobiles*, the Druids and the Horsemen, and a single lower class or *plebs*. The Horsemen or lay nobility made it their ambition to multiply the numbers of their dependents, whom he describes by the word *clientes*; we shall come back to them, as also to the Druids, who were the Gaulish clergy. But note meanwhile that in their religion again Caesar takes all the Gauls as one (*BG.*, VI, 16–17); and he goes on to testify (18, 1) that the Gauls all declare themselves, on the authority of the Druids, to be descended *ab Dite patre:* from a father-deity, in other words, who was god of the Underworld— the Romans' Dis (our 'Pluto')—not of the sky. To these religious matters we shall return after seeing more of the prehistory: what it will have to show us bears on them too. We can expect altogether, indeed, to find that the old French claim for its importance is still good, even though French archaeology, and I must repeat this, has as yet much digging on the claim to do. In fact, one day, it may be old Camille Jullian's detractors—who, to be frank, have met his exuberance by a certain belittlement, even derision, of 'la Gaule éternelle'—that are found to have gone too far.

The case for any such *péripatie*, I know, must be authentic. With time, I think this one can be made so; but we shall see.

Europe is as a whole populated by descendants of three series or sets of peoples, of which one set, hunters and fishers, was already in it in the Old and more palpably the Middle Stone Age, a second series entered variously on the south-east and south, before and after 3000 B.C., bringing from the Near East the Neolithic or New Stone Age mode of life by farming stock and cereals, while the third, also knowing the Neolithic arts but disposed to rate the herding above the cultivation, spread out in the centuries before and just after 2000, from homes in the region of the Black Sea (not excluding Asia Minor) and of south-east to mid-eastern Europe. This division is not quite exhaustive —it ignores later comers out of Asia—nor fully logical, in that its third set of peoples will have originally been easterly portions of the first, and in their homes already in the Middle Stone Age. Adopting, however, on those mainly grassland plains, the Neolithic arts in mainly pastoral and mobile form, and accentuating, perhaps, a certain distinctiveness in their range of physical type, they were differentiated at least in some things from the peoples among whom they spread. Seemingly, too, they spread often in warlike fashion; and they achieved a dominance all the more successful since during those same centuries knowledge of metal-working, of which they took all advantage possible, was being brought to Europe from the Near East. From their archaeological distribution compared with those of historically known peoples and languages, from the comparative philology of these, and from linguistic evidences for economic and social order and religion compared with those drawn from archaeology, the belief most widespread today is that they or their prevailing components were 'Aryan' or 'Indogermanic', that is, Indo-European peoples.

From among them—we need not dwell on Asia—Greeks were in and near Greece at latest soon after 2000, and Italic folk in parts of Italy and elsewhere near the Adriatic but little later, whilst the ancestors of Celtic and Teutonic, Illyrian and Thracian, and Slavic peoples (to go no further) were all present in one part or another of the remaining Continent. And well before 1500 parts of Gaul, as of the British Islands also, were certainly invaded by peoples of this kind. The Early Bronze culture of the upper

Rhône is perhaps one result, and undoubtedly other regions in the east were entered. Farther west, however, Brittany alone appears strongly colonized: elsewhere the signs are sparser, and point rather to infiltration—where they exist at all—among the earlier inhabitants. Those inhabitants were divided, or compounded, between the primary Neolithic farmer-settlers and further entrants from the south (where e.g. makers of the so-called Bell-beaker pottery are mainly found), and the more ancient natives, converted now from their former hunting life to secondary versions of the Neolithic culture. The primary Neolithic folk seem to have been of what has been called the 'Mediterranean' race; the secondary Neolithic peoples certainly included the short and round-headed type known as 'Alpine', but within a range of physical characters which as a whole was wider. The new intruders in whom we are seeing Indo-Europeans tended to long- and high-headedness (though a round-headed strain was somehow present also), at least towards the Rhine (where an element making Bell-beakers again appears, and spreads thence to Britain); their typical form of burial was by inhumation crouched in single graves, normally in or beneath round barrows.

Now this burial-rite makes sharp contrast with that which had for some time prevailed in one form or another amongst most of the earlier inhabitants for whom distinctive burials are known at all, namely, the collective interment of the dead in megalithic stone-built chamber or gallery tombs, or sometimes natural caves. With that, there may be signs of a tradition also—it is clear in Britain—of cremating the dead and depositing the ashes in a cemetery, which can thus be viewed likewise as a place of collective burial. Where symbolism is associated with these rites, as in Brittany, or the south slopes of the *massif central*, or the chalk lands of the Marne, it is the symbolism of a female divinity, a Mother-goddess—we may say, an Earth-Mother; and whether or no the dead collectively entombed were thought to have thus re-entered her protective womb, it seems certain that ceremonies were enacted before the tombs, and in the stone circles or alignments, or at the menhirs or single standing-stones, of which the cult likewise called for the erection. The religion, it thus appears, was what in Greek studies would be called a 'chthonic' one, with the Underworld giving fertility and birth and embracing the community of the dead, through whom the community of the

9

living, by ritual observance, was made strong to live. The west-ward penetration of Indo-Europeans, on the other hand, will have brought in the quite different religious ideas which everywhere appear primarily associated with their speech and their warlike, man-ruled social order. For these are peoples with a sky-god; in many regions we find them attached to sun-symbols, and they revered the masculine force of heaven in thunder; femininity they exalted always less, save where they made contact and accommo-dation, as in Aegean regions, with one form or another of the chthonic fertility-religion.

Thus Mr Stevens in our Classical Dictionary is quite right to say of that chthonic religion, in the form we know from the megalithic tombs and monuments of France and the British Isles around 2000 B.C. (and after), that it was a unifying factor in the West, which we can see at work in Gaul. And in many parts it lasted, as he further says, till the coming into Gaul of further Indo-Europeans, from the direction of the Rhine: those who mainly, in the first millennium and after, become represented for us by the folk we know as Celts. Only we have seen that before these, well back in the second millennium, there had arrived already some earlier apparent Indo-Europeans; and these also, as well as the peoples of the megaliths in Gaul before them, and as the Celts we can recognize there after them, must be reckoned with in the ethnology of the Gaulish *protohistoire*.

It has been a favourite tenet of the French, and of none more emphatically than Jullian, that the leading folk of Bronze Age Gaul were Ligurians, whose presence in classical times in the south-east, and the adjacent corner of Italy, can be thought the residue of a far wider Bronze Age distribution. From what appear scraps of their language preserved in place-names, notably with terminations such as the *-asco* in Tarascon, they have been believed non-Indo-European; more modern conjecture has supposed them Indo-Europeanized, within anyhow the first millennium B.C., through admixture brought by the invasions that in the main will have been Celtic. As Professor L. R. Palmer has lately indicated in his book *The Latin Language*, the means for a sound solution of the Ligurian problem are not yet to hand. However, a wide former distribution for them is attested much better in Italy than in Gaul; and if their language was indeed Indo-Europeanized, or Indo-European outright as maintained by Dr Joshua Whatmough, we must remember the archaeologists' case for accepting as Indo-European right back in the Early Bronze Age, before the middle of the second millennium, peoples not only elsewhere in Gaul, but as near to classical Liguria as the upper Rhône. The Gaul of 1500 B.C. need not—I would say should not—be called Ligurian at large: it was a patchwork of peoples of surviving Neolithic and of Early Bronze material culture, among whom the former were strongly rooted in what one may call the 'megalithic religion', and the latter included, in some parts at least, some Indo-European groups.

It was with this patchwork Gaul, between the sixteenth century B.C. and the twelfth, that seafarers from the Aegean or Mycenean end of the Mediterranean had the contacts which are indicated by various rare but significant features of its archaeology. Through it, by the gap of Carcassonne between the north-west Mediterranean and the Atlantic coast, those contacts were shared (even if others were passed across Central Europe and the Rhine) by the Britain of Stonehenge and the contemporary 'Wessex culture', and by parts at least of Early Bronze Age Ireland. And so, when the Mycenean world sank and collapsed, Middle Bronze Age chiefs in Gaul, as in Britain and Ireland, were left with smiths who could make gold ornaments, for example, in a technique first known in Cyprus, and long bronze rapiers which adapt into new Western forms the old thrusting weapons of the Aegean warriors.

Now in the east of Gaul and away beyond the Rhine, in the centuries from the fourteenth B.C. on, which form our Middle Bronze Age, there were growing continually the strength and resources of those Indo-Europeans whom we can connect, by a chain of culture-stages archaeologically continuous, with un-doubted later Celts. Along that chain runs the long story of their pushings and penetrations into Gaul at large, fusing much, without doubt, with the previous populations. The story takes us into the first millennium through the Late Bronze Age, when the rite of cremation-burial in 'urnfields' came in from the east, in great part eclipsing barrow-burial; with this from Central Europe came new forms of pottery and bronze equipment, and new skills, in agriculture, in building and all woodwork, and in using horses and wheeled vehicles. If the primary hands in this 'urnfield' mode of culture were non-Celtic—one school has argued them Illyrian—it was second-hand by the time it crossed the Rhine, and the cultural forerunner of the Iron Age of known Celtic dominance. The tale is not complete, in fact, till the Iron Age culture had spread in after, again from the Rhine, and gradually over to the Atlantic, through the seventh to fourth centuries B.C. For its fullness, stage by stage, we must await Miss N. K. Sandars' book *The Bronze Age in France*, to be published before long by the Cambridge University Press. The idea that it began only at about 900, and was mainly an Iron Age affair, is no longer good prehistory: only after it had run from the Middle through the Late Bronze Age for a good five hundred years did there spread into it, towards 650, the first Iron culture of Central Europe, named Hallstatt after the type-site in Alpine Austria. But the result, the first Hallstatt culture of the Gaulish Iron Age, brings us into a brighter twilight: that of the West-Mediterranean dawn of ancient history.

With this first Gaulish-Hallstatt culture, from towards the mid-seventh to the late sixth century B.C., we can see Celts established from Switzerland and the Jura, the Rhine and central Belgium, over Burgundy and all the middle of the country. Moreover, it was carried southward also, to the Mediterranean coastal belt. And there, by now, Greek mariners, Rhodians and others come by Sicily, had arrived to traffic and begun to colonize; there, close to the year 600, was founded the Phokaean Greek colony of Massalia, which would be Massilia to the Romans, and is today Marseille. In the hills behind, on this east side of the Rhône, were Salluvii and other tribes who were Ligurians, and remained perceptibly distinct; but in Languedoc west of it the folk the Greeks would meet were of the Hallstatt culture that we can take as Celtic, and from datable Greek vase-sherds found among their leavings the archaeologist can stiffen his chronology. It was this Greek sphere of influence, and the districts next behind it, that we have seen become the first Roman province of Transalpine Gaul. But of the three parts of Caesar's 'Gallia omnis', Gaul as a whole, beyond that, the South-western or Aquitanian region is distinctive. It was not reached by Hallstatt immigrants till after or about 500, so that the substratum of its old inhabitants, partly now extant in the Basques, could stand thinly enough blanketed by Celtic Gaulishness to make Aquitanian culture as different, within Caesar's whole, as he says in fact it was.

The great middle tract of Hallstatt Gaul, if we look past 500 through its culture's second stage, is found extended west right to Brittany, thus filling already the bounds of Caesar's Celtae. Its culture there succeeded a 'Final Bronze' one, which had ensued, albeit at a long remove, upon that of the former Early Bronze colony in those parts, which at its outset we claimed could already have been Indo-European. Was that colony too early to be in any sense Celtic too? It had been closely parallel to the British 'Wessex culture'; and from this same quarter possibly, in the Late Bronze Age, migrants went over to our Wessex counties and set up there a culture, known as 'Deverel-Rimbury', in some things quite like that of their Iron Age successors who were clearly Celtic. These Brittany-Wessex connexions let one guess, in fact, that second-millennium Indo-Europeans in the west at large, wherever scattered, were in some sense Celts or Celtic forerunners. That would fit the idea of continuity between those in East Gaul and on the Rhine, and the Late Bronze and Hallstatt peoples from there, who went west to make the Celtae of the first millennium. The Celticity of Gaul and the British Isles at large, then, will have been produced by first-millennium migrants who had been preceded, in some parts, by second-millennium off-shoots from their own stock. I believe this idea has truth in it. Nevertheless, the interval of time is long; the earlier migrants, certain in some degree to fuse with the folk they came among, can during it have often become quite merged in them. As late as Early Christian times, in the language of the Picts of northern Britain, its Celtic components had failed to efface a non-Celtic one that was not Indo-European at all; and it is not fanciful, but rather prudent, to ascribe that component to a local Bronze Age language. Any such ancient tongue, then, no more Indo-European than is Basque, can have swamped the speech of second-millennium Indo-Europeans, scattered in the west too far beyond their kin, well before their kin began moving west again. That may have happened in Brittany; and what tongue the Deverel-Rimbury people spoke, we can only guess. What we can properly feel sure of, however, is at least this much, that the Celtic movements of the first millennium, anyhow in Gaul as a whole and Britain, spread over a prior ethnic and cultural amalgam, in which ancient native elements, whether in language, in economy and society, or in religion, were often strong.

It is time we turned lastly to the Belgae, who in Caesar's time occupied Gaul from the lower Seine and the Marne north-east and northwards. They were made up, it seems clear, of people with a like Bronze Age and Hallstatt ancestry to their southward neighbours, only mixed with late-comers from the Rhineland. Their boast of a German origin across the Rhine (*B.G.*, II, 4) need not mean an ancestry that we should call Teutonic: the Teutonic Germans of Caesar's Rhineland were in large part recent arrivals. Its older folk were in the broad sense Celtic; and this can be said also of the Belgae, only with some difference. For it was the lower Rhine that they adjoined (*B.G.*, I, 1, 6), and ethnology on and beyond that has been confused, not only by classical writers using 'German' and 'Celt' ambiguously, but also by an archaeology easy to misconstrue because so drab. It is clear and is becoming clearer, however, that the background to the Belgae here is a differentiated Celtic one, and that the *Germani* of their ancestry do not mean just the same *Germani* whom Caesar (*B.G.*, I, 1, 3) found them perpetually fighting. But we must resume our main concern.

In the late fifth and earlier fourth centuries B.C., among the Celts of the central territories from east Gaul to Bohemia, there was a rapid development from the Hallstatt culture, as we know it in material remains and art, to the new culture and art that is called La Tène. This name, taken from a site in Switzerland, is used in archaeology thenceforward to the Roman conquest. La Tène art is truly moving and exciting, in the rich phantasmagoria of imagery and ornament that it created from Oriental and Classical elements, together with the older Hallstatt repertory. And in its purely material accomplishment, especially in all crafts to do with fighting, La Tène culture is undeniably impressive. Yet, for such prehistoric and historical ethnology as we are here looking at for Gaul, the significance of the whole culture seems in great measure only supplementary—a finishing touch to the prehistoric Celts' achievements—and not fundamental. The foundations of the Gaulish world were already laid. That is without doubt true; but there is more that must still be said. The finishing touch of the La Tène centuries, directly before the Roman conquests came, did give Gaulish society the final form in which it was observed and set down by Caesar, and from which it was after him Romanized into the Provincial Gaul, of the place-names and the *fundi*, the nobles in their families and the peasant *plebs*, whence the medievalist must draw the irreducible elements in his seigneurial institutions. Those Horseman chieftains, with their dependent clients and communities, are at once the richly furnished dead excavated by the archaeologist, and the holders of the ancient rural chiefdoms discerned behind his *seigneuries* by Bloch. Prehistory and history are here truly meeting. And so will not old Camille Jullian, purged somewhat of his extravagances but all the more *bon gaulois* for that, be vindicated after all?

If he is, it will not be without the testimony of those other Gaulish *nobiles* of whom Caesar tells, the Druids. For what is this curious clergy—priests, judges, mythologues, astrologers, bards, wizards and philosophers of religion—doing in Gaul amongst the Celts, while in the historically invaded Celtic lands, North Italy, South-east Europe, Spain, we hear absolutely nothing of them, nor yet see any sign in Celtic Central Europe? Outside Gaul, their only known homes are the British Isles; and what does Caesar say of Druidism in Britain? That it was said actually (*B.G.*, VI, 13, 11) to have come from there—*disciplina in Britannia reperta*; to have been brought thence to Gaul; and to have its authoritative seats there still!

How could that have come to be believed of it, unless it was something that Gaul had had in common with Britain, in its fundamentals, long before the La Tène and the Hallstatt and Late Bronze centuries in which the movement had been all the other way? And from what could those fundamentals have been derived, unless from an accommodation reached by Celtic forerunners, long before those centuries, with the ancient religion with which in these lands alone such an accommodation is archaeologically indicated? Are not the Druids the nameless priests of the old megalithic religion Celticized, through a long tale of stages only ending, at last, in the La Tène world in which Caesar came to know them? If so, it will explain the repeated association of Gallo-Roman religious relics—even built temples— with megalithic remains in France; it can explain the Iron Age potsherds scattered within stone circles in Britain, on the one hand in Scotland, on the other at Stonehenge itself; it can explain yet other things—and not least, perhaps, that Gaulish deity of the Underworld whom Caesar called Dis and said the Druids taught all the Gauls they were descended from. For to the unmixed and pristine Indo-European it is the sky-god—Diespiter, the bright-sky father, Jupiter—it is Zeus, dwelling in aether, who is father of gods and men.

And if this seems momentarily over-far from Government and Society in France, the proper subject of these lectures, let me remind you that Bloch found it characteristic of the rural lord and his villagers that they owed him strange ritual gifts, and that in the games, dances, inexplicable rites and services that French lawyers came to call *droits ridicules*, the *seigneur* was acting 'the probably very ancient part of a kind of president over ritual practices, which have come down, there can hardly be any doubt, from an immense antiquity'. 'Natio est omnis Gallorum' observed Caesar (*B.G.*, VI, 16) 'admodum dedita religionibus'. He found Britons who differed from them little; and he might have said something similar of the Irish, if he had beheld the gruesome Iron Age remains excavated in 1953 on the Hill of Tara—the bushels of cremated and buried human skeletal relics recall at once the Gauls' victims burnt alive in that same chapter—in front of deep post-holes wherein had stood stakes and perhaps tall idols, like that found once in Scotland at Ballachulish. There are Bronze Age burials at Tara too; and what are its earthwork sanctuary-circles but later renderings of such circular 'Henge'-monuments as we know from the second millennium in Britain, scattered from the Channel to the far north? It is in them that we find our Stone Age cremation-cemeteries; to them are related the stone circles that we share with Ireland and Gaul; at the foot of every stone in the Breton circle of Er-Lannic were cremations; and these monuments in their turn, with Dis receding before the more primitive femininity of the nether Earth, bring us back to the great stone tombs—represented at Tara likewise—and to their goddess.

As I see it, both in Gaul and in these islands, it was the Indo-European immigrants of that same second millennium, whom I have called Celtic forerunners—whether they were early-Celtic or pre-Celtic or just near to Celtic, and whether they kept their language alive or not—who made that accommodation between their own masculine sky-religion and the old chthonic megalithic one existing here before them, which could descend through the Bronze Age to their undisputedly Celtic successors. Thence came the religion that the Druids administered, and that was so closely bound up with the social order of La Tène times. That social order passed in Gaul into Roman hands with Caesar, and lasted on as the embryo of the rural system of medieval France. 'C'est elle'—for we are back with Camille Jullian—'qui des débris romains, a fait notre France'. Put that way, an old man's romantic exaggeration, no doubt. But had not the old man there something worth exaggerating? To the *bon gaulois* of today who would like a clear reply brought closer, in the excavation-field or elsewhere, and for the *protohistorique* of whatever period, good chances still lie open.

BIBLIOGRAPHICAL NOTE[1]

To the older writers—himself of course one of them—the best English guide is T. Rice Holmes, in his *Caesar's Conquest of Gaul*, 2nd edn. (Oxford, Clarendon Press, 1911). Camille Jullian's *Histoire de la Gaule* is in 8 volumes (1908–26); for his life, see *Camille Jullian*, by A. Grenier (1944). J. Déchelette's *Manuel d'Archéologie* (4 parts, 1908–14) was reissued (4 vols.) in 1927. H. Hubert's two volumes on *Les Celtes* (1932) appeared also in English, as *The Rise of the Celts* and *The Greatness and Decline of the Celts* (1934). These had full bibliographies. A. Grenier's *Les Gaulois* (2nd edn., 1945) was somewhat more compact.

Progress may be followed annually in the Paris periodicals, *L'Anthropologie, Bulletin de la société préhistorique française, Revue archéologique, Revue celtique* and (since 1943) *Gallia*, with its companion *Gallia-Préhistoire*); also *Ogam* (Rennes), with its *Celticum* supplements. *Helinium* (Wetteren), for Belgium and all 'Benelux', succeeded in 1961 to the section *Archéologie* in the annual *L'Antiquité Classique* (Ghent). Much is published in French regional periodicals.

For Neolithic France, with the beginnings of its Metal Age, see G. Bailloud and P. Mieg, *Les Civilisations Néolithiques de la France* (1955); G. Bailloud, *Le Néolithique clans le bassin parisien* (supp. to *Gallia-Prehist.*), 1964. For the Bronze Age and early Hallstatt, N. K. Sandars's *Bronze Age Cultures in France* (Cambridge, 1957) and J. Briard, *Les Dépôts Bretons* (Rennes, 1965). For the earlier periods more generally, V. Gordon Childe's *The Dawn of Euro-*

---

[1] Works above cited for the Roman and Medieval Periods will be found, if not here, in the Bibliographies to Lectures II and III respectively. Julius Caesar's *Commentarii De Bello Gallico* is cited as *B.G.*

pean Civilization had its last edition in 1957; C. F. C. Hawkes's *The Prehistoric Foundations of Europe* dates from 1940. S. Piggott's *Ancient Europe* (Edinburgh, 1965) has fullest bibliography.

From the Bronze through the Iron Age, Gabrielle Fabre dealt with south-western France in *Les Civilisations protohistoriques de l'Aquitaine* (1952); for the Bronze and Iron Age barrows of Alsace, see C. F. A. Schaeffer, *Les Tertres funéraires préhistoriques de la Forêt de Haguenau* (Haguenau Museum, 2 vols., 1926–30); of Burgundy, F. Henry, *Les Tumulus du dépt. de la Côte d'Or* (1933). For the all-important Hallstatt period, centred on the sixth century B.C., see the trilogy by R. Joffroy (Paris): *Le Trésor de Vix* (Monuments Piot 48, i, 1954); *Les Sépultures à Char du Premier Age du Fer en France* (1958); *L'Oppidum de Vix et la Civilisation hall-stattienne finale dans l'est de la France* (1960). For the N. and N.W., R. E. M. Wheeler and K. M. Richardson, *Hill Forts of Northern France* (London, Soc. of Antiquaries, 1957); P. R. Giot, *Brittany* (1960); the S. and S.E., J. Jannoray, *Ensérune* (Paris, 1955);

F. Benoît, *Entremont* (Aix, 1957), and *Recherches sur l'hellénisation du Midi de la Gaule* (Aix, 1965); G. Barruol, *Les peuples pré-romains du SE. de la Gaule* (Paris, 1969); F. Villard, *La céramique grecque de Marseille* (1960); M. Louis and O. and A. Taffanel, *Le premier age du fer languedocien* (Montpellier, 3 vols., 1955–60).

Celtic art was treated fully by P. Jacobsthal in *Early Celtic Art* (2 vols., Oxford, Clarendon Press, 1944, reprinted 1969). See also (Paris) A. Varagnac and G. Fabre, *L'Art gaulois* (1956); L. Lengyel, *L'Art celtique dans les médailles* (1962); F. Benoît, *Art et dieux de la Gaule* (1969); J. Moreau, *Die Welt der Kelten* (Stuttgart, 1958); F. Benoît, *L'Art primitif méditerranéen de la vallée du Rhône* (Gap, 1955). In the field of religion *The Druids* by Stuart Piggott (London, 1968) is by far the best modern treatment. On Temples and sanctuaries, its bibliography extends that in O. Brogan's *Roman Gaul* (cited above), p. 243.

Finally, the Indo-European question, archaeological and linguistic was freshly reconsidered by Hugh Hencken, in the *American Anthropologist,* 57, 6, Memoir 84 (December, 1955), and by P. Bosch Gimpera in *Le problème indo-européen* (Paris, 1960).

C. E. STEVENS

Roman Gaul

The period that I describe will bring Gaul—we cannot yet call it France, and our area includes Belgium and Rhineland Germany—from barbarism into civilization and take it back to barbarism again, but a barbarism, to use a word of which R. G. Collingwood was fond, that 'incapsulates' civilization. The manner in which the changes are effected is typical of it. Roman rule comes to Gaul by formal treaty arrangements and the establishment of recognized governmental forms: it leaves so gradually that there is hardly a moment at which a Gaul could say: 'Today I am not a subject of the Roman emperor as yesterday I was.' The period can begin, therefore, sharply, with the entrance of *Gallia Narbonensis* into the Roman provincial system· in 121 B.C.; its end must be arbitrary—we may place it at the accession of Clovis to power with the defeat of Syagrius in 486 A.D., though a formalist might prefer the reigns of his sons, when their heads, not those of reigning emperors, appear on the coinage and their regnal years are used for dating. It is thus a span of some six hundred years—as long as separates the Hundred Years War from our own day.

The Romans did not at first come to Gaul as conquerors at all: the aristocratic senate that ruled them was as averse as all aristocratic governments to overseas adventures. They came to protect their ally Massilia (Marseille) against the great empire of the Arvernian kings (Auvergne) that was molesting her. The maintenance of Massilia was essential to Roman policy, since it controlled both land and sea routes to Spain, whose mineral wealth (as Judas Maccabaeus in distant Palestine understood) was vital. Rome therefore annexed simply what was necessary to provide a glacis for its ally, the lower Rhône basin in fact, an area bounded by the middle Rhône (from the Lake of Geneva to its junction with the Saône) on the north, the Cevennes *massif* to the west, the Mediterranean and the Alps to south and east. The whole Arvernian empire, extending, as it seems, to the Atlantic and the Rhine, might have been annexed too. Business men with their eyes on the tin trade might have liked that, which was a fair reason why senators might not; but the Romans claimed a kind of equity of annexation—if they felt like it.

It was not long, however, before the business men forced, in the teeth of senatorial opposition, the foundation of a colony at Narbo, to tap, if not to control the tin route, which ensured, even before Julius Caesar, that the main influence throughout the country should be Latin and not Greek. Otherwise the Roman government showed as little sense of responsibility in this province as elsewhere. Nevertheless the fact of the Roman Peace could not be outweighed by the usual malfeasance of governors: it should not surprise us, for instance, that the inhabitants of a native town, Glanum (St Rémy-en-Provence) began to erect more sumptuous houses and habitually use imported pottery at table. Indeed, its century's start in Romanization made certain permanent differences between the *provincia* and the rest of Gaul, which perpetuated themselves in a contrast between the *Langues d'Oil* and *d'Oc*, though the contrast was more profound between the hinterland and the coastal strip along the Mediterranean, to which Celtic cultural influences from over the Rhine had penetrated less strongly in the epoch of the invasions. Of this coastal strip rather than of the *provincia* as a whole it is true to say with the naturalist Pliny, two centuries from the annexation, that it was 'more like Italy than a province'.

The equity of annexation in northern Gaul might have been long unrealized had not Julius Caesar acted in 58 B.C. It is strange to reflect that not only did he not desire a Gallic War, but had taken diplomatic measures to prevent one. There had been, however, a fresh demonstration of German pressure across the Rhine, and he did not wish Gallic nationalists to enjoy the credit of their own salvation from it. He took over the old Arvernian empire at first indeed without any battles and went on in fighting campaigns to extend Roman annexation to its logical limits of Rhine and Ocean, announcing officially the conquest of a Gaul included within these limits.

It is legitimate, indeed, to wonder whether to the inhabitants, at least, such an area would be recognized as Gaul and its population one and all Gauls. Certainly Aquitanians were able later to persuade the central government that they were not Gauls, and the Belgae of the north-east were at least half-German. There may have been some kind of religious unity outside the central area of true Gauls, based on Druidism, which seems, as far as we can sift the evidence, to derive from pre-Celtic cultures; certainly Caesar's great antagonist, Vercingetorix, from the Auvergne that had been annexed without a blow, was able to call for aid from this wider area. It may not be wrong to suggest that it was the dream of a patriot, and the sales-talk of his conqueror anxious to justify the extents of his conquests, that gave a unity to the area which, after eight years of struggle, came finally under Roman domination in 51 B.C.

It fell to Augustus, the adopted heir of Julius, sole master of the Roman world after the Battle of Actium (31 B.C.) and founder of the system that we call the Roman Empire, to consolidate the conquest. The *provincia*, long familiarized with Roman rule, could be allowed to perpetuate the traditional governmental arrangements of the Republic, with continually shifting governors appointed by lot, often as a consolation prize for less competent members of the senatorial body. The coastal strip had been heavily colonized by discharged soldiers from the Gallic wars, and the capitals of tiny, non-Celtic tribes, only commemorated by technical geographers, could fit easily into the Mediterranean idea of the city-state, as preached by Aristotle, but standard in Italy too, in which each citizen could hear the voice of the herald. These towns, with their small areas of territory attached, early enjoyed the titles of Roman colonies, and the emphasis on the town is said still to colour the composition of *Conseils départementaux* in the Bouches-du-Rhône and neighbouring *départements*. The hinterland, conspicuous, on the other hand, for large tribal areas, whose Celticity is betrayed by their names—Volcae (the same, they say, as Welsh and walnuts) and Allobroges, may well have caused embarrassment to administrators of Republican days, who could only pay tribute to the Aristotelian idea by assuming territories of vast size attached to capital towns, and even penalizing the countryside against these towns—measures appropriate enough in Rome's eastern conquests, where Hellenized towns were very often opposed to lesser breeds of natives in the country around, but hardly appropriate for Celtic lands. Nevertheless such inferiority soon seems, in the epoch of the empire, to have been a matter of theory alone. Nemausus (Nîmes) might be the capital of Volcae, and Vienna (Vienne) of Allobroges, privileged with mighty buildings and virtually extinguishing the tribal names. Yet it would appear that even among the 'ignoble towns' in their territory everyone who mattered (which meant local landed magnates and the principal merchants) enjoyed by the first century A.D. the privilege of calling themselves Roman citizens, which entitled them to enter Roman public life. The *provincia* was soon producing orators, consuls, even emperors, illustrating, from another angle, Pliny's 'more like Italy than a province'.

Caesar's conquests are, however, differently treated, as 'imperial provinces', three in number (Belgica, Lugdunensis, Aquitania), with their governors appointed directly by the emperor for periods always, and sometimes much, longer than a year. And the treatment of the large tribal areas too is essentially different. It was certainly unhandy and might be politically dangerous to treat them as city states along Aristotelian lines, when they were clearly nothing of the sort. Rome found once in its history a great genius of administrative reform, a Madison or Lord Durham, the conqueror of Gaul itself, Julius Caesar, and one would gladly credit to Julius a solution simple when found but needing a genius to transcend the ideas of the time and find it. The tribe is treated as a kind of imaginary city, as though the town-wall enclosed the whole area of the tribe. The capital—we really need the French *chef-lieu*—is merely one of the villages (*vici*) of the tribe, merely the local repository of its government. This is what scholars have called the 'cantonal system', and we can follow its adaptation to special circumstances and the varieties of evidence from which the totality of the system has been inferred. The Périgord gives us, for instance, some neat demonstrations. The Petrucorii are a tribe whose name in Gaulish denotes 'the Four Kinship-Groups' (*coriae*—we can find the word in Irish as *cuire* for a population-group). Rome provides a *chef-lieu* on a ᵥacred site at their centre, where a Roman town is built around and called from the goddess Vesunna. The tribe becomes the Roman *civitas Petrucoriorum*, and the tribal feeling is strong enough to transfer the tribe's name to the bricks-and-mortar of the Roman town, that as early as the third century will be called simply 'Petrucorii' from which the modern Périgueux derives.

The Christian episcopate will base itself on the Roman civil administration, so that the pre-revolutionary boundaries of the see of Périgueux will give us those of *civitas Petrucoriorum* (Roman names such as *fines* and Celtic ones as Icoranda, disguised as Eygurande or even more strangely as La Délivrande, on the boundaries of these bishoprics show that the principle is sound). So far Périgord has merely been a case among many others; one thinks of Parisii–Lutetia–Paris: Bituriges–Avaricum–Bourges and scores more; but it has its own peculiarity in respect of 'cantonal' evidence. The bishopric had five archdeaconries, one for Périgueux town, the others divided over the territory of the diocese. Clearly we have the Christian adaptation of the four *coriae* and the Roman *chef-lieu*. This is but one example of the manner in which, by the 'cantonal system', the Romans secured continuity between their own arrangements and those of free Gaul before them.

Both in the political form and in the maturity of its Romanization, then, there is a certain distinction between the *provincia* and the newly acquired lands. Yet the essential unity of the country, which, as ancient authors observed, seems imposed on it by nature, persists. It is appropriate that Gaul is treated as a whole by Roman tax-gatherers and Gallic grumblers. For taxation purposes, the whole country, *provincia* and the rest, is administered from a central bureau at Lugdunum (Lyon); while the grumblers who speak for all the 'magnificent Gallic provinces' are—typically—appealing to the emperor against blackmail prices charged by such truly Roman phenomena as gladiatorial syndicates.

Augustus rounds off the Gallic picture partly on the administrative, partly on the architectural side. Administratively Gaul is now exactly surveyed for taxation purposes, and the bases of the survey are the estates of the local magnates. Their names, often commemorating proprietors with Celtic names, are the backbone of *commune* names today. It is significant, however, of the comparative rate of Romanization that the purely Celtic suffix -*acum* which we meet disguised as -y (Antony=Antoniacum) in the north or -ac (Brennac=Brennacum) farther south, changes to the Roman -anicum (Sauxillanges=Celsinianicum) or -anum (Aubignan=Albinianum) as we approach or enter the more early Romanized *provincia*. These magnates must pay taxes to keep the empire of Rome in being, but they keep their estates as Gallo-Roman nobles (a later governor could remind them of both facts). Free Gaul had been, as Caesar said, a land where the nobility controlled all and the common people were 'almost in the condition of slaves'—a land admirably adapted to the Roman recipe for maintaining Rome's conquests—to support the rich and hope for the best, and in Gaul the hope was in the main realized. Josephus at the end of the first century A.D., putting words into the mouth of Herod Agrippa, dissuading the Jews from revolt, commented that though Gaul had the traditions and inducements for an independent movement, the Gauls did not revolt. The emperor Claudius had said much the same thing some twenty years before him.

Thus the grandson of a Gallic chief with broad, if ill-defined, acres, and a mass of obedient serfs to till and, in factional brawl or tribal warfare, to fight, took on with ease the lineaments of a Gallo-Roman squire, removing (as we can prove at the site of Mayen in the Eifel) his rude hut to construct a Roman villa of standard pattern; and when we think of the social background, we should not find it surprising that the plan of a great villa with its extensive adjuncts, Chiragan, near Toulouse, or Anthée in Belgium, reminds us strongly of the layout at Washington's Mount Vernon. The Gallo-Roman noble was forbidden to fight but encouraged to prosper. Strabo, the contemporary of Augustus and universal interpreter of natural and human geography to his age, saw the prosperity coming 'now that the Gauls have stopped fighting and started working'. To the Gauls, Augustus could make the same appeal as was made to Frenchmen also after an epoch of war and revolution: 'Enrichissez-vous'. The two elements of *enrichissement* were there—fertile soil with natural avenues of communication along the great river valleys (Strabo noted these too) and an appreciation already reached of law, sanctity of contracts and property rights. Cicero might ask a Roman jury what the Gaul of the *provincia*, Indutiomarus, might 'know of the nature of an oath'. The unassisted progress realized by the *provincia* under the Republic showed up the jingoism of his remark. In the areas newly conquered, the progress could be faster precisely because it could be assisted.

The *de facto* control of one centralized financial authority in the presence of the emperor enabled capital resources to be pumped into backward areas of the empire. If Augustus found his capital brick and left it marble, it is true enough to say that he found Gaul (even much of the *provincia*) wattle-and-daub and left it stone (sometimes marble). The *chef-lieu* of a tribe is given the architectural likeness of a Mediterranean city. Free Gauls of the Aedui (Burgundy, more or less) had their capital on the wind-swept Mont-Beuvray (Bibracte) with winding streets and houses vaguely suggesting Mediterranean house-plans but with archi-tectural possibilities limited by the absence of mortar. Augusto-dunum—'Augustusville'—if we can go to America for our parallel—is located on a new site, down in a river plain, so much more convenient, but so much less easily defensible too by potential last-ditch resisters. It has its chess-board street plan, invented by Hippodamus of Miletus, which takes Gaul in its stride on the way ultimately to Philadelphia and Cincinnati; it has gates embodying the most modern Greek thinking on fortifi-cation but adapted for customs' collection rather than combat. Within, the public buildings make the finest show, above all the *forum*, centre of marketing, and the *basilica*, where the Gallic chief turned Gallo-Roman magnate meets his fellows in the local senate, while for amusement there may be an amphitheatre in the Roman style or a theatre or both, though it is interesting to observe that the Gauls usually adapt the plan of a Greco-Roman theatre to be more suitable for cock-fights and the like. Actors who were failures on the Roman stage might do well with the less sophisticated Gallic audiences.

What is true of Augustodunum is true for town after town provided for the Gauls as centres for their *civitates*; it is rare to find a town still left on its hill, like Langres, the situation of which is rather an embarrassment to its citizens today. A modern scholar, Goodchild, has demonstrated that *forum* and *basilica* in towns all over the country, from Paris to St Bertrand de Comminges under the shadow of the Pyrenees, seem to have been constructed from the same blue-print. The identical *Hôtels-de-Ville* of the Third Republic make a curious parallel. And the towns are linked by a national road system and develop their tribal com-munications. No more striking and strange demonstration of their adequacy can be given than that of Pliny, who tells us that geese were driven on their feet from the Morini (around Boulogne-sur-Mer, that is) to Rome.

With such a background of capital equipment, 'enrichissez-vous' was a command easy of obedience. The evidence cannot be

statistical but can be deduced from literature, architecture and
such widely circulable and imperishable products as reach the
archaeologist. The poet Martial—with no real or sentimental ties
to Gaul—could urge gold-digging girls to leave him alone and
go where they belonged, and with the whole empire to choose,
he picked for their destination the fat business men of Bordeaux.
One of these business men brought a water supply to his town;
it cost him two million *sesterces* (twice the census figure qualifying
for membership of the senate of Rome). Britain indicates how
these business men earned the sums for aqueducts and girls. Used
wine-barrels became well-linings for the water-supply of
Silchester, and the wood, the experts tell us, must be fir from the
Landes. It is appropriate that a man from Bordeaux recorded
honorary distinctions granted to him by the towns of York and
Lincoln. Pottery tells an even louder story than cooperage.
Figures of pots thrown by companies or guilds are extant on
waster sherds at La Graufesenque near Albi; amounts up to
80,000 in a batch are figured, and the works at Lezoux near
Clermont-Ferrand with more than two hundred furnaces were
still larger. We need not be surprised that by the middle of the
first century A.D., Gaul began to capture the *bourgeois* and officers'
mess table-ware throughout the western world. Claudius'
invading army at Richborough (43 A.D.) were dining off Lezoux
ware. In 61 A.D. Boudicca's hordes burned a shop at Colchester
crowded with it, and—more remarkable still, in Italy itself,
Vesuvius in 79 A.D. overwhelmed in a store an unopened crate
from Gaul. Small wonder that Caligula could hope to squeeze
Gauls by enforced bids at an auction of old imperial furniture,
that Lyon could contribute voluntarily four million *sesterces* for
the building after Nero's great fire of imperial Rome. How can
Jews hope to succeed in rebelling against the might of Rome,
asked Herod Agrippa: 'Are you wiser than Greeks? Are you
richer than—Gauls?'

He also invited them to note that Gauls remained content with
a garrison of no more than twelve hundred soldiers at Lyon to
keep them so. This was not altogether true; the sixty thousand
troops of the Rhine army could look over their shoulders as well
as keep the watch. Nevertheless in spirit his observation was true
enough. The discovery that taxes had come to stay and that
the borrowing necessary to 'keep up with the Jones's' of Italy

demanded its price was responsible for a wild rebellion of chiefs
in 21 A.D., which was swiftly suppressed by these armies of the
Rhine. In 69 A.D. Gauls were able to observe that no army—the
Rhine army included—was loyal to any agreed superior, and
illicit congregations of Druids reminded them that if Rome's
Capitol was burning now, free Gauls had burned it before, which
meant that now was the time to strike for freedom. But Gallic
nobles were disinclined to strike. They were too rich, and which
group would seize power if they won? Perhaps the Last Testament
of a Gallic chief of this time gives the background to their
reluctance. We do not know his name—his Testament, a flawless
example, they tell us, of Roman conveyancing, was copied we
know not whence or by whom in the ninth century, to lurk in a
Basel library until 1863. He remembers his Gallic ancestry by the
savage request to burn his spears and hunting gear with him on
the pyre, but he is ultra-modern, like an American 'coal-oil
Johnnie', in his demands for the mausoleum: everything of the
best and overseas material, the portico to be fashioned of the very
best Carrara marble. It is the world of the 'Loved One' indeed.
But men of this stamp are not often found in the *maquis*—either
in 69 A.D. or millennia later.

Rome had done its work too well. Bruce and William Tell
have been lanterns of patriotism; but the men of 69 A.D.
found leadership not in the name of Vercingetorix but in
one who boasted descent from Julius Caesar, his conqueror.
Gaul was not at all like Scotland or Switzerland. The work was
done not least, as the evidence of modern culture-transmission
to backward areas shows, because it is so easy to do, almost does
itself. A Gaul whose grandfather worshipped the horned Cernun-
nus would probably for very shame before Roman civilization
call the horned one Apollo (and then often omit the horns).
The Gallic chief takes a Roman name—we can see it happening
with the dedicator of a triumphal arch at Saintes. His father and
grandfather are Roman citizens though with the outlandish
appellatives, Otuaneunus and Gedemo (his great-grandfather,
Epotsorovidus, was probably a free Gaul before the conquest);
he himself is plain C. Iulius Rufus. Such men were probably
talking Latin as their normal speech. Certainly Latin has moved
to French through a Low Latin vulgar language, which develops
with similar phonetic principles all over the west. Backwoods

peasants in the Eiffel, medical quacks and witches (a significant trinity) clung in the later empire to Gaulish. We can contrast the survival of British into Welsh.

Naturally the Roman government added to the movement some discreet pressure. Worship of the quasi-divine majesty of Rome and the emperor, extended sometimes to the imperial family, was customary in Gallic towns; freedmen and their families, engaged in commerce rather than land-holding, and thus less likely to be members of local senates, were given a chance of social position and activities through their conduct of the ceremonies. But it was among the tribal magnates that delegates were invited to a virtually national worship of Rome and the emperor at the junction of Rhône and Saône, on the opposite side of the rivers to the colony of Lyon. The difference of locality is important. While upon the hill, Augustus' governor, a senator of Rome, sends orders and gives judgement, while therefrom his procurator settles matters of revenue, while money to pay those taxes is there coined under protection of troops from Rome, all surrounded by Italian colonists looking down in more than the literal sense upon the natives, the leaders of these natives, separated from them by the river, have in a manner a direct line, through this imperial religion, with the emperor himself. They may indeed find that, if they have come for religious ceremonies and banquets, they may stay to discuss governors and taxes, forming a kind of critical assembly with mandatory powers from their tribes to give and withhold the criticism. Meanwhile in the details of the assembly Augustus misses no propaganda trick. The day of dedication is that on which he had completed, by capture of Alexandria, the holy war against Antony and his Egyptian queen. The year of dedication (12 B.C.) is that when Augustus reversed Caesar's policy of a 'Watch on the Rhine'. Rome will lead Gauls in avenging war against the ancestral foe across the river. Moreover among the leaders are singled out for decoration men of the Nervii, on the one hand really rather more akin to Germans than Gauls, on the other among the most pertinacious opponents of Julius. Among the delegates, a certain M. Lucterius Leo has recorded the fact in an inscription from his town, Divona of the Cadurci (Cahors). Not very interesting this, we may think, until we remember that a Lucterius of the Cadurci, presumably an ancestor, was the actual last resister in the field against Julius and at the end was handed over to him, bound, by a renegade. It is as though Hitler had won and among celebrants of his New Order in Berlin was found a deputation from Oradour-sur-Glane.

Here then we find the background of Herod's argument. A Roman governor, seeing the failure of the nationalist movement in 69 A.D., would find much for smiles and little for apprehension. He would notice that ultimately stability rested on the exploitation of a servile peasantry, but with the landlords backed by a prosperous trading class in the towns, there was little to worry from here. An attempt of a local peasant leader to head a movement compounded of religion and nationalism in the turmoils of 69 A.D. had received short shrift from locals before detachments from the army needed to go into action. Gallic peasants were not likely to behave like zealots in Judaea.

It was perhaps slightly a matter of apprehension to note that Gauls seemed disinclined to serve Rome, more ready to take from Rome than to give back. Though permitted by Claudius to serve in the senate of Rome, they hung back, and are not conspicuous in the 'lesser nobility' of the revenue officials, the equestrians, nor in the legions either. Men, it was said, will not die for the meridian of Greenwich. They might not want to die for aqueducts or Samian pottery.

If such apprehensions were proved to have their grounds, this is the result of causes affecting the whole empire, notably the great plague under M. Aurelius, accompanied with simultaneous barbarian attacks on all frontiers: population and capital resources were alike disastrously diminished. The subsequent phenomena of fiercely increased taxation, inflation and lowering of military discipline and morale, at once let the barbarians in and crippled the trading classes. Seventy towns of Gaul are said to have been destroyed in a barbarian raid of 276 A.D., and it looks as though the feeling that Gaul had better look to itself had revived old nationalist feeling and memories of a 'Gallic empire'. The outward signs of a change in the structure of social and economic life are seen in the vast shrinking of areas enclosed within the walls that were hastily erected for urban defence for the most part from torn down buildings, temples and even tombstones. These areas, which cannot have enclosed much more than the offices of administration, vary between fifty and as low as twelve acres (Périgueux—no larger than a College sports' ground!). The landowner faced his peasantry without the buffer of an urban middle-class; and it is not surprising that an aftermath of the great invasions was a general revolt of the peasantry under the Celtic appellation of Bacaudae, with difficulty suppressed.

It was possible for the restored monarchy of Diocletian, Constantine and their successors in the fourth century to succeed more or less in ejecting the invaders by war. Nevertheless the government, faced with the chronic manpower shortage, was forced to let them return, in a manner, by the back door. The army was increasingly recruited from barbarians, partly by direct enrolment across the frontier—the commander of the Rhine armies who made a bid for the empire in 355 A.D., Silvanus, was a Frankish recruit—partly from barbarian captives whose strong arms became more and more necessary to keep the fields tilled. An orator, addressing Constantius, father of Constantine, speaks of virtual 'concentration camps' where Frankish captives sit, awaiting their allotment for cultivating deserted fields of land-owners or compulsory recruiting in the army. Many such settlements have left their traces in modern place-names, Sermais and Charmasse commemorating Sarmatians, Allemagne, the Alamanni, Tiffauges in the Vendée, the pagus Theofalgicus, the Taifali. It was a kind of combination of these procedures when whole tribes of Franks were settled by Julian in 358 A.D. along the Meuse and eventually given the responsibility of defending the frontier instead of regular units of the army. It will not surprise us, then, to learn from a contemporary that in the reign of Valentinian II in Gaul (388–392 A.D.) 'the emperor was almost reduced to a private citizen, all military matters were in the hands of the Franks, and even civil administration was in the hands of their leader and his associates'. We are not far from Clovis now.

We are soon to come nearer. On the last day of 406 A.D. a horde of barbarians crossed the Rhine and spread such devastation that organized life nearly broke down. It looks as though it were truly 'every man for himself'. The strong barricaded themselves in fortified places where their dependents could find refuge. The background of this 'time of troubles' was painted in touches sombre and skilful by the presbyter Salvian of Marseille, and his language reminds us of the description of anarchy in Stephen's reign from the *Peterborough Chronicle*. The central government still tried to enforce its harsh taxation which each man strived to push on to the shoulders of weaker than he. Some of the weaklings virtually surrendered lands and liberty to great lords for their protection. Others joined either the barbarian invaders or the bands of peasants in revolt, calling themselves again Bacaudae: a contemporary document pictures to us a veritable republic of these brigands on the Loire, where justice was done 'under the greenwood tree'. Modern Russian scholars have studied such phenomena with natural enthusiasm, but it would be wrong to romanticize them. The physician Eudoxius who had become a 'Bacauda' and then fled to the Huns, is an interesting pointer to social despair and collapse, but we must not forget that these outlaws had neither serious programme nor leadership, as well as we can see. Moreover, though Salvian could speak of co-operation between Roman subjects and barbarians and Eudoxius illustrate it, the barbarians themselves were not slow to realize that their material interests were better secured by infiltrating themselves into the established order than by co-operating in its overthrow. It is in this light that we must see the establishment of whole barbarian tribes, Visigoths and Burgundians, no longer on the frontier, but in south-western and central Gaul. Their tenure is military, literally so, involving the allocation to them of a portion (two-thirds or one third according to circumstances) of the land of their noble hosts—a condition directly derived from the rules for billeting Roman troops in the days when Rome had still a Roman army in the field. In this fashion of agreements with tribes—*foedera* as they are called, and the tribesmen *foederati*—veritable national units could imperceptibly come into being, so that it was hard for a 'Roman' civil administrator in an area occupied by a Visigothic king and his 'billeted' tribesmen to be sure whether he was in the Roman empire or not.

This is the background of Sidonius Apollinaris (*c*. 430–80 A.D.) who wrote of Gaul when the danger of barbarian destruction and peasant revolt had been checked—by the barbarians. Sidonius did not like them—they smeared butter on their hair, even the best were unpleasant; yet they were underwriting a still civilized society; and what is significant is that Sidonius has no idea that his society, thus underwritten, will not be permanent.

In fact, the destiny of history decided that this Gallo-Roman society would be underwritten not by the relatively Romanized Visigoths and Burgundians, but by Clovis and his Franks who moved in from the Belgian forests to take over the control of the country. The Franks were far less savage than the Saxons invited by Vortigern on a similar mission, but they were pagans with relatively small Roman contacts in an area from which the forms of civilized life had been steadily shrinking. It is fascinating to read the letter with which Remigius, Bishop of Rheims, welcomed the appearance of Clovis in 486 A.D. on the Gallic political scene. It is as though he addresses a wild 'child of nature', whom he can hope to influence nevertheless. 'You had better put yourself under the advice of the bishops', he says, 'then providence will see you through.' Wild children of nature—the wheel appears indeed to have spun full circle, and we see ourselves returned to the days when Caesar spoke of continual faction and violence in free, Celtic Gaul, as yet uncivilized by Rome. And yet, of course, it is not the same. The Roman empire has been there and its gifts remain, not only roads and town-walls, but gifts of the spirit— though in decay, the Latin language; though deformed, the face of Roman Law and above all, the empire's gift of a universal religion, Christianity. Its origins and diffusion in Gaul are obscure, but by the end of the fourth century it had driven pagan cults from the field. It is there both to bind society together and to insist with however uncertain and compromising a voice upon a moral code. Moreover the Christian church with its organization of metropolitans in the provincial capitals and subordinate bishops each in his city, the *chef-lieu* of a tribal area, provided tenuous but real links of organization and justice, of art and architecture between the old world and the new. It is no accident that Sidonius Apollinaris, hoping for the survival of the old life, and Remigius, welcoming the harbinger of the new, had chosen the episcopal career. There is point in citing at the end of my lecture the Carolingian Walafrid Strabo, to set by strange coincidence alongside the Asian Strabo that I cited at the beginning:

> Felix Gallia, fortibus tropaeis,
> Ubertate soli, virum nitore,
> Regni nomine purpurata magno,
> Romanae soror urbis atque consors

and, as he adds a few lines later:

> omne Galliarum
> Regnum de nece martyrum coronans.

BIBLIOGRAPHICAL NOTE

Original Authorities

Texts. There are few authors, Greek or Latin, from at least the second century B.C. onwards, who do not mention Gaul somewhere. Five authors, however, stand out, as devoting themselves on a large scale to its history, anthropology, administration, etc. Most are accessible with text and English translation in the *Loeb Classical Library* (Authors included there are italicized).

1. Posidonius of Apamea, *flor.* 70 B.C., devoted important parts of his *Histories* to Gaul, in which he had travelled. They are now only extant in fragments (collected in Jacoby's *Fragmente der Griechischen Historiker,* iiA 87), but were largely used by *Caesar* (evidently, though not explicitly) and by *Strabo* (*flor.* 10 A.D.) for his account of Gaul in Book iv of his *Geography.*

2. *C. Iulius Caesar* wrote his commentaries on his Gallic campaigns (*de Bello Gallico,* i-vii. Gallic religion, organization, etc., are particularly treated in Book vi) probably in the winter 52–51 B.C. An eighth book, describing the final campaign of 51 B.C., was added by A. Hirtius. In addition to the Loeb edition, there is a translation (without Latin text) by S. A. Handford in the *Penguin Classics.*

3. Among incidental references to Gaul, there are accounts of the rebellions of 21 and 70 A.D. (with the abortive proposals for an *imperium Galliarum* in the latter year) in the *Annals* and *Histories* of *Tacitus.* Penguin classics have translations of *Annals* (Michael Grant) and *Histories* (Kenneth Wellesley).

4. There are numerous references to Gallic affairs in the *History* of *Ammianus Marcellinus* (*flor.* 390 A.D.). In Book xv there is important matter on Gallic administration, national character and ethnology, the last mainly from Timagenes of Alexandria (*flor.* 20 B.C.).

5. The transition between Roman and Frankish Gaul forms the substance of the first two books of Gregory of Tours, *Historia Francorum* (*flor.* 575 A.D.). There is an English translation by O. M. Dalton (Oxford, 1927).

Inscriptions

Complete collections up to the time of publication are to be found in *Corpus Inscriptionum Latinarum,* vols. xii (Narbonensis—Berlin, 1888) and xiii (Tres Galliae et Germaniae—Berlin, 1899–1916). Supplements have been produced by E. Espérandieu, *Inscriptions latines de la Narbonnaise* (1929) and P. Wuilleumier, *Inscriptions latines des Trois Gaules* (1963). Celtic inscriptions are collected in G. Dottin, *La Langue gauloise* (1918).

Any Gallic name, whether of place or person, has appended to it all the literary and inscriptional references in the *Alt-keltische Sprachschatz* of A. Holder, 1896.

Sculpture. The photographic record commenced by E. Espérandieu, *Recueil des bas-Reliefs, statues et bustes de la Gaule romaine* is being continued by R. Lantier (early volumes reprinted). A useful selection, with new photographs, appears in *The Art of Roman Gaul* by Pobe and Rouhier, London, 1961.

New discoveries are regularly announced in the periodicals *Gallia* and *Revue des Etudes anciennes*. A record of site finds is being shown on the *Carte archéologique de la Gaule romaine* (in progress).

Modern Works

Virtually all studies of Roman Gaul depend on Camille Jullian's magnificent *Histoire de la Gaule* in eight volumes, completed in 1926, which takes the story from the earliest times to the revolt of Eugenius in 394 A.D.

There is a somewhat quaint pro-Gallic nationalism running through the whole work, and Jullian was not very well equipped to understand purely archaeological evidence. Nevertheless, for its sensitive use of texts, both literary and inscriptional, it remains a magistral study, truly entitling its author to a chair among the 'Immortals' of the *Académie française*.

The archaeological material is—somewhat unevenly—supplied by the *Archeologie gallo-romaine* of A. Grenier (1931–1960; Grenier died before its completion).

English readers will find O. Brogan, *Roman Gaul* (1953) of value, not least for its bibliography. Recent French studies, all more or less popular, but all good, are P.-M. Duval, *La Vie Quotidienne en Gaule* (1953); H. P. Eydoux, *Monuments et Tresors de la Gaule* (1958) and *La France antique* (1962); and J. J. Hatt, *Histoire de la Gaule romaine* (1959). There are many recent local monographs of value, of which may be singled out Edith Whiteman, *The Treveri* (1970) (particularly important since *Augusta Treverorum* (Trier) was the virtual capital of the Roman Empire in the West for much of the fourth century); P.-M. Duval, *Paris antique* (1961); R. Etienne, *Bordeaux antique* (1962) and M. Labrousse, *Toulouse antique* (1968). A valuable contribution to the very difficult study of Gallic religion and the impact on it of the Roman empire is P. Lamprechts' *Contributions à l'étude des divinités celtiques* (Bruges, 1942). For the transition from the Roman empire to the Frankish kingdoms, the most important study is Lot, Pfister and Ganshof, *Les Destinées de l'empire en occident de 395 a 888* (2nd edn., 2 vols., 1940).

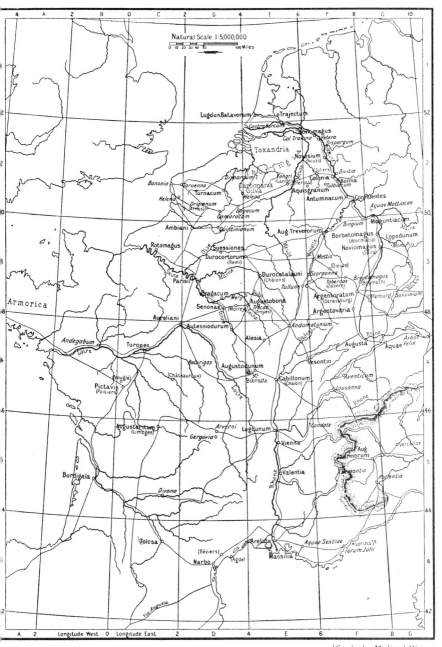

GAUL IN THE FIFTH CENTURY

J. M. WALLACE-HADRILL

Frankish Gaul

———◄>✦◉✦◄—————

W ho were the Franks, 'the underwriters of Roman
Gaul'? They were a group of West German tribes
from across the Rhine, tribes that had been in contact with Roman civilization for centuries, the trusted soldiers of
successive emperors. They were good soldiers, especially on foot,
and clever in making and using arms (we know exactly what sort);
they were good husbandmen, too; in brief, no fools. The only
strange thing about them is that they were not Christians years
before they set foot in Gaul; but such is the fact. Notice, further,
that even combined with all the Visigoths and other barbarians,
their numbers can have been only a small fraction of the total
population of Gaul; and that they had neither the desire nor the
means to resist the process of Romanization. They wanted to be
Gallo-Romans, though in actual fact they became French; not,
however, overnight, for what follows Gaul is not immediately
France but sub-Roman Gaul, and sub-Roman it remains throughout certainly the first 150 years of Merovingian rule, and perhaps
beyond. It is a society to which, a century after the coming of
Clovis and his Franks, Gregory of Tours does not deem it
necessary to explain what he means by *civitas*, *pagus*, *territorium*,
vicus, *villa*, *exactor*, *fiscus*, *indiculus*, *privilegium*, *rescriptum*, *testa-
mentum*: the administrative shape of Frankish Gaul is sub-Roman,
and it uses the old Latin terms sometimes inaccurately but never
with any sense of constraint. And what is true of Frankish Gaul
in the narrow sense (the greater part, that is, of old *Gallia Comata*)
is true also of Burgundian Gaul and Visigothic Gaul. All three
are sub-Roman and the differences between them have more to do
with degrees of Romanization than of barbarization. All three,
moreover, are held together, however loosely, by common
experience of the forms of Roman rule, most particularly as
expressed by Roman Law. For this reason, and because I think

it too often neglected, I propose to pay rather more attention to Gallo-Frankish law and its social implications than you may consider altogether usual.

Look at this sub-Roman society as it appears in its most famous legal pronouncement, *Lex Salica*, the Salic Law. This Law is transmitted to us in no very good shape, but it is more than a fair guess that it gives a true, if partial, picture of how the Salian Franks ordered their lives in sixth-century Gaul. (The Law does not apply only to northern Gaul, but is binding on Salian Franks wherever they may live in the *Regnum Francorum*, by the banks of the Loire or deep in the Ardennes, as well as in the Paris basin.)

Lex Salica reveals not a mobile, pastoral but a settled, agricultural society, far advanced from the Germanic world of Tacitus. The Franks are farmers. They are not simple cattle-raisers but owners of orchards, cornfields, beanfields, lentil-fields, vineyards. They are concerned about the inviolability of standing corn, about the cutting of hay and rights over fishing, and they know something about what medievalists would call 'vert and venison'; they have adapted themselves to the *villa*-economy of a Roman province, and that over a wide area. The Gallo-Roman *villa* survives: the Romano-British does not. What consequences may not flow from this vital distinction? But to return to our law, the assumptions of *Lex Salica* are peaceful, not warlike. Nor is this surprising when we remember that, for all their paganism, the Franks were no savages; they were *foederati* with a long experience of Roman ways and a taste for Roman things. The grave of their chieftain Childeric, buried at Tournai in 482, contained possessions that suggest the successful business man as much as the ruthless warrior. His followers were not wild horsemen, like Attila's Huns, but for the most part plodding foot-soldiers. We have their graves by the score, where they lie quite often cheek by jowl with Gallo-Romans. It is difficult, at this remove of time, to appreciate that the vendetta (the normal Germanic way of settling differences arising from bloodshed) was not the law of the jungle but a duty regulated by custom that one owed to the community for the maintenance of order (the phrase is Miss Whitelock's). It was horribly bloodthirsty and not very efficient; it was even rather wasteful; but it was all that the Germanic tribesmen had till, as in the case of those who settled in Gaul, they had had time to learn other and better ways from their hosts. But if the first Franks were rather tamer than Gregory of Tours believed, the Gallo-Romans were not all aristocrats like Sidonius. We use the term 'Gallo-Roman' to describe a mixed society already highly barbarized before the Franks arrived in Gaul. Their *villae*, to say nothing of their towns, had long been crying out for more men, more labour, and there cannot have been much forcible dispossession of Gallo-Roman gentry to make room for the Franks. One reason for accepting the social implications of *Lex Salica* is that they are also the implications of archaeology and of place-name study. They all three point to the peaceful absorption into the countryside (the Celtic, Roman countryside) of one more group of tribes, soldiers at a pinch and better led than the Goths south of the Loire, but essentially farmers.

Yet there is more to *Lex Salica* than this. It is full, too, of assumptions about government. Of these, one, though not perhaps the first, is that there is a king, the *Rex Francorum* (*caput populi* Avitus called him), the ruler of all free men who acknowledge him, whether of German or Latin stock. He is still a war-leader who keeps about him a devoted body of henchmen, his antrustions. These not only protect him with their lives but are the nucleus of his field-force. In return for their devotion, he provides for their upkeep and protects their lives with a specially heavy *wergeld*, or man-price. In one form or another, the antrustions remain at the king's side to the end of this period. However, the kings who sanctioned *Lex Salica* liked Gallo-Romans as well as Franks, for their company also included a type of antrustion classified as *Romanus homo, conviva regis*. The Frankish king's authority as a judge is direct and far-reaching; non-attendance at his court, or at the courts of his officials, is a serious matter—it costs 15 *solidi*; his officials (laymen, as under the Empire) issue *cartae de rege* for those who wish to move from their land; before him come those who have accusations to make against their fellows, and it proves expensive if the accusation is false; before the king, freedom is bought; a count who fails in his duty to those he governs will be punished, unless excused on the ground of royal business. Moreover, the king can delegate his authority to counts and other officials who rule, much as in Roman times over the *civitates* and districts (*pagi*), but he is clearly expected to resume that authority as and when he wishes. What is the basis of all this power? It is, quite simply, wealth—and wealth far in excess of any rival's. It is both landed wealth and wealth in the form of movable treasure, amassed by taxation, confiscation, subsidies, bribes and plain loot. Numismatists tell us that the gold coinage of the earlier Merovingians is of excellent quality. The landed wealth is the old imperial fisc in Gaul, an enormous area of scattered estates that only centuries of alienation in the shape of lavish gifts seriously reduced. But the point is this: the distinctive features of royal Frankish power, as they are revealed or implied in *Lex Salica*, do not come direct from the forests of Germany but are for the most part indigenous to Late Roman Gaul. Here is no mystique of barbarian kingship. I do not for a moment suppose that Clovis knew his own genealogy further back than his great-grandfather, if so far. His prestige rested on his unique achievement of seizing the kingdoms of Syagrius and Alaric, northern and southern Gaul, and then ruling them much in the way they were used to. *Lex Salica* may not be recognizable as a piece of Roman Law, but it is unthinkable without a Roman background.

In the course of the seventh century, and probably in its first half, a certain Marculf, who labels himself 'least and vilest of all monks', made a collection of documents, royal and other, and presented the resulting formulary to a bishop Landericus. He did not mean it to be useful for scribes nor, he says, was it meant for clever men, skilled in composition; it was merely *ad exercenda initia puerorum*. Marculf clearly had access to important deposits of documents, perhaps in the Paris region. There is no evidence that he had access to the Merovingian court itself and he certainly did not regard his collection as in any sense officially sponsored; and this makes it the more remarkable as evidence of royal authority in the century after Clovis' death. Marculf divides his ninety-two documents into two books, which he calls *cartae regales* and *cartae pagenses*. The former, taken as a whole, leaves the impression that the Merovingian kings were even stronger than they had formerly been. They corroborate the picture that the historian Fredegarius gives of King Dagobert on one of his great tours of justice; his coming into Burgundy, writes the historian, caused profound alarm among the bishops and magnates, though his justice brought joy to the poor; neither bribes nor respect of persons influenced him, and for a time he neither ate nor slept lest anyone, rich or poor, should leave his presence without having obtained justice. Fredegarius did not love Dagobert and I doubt if he exaggerates common report here. But to return to Marculf, the tone as well as the format of his *cartae regales* is Roman, not Germanic. We learn from them how a duke or patrician or count was appointed; what provision was to be made for royal agents on the king's business; how a *beneficium* was granted, under the royal hand; how a man became an antrustion; how royal permission was given for receiving the clerical tonsure; the conditions under which royal *missi* were sent to supervise the division of land; how slaves were freed in the royal presence; how royal protection or *mundeburdium* was granted to those who sought it; how a bishop could be ordered to give up property to which he had no right; how a count could be ordered to enforce the restoration of lands unjustly seized; how a rebel was deprived of his possessions and pursued; and how the count assembled all free men from his *civitates*, *vici* and *castella* to swear fidelity, before the Merovingian *missi*, to a new royal prince. Certain cases could be terminated by oath in the royal chapel, on St Martin's cloak (the greatest Christian relic of Roman Gaul appropriated by the Frankish kings); and we are given the prologue, very grandiloquent, to a royal judgement. Throughout, the accent is on judgement, decision, action; the king, *in palatio nostro*, is a very busy man, constantly being sought out by suitors from all over his kingdom. 'Le roi, lorsqu'il juge', wrote Fustel, 'est toujours chez lui', and it would be equally true to say that when a weakling or a minor reigned, there was still this need for royal action that somehow or other went on being expressed in legal forms and official documents. Perhaps the most characteristic sort of Merovingian document is the concession or the confirmation issued in the form of a judgement. Landowners of all kinds will come to the king and beg him to confirm in writing his gift, or that of his ancestors, or even that of a third party; and this is done because it is worth doing. The power of the royal *palatium* is a reality that can be made to be felt not only through its writing-office but through its control over royal officers everywhere. There is no count and no bishop who may not find himself summoned to explain his conduct to the king personally or to surrender to the king in his court a case, civil or criminal, in which the king has decided to show interest. All this, however, takes place against a background of the steady giving-away of royal estates to the church and other beneficiaries that increases snowball-wise as the centuries pass. Lands so given remained as a rule directly under royal protection; the count and his officers were excluded from them; they enjoyed, in brief, immunity. Judicially, and often fiscally, the immunist is himself the substitute of the count, though not of the king. But not all royal gifts were grants of vast Roman *villae* (and the Gallo-Roman variety were vast) to churches; a smaller, but very significant, kind of gift, made in lieu of a stipend, was a direct descendant of the old Roman concession of land made for the same reason. A landowner —it might be a king or a church or a lay magnate—would make a grant of land to a follower (a *miles* or *bucellarius*, perhaps, or a *fidelis* or *amicus*). The grant was freely bestowed without any sort of contract; it was revocable and lasted just so long as the service of which it was payment lasted. Strictly speaking, it was a benefice in return for service, the beneficiary being further tied to the donor by the personal bond of fidelity. That there is little written evidence of these concessions *in stipendio* is probably to be explained by the fact that they would as a rule have been bestowed verbally. But here at all events seems to lie the root of that union of land-as-salary and faithful service in return that a later age was to generalize in use. It is, if you like, incipient feudalism—but of a kind that only increases the power of its practitioners: the king can pay his bodyguard or *amici* in land, but he can, and does, get it back again. His estates are not permanently the poorer.

Now, it would be wrong to give the impression that Merovingian Gaul was ever a close-knit administrative or political unit, or that its kings ever commanded sufficient resources to enforce their will everywhere at the same time; it is the lack of efficient administration rather than the presence of it, that first strikes historians. Undeniably the Merovingians could never have run Gaul at all without leaning heavily, like their Roman predecessors, on the local authority of magnates, lay and ecclesiastical; and there was always a tendency for local families to assume local public office if possible, and to make it hereditary. But a tendency is only a tendency, and when all is said and done, one must take account of Merovingian success, not simply in settling a shattered Roman province but in quietly assuming so many of its forms of government: the *palatium* and its officials, including the *maior domus*, are Roman; and so are the form and language of the documents they issue, the *civitas* and *pagus* and their officers, the occasional municipal *curia* with its senators, the taxation they vainly try to perpetuate, and much of the justice they mete out. ('The judicial system of the Merovingians', writes Dill, 'paid slight heed to old German ideas of justice'.) But above all, the Merovingian church is Roman; its diocesan boundaries, coterminous with the *civitates*, have been disturbed hardly at all by the Germanic settlers; its bishops, so far from disappearing like those of the Romano-British church, remain to deepen their control over provincial administration (many a Merovingian bishop's *Vita* could be cited in illustration); and if, on the one hand, the Merovingians will stand no nonsense from men they have appointed to positions of terrible power, on the other hand the smooth transition from Gaul to France owes infinitely much to unbroken episcopal rule. The Gallo-Roman episcopate, without entering into the inmost recesses of the Frankish *comitatus*, does, so to say, groom the new barbarians for their rôle of underwriters of Gallo-Roman civilization; and in return, to its enormous landed possessions the Merovingians are willing to make additions for nearly three centuries. Only towards the end of this long time do they find it necessary to take back something of what they had given, by regranting church lands to their warriors—a makeshift that the early Carolingians were greatly to develop. Unlike the Carolingians, however, the Merovingians did safeguard some of their rights over churches, and what affords them a certain independence of the church is not barbarian aloofness but a sense of being heirs to a Roman administration still run by secular officials and backed by the resources of innumerable estates.

I said that the legal assumptions of *Lex Salica* and, still more, of Marculf's formulary, were Roman. But in what way are they Roman? They plainly have nothing in common with classical Roman Law, the Law of the Republic and of the Empire in its prime. Their background is Vulgar, not classical Law, but it is still inescapably Roman. For example, the barbarian law of possession or seisin can now be shown to be derived from the Vulgar Roman law of *possessio*, and this is only one of many instances within the Law of Property where what was once thought Germanic, just because it was not classical Roman, can now be proved to be not Germanic at all. The idea of unrestricted donation is Roman and so, too, is the structure of the transaction for the transfer of property. Something of all this the Franks must have absorbed when they first settled as neighbours of the *coloni* on the Roman *villae* north of the Loire, if they had not already done so much earlier; but one obvious effect of the conquest of Visigothic Gaul by Clovis and his sons was to open the north more fully to the Roman legal usages of the south. Roman Law schools still existed in Aquitaine (the Clermont school still flourished in the seventh century) and their resources had enabled Alaric II to produce a Roman law-book with some claim to style and subtlety. It is real law-making. Alaric's book lies behind the law-giving of the Burgundians in eastern Gaul, and it was known and used by Romans in the north. Even as early as 596, the Frankish King Childebert is borrowing from the *Lex Romana Burgundionum* for a famous decree that survives as an addendum to *Lex Salica*. But this is a technical matter which I mention in passing merely to serve as a warning against putting any trust in the theory of a sharp break with the Roman background of Frankish Gaul. The Franks may well have misunderstood and failed to use much of what they found of government and administration in Gaul, but they certainly brought no alternative with them. Their rule was Roman-derivative.

Some notable changes occur in the years that follow the death of the great King Dagobert. From the late seventh century onwards we are among the 'rois fainéants' who, for one reason and another, can no longer make their power felt practically, although it is still often expressed theoretically in traditional forms. Family degeneracy may have played its part in the failure of the Merovingians, but the historian will do better to focus his attention on their lack of means. For one thing, the giving away of royal estates was beginning to tell, and, for another, the *teloneum*, the Roman tax on commerce that made the early Merovingians so rich in movable wealth, was drying up with the Mediterranean trade that fed it. The later Merovingians had less land and less money than had their predecessors and consequently their power was less felt and less relied on. What were the consequences? First, that the prestige of kingship suffered, and was not made good by the early Carolingians, despite their attempt to bolster it with sacerdotal pomp. Secondly, with this deflation went a drying-up of the supply of trained officials, secular and ecclesiastical, and the consequent need of the crown to develop emergency measures to ensure any sort of administration; and here we should be on our guard against tales of the extraordinary initiative of the early Carolingians, and particularly of Charlemagne, in overhauling and centralizing Frankish government. They were men of personal authority and power but not of administrative genius; in most respects Charlemagne's reign marks no sharp break in the story of the development of Frankish government within Francia. The significant domestic achievement of the early Carolingians was the reduction of the Roman Midi, a world of which the Frank had hitherto had only occasional direct experience. This reduction cannot be laid wholly at the door of the Arab invaders from Spain, for you have only to turn to Fredegarius to read of repeated raids by Charles Martel and Pippin III into the Midi, when towns were sacked, walls demolished, people driven away and the vineyards and countryside laid waste. Nothing approaching this systematic penetration had ever been undertaken by the Merovingians, who were generally content with control of those Mediterranean *civitates* from which came wealth and the good things of life. This reduction, however, was economic rather than political. No barbarian ruler, whether Merovingian or Carolingian, could have devised a means of keeping the men of the Midi under permanent control; they lived, as they had always lived, their own lives under the forms bequeathed to them by Rome.

Let me now move on half a century, to a time of great change. In the year 843, a lady named Dhuoda, wife of Bernard, marquis of Septimania, addressed a letter to her son William, urging on him the importance of fidelity towards his lord the king, to whom he had, or should have, commended himself. It is an enlightening document and I will give you part of it (the translation is Philip Grierson's):

'An admonition relating to your lord.
Since God, as I believe, and your father Bernard have chosen you, in the flower of your youth, to serve Charles as your lord, I urge you ever to remember the record of your family, illustrious on both sides, and not to serve your master simply to satisfy him outwardly, but to maintain towards him and his service in all things a devoted and certain fealty both of body and soul. . . . That is why, my son, I exhort you to maintain

faithfully all that is in your charge, with all your strength of body and soul, as long as your life shall last. . . . May the madness of infidelity be ever far from you; may evil never find such a place in your heart as to render you unfaithful to your lord in any matter whatsoever. . . . But I do not fear this on your part or on the part of those that serve with you. . . . Therefore, my son William, you who are of our blood, show yourself towards your lord, as I have already urged, true, vigilant, useful and most prompt to his service. In every matter which concerns the power and welfare of the King, both within the kingdom and without, show that wisdom with which God has plentifully endowed you. Read the lives and words of the holy men of former times, and you will find there how to serve your lord and be faithful to him in all things. And when you receive his commands, apply yourself faithfully to execute them. Observe also and regard carefully those who show the greatest fidelity and assiduity in his service, and learn of them the way in which to act.'

Now, it has been said that the interesting things about this letter are the religious character of the vassal's oath of fealty (or fidelity) to his lord, and the fact that the lady is only urging her son to behave to the king exactly as any vassal would behave to any *senior* (or lord). What I find strange about the letter is the possibility, repeatedly harped on, of unfealty, *infidelitas* (the word is used more than once); a great man's son needs such a warning at the outset of his career. *Fidelity* can be dug out of the lives and words of the old holy men: *infidelity*, not fidelity, is the new general feature of social relationships under the Carolingians. How did this come about?

The late eighth and ninth centuries are the era of Viking attacks along the entire length of the Frankish coastline and deep into the interior, up the rivers. The people of Gaul had always been sensitive about attack from the sea; Sidonius was most perturbed about the Saxon sea-pirates and thought that even the Visigothic settlers in Aquitaine were better than no protection. But the Viking danger was more formidable, because more continuous. We know very well of monastic communities uprooted or destroyed by the plunderers, but the monkish historians were not concerned to explain what became of the countryside and of its villages and manors. Yet there is enough evidence to let us guess at widespread local dislocation. For example, in the Toulonnais the old boundaries between properties were no longer recognizable; at Vontes, in Touraine, five men of servile rank 'could have the land if there were peace'; at Martigny, many men were recorded as having neither wives nor families; in the Limousin and Burgundy, whole villages were abandoned by people seeking safety in the hills. The fear of destruction seems to have been almost as devastating as destruction itself. At all events, the effect of the two was to depopulate the countryside and allow good agricultural land to lapse; and to these should be added the effects of what looks, now and again, like scorched earth policy. Small wonder that Marc Bloch sums up the demographic problems of the age in the phrase 'absence de densité'. For at the very time when, because of troubles in the Mediterranean world, land was becoming increasingly the one possession worth having, its defence and its upkeep became more difficult than before. More men than ever were seeing the necessity of seeking a lord's protection, not, as in Roman times, against an exacting State but against attack and insecurity; and this protection, in its turn, was seen as part of a contract (since free men were involved) highly personal in its nature and based on the working and protection of land. Nothing is implied as to the relations of either lord or man to the king; it is simply the natural drawing-together and extension of two things that have been known since Roman times: the lord-man relationship and the holding of land in return for service. The king can do little, for he lacks the means to defend all his people everywhere at the same time; they must look after themselves against a menace the chief characteristic of which is that it is irregular, unpredictable. The king has enough to do looking after his own without bothering about other people's property. As the West is attacked, so it becomes intensely local in its outlook. The attacks of the ninth century did not unite Frankish Gaul; by their very nature they dissipated effort and compelled men to concentrate on the local, not on the national, aspects of their tribulations. There was no continental King Alfred.

Though the Carolingians took more notice of the general peril and more steps to combat it than is sometimes thought, their chief concern was a weakness that had nothing to do with the Vikings, namely, the dispersal of royal estates by the later

Merovingians, the virtual impossibility of reclaiming them and the difficulty of adding to them. These estates, the fisc, were not primarily a source of movable wealth to the kings; much, we know, was rough and uncultivated land. The great value of the fisc was as a reservoir for the rewarding of followers and the endowment of churches. The crown generally lost nothing tangible when an alienation was made; but what it did do, apart from lowering the reservoir, was in effect to invite the recipient to extend the privileges of his new immunity over all his other possessions; and this did involve loss to the crown. When the later Merovingians made presents of domains of the fisc, mostly to churches, they did so unconditionally. The gifts were absolute even if the kings still kept some kind of judicial control within them. The Carolingians not only had more trouble in keeping such control but failed to keep clear the distinction between land given as a personal reward and land given as salary for public office held temporarily; the two kinds tended to be fused, and here was the basis of the great territorial principalities of the Middle Ages. This last, I think, more than outweighs the benefit of the Carolingian resolve never, if they could help it, to grant away their lands unconditionally but always to leave a loophole for reclaiming them as royal.

The Carolingians started their career in possession not only of the rump of the Merovingian fisc but also of their own huge estates in north-east Francia and the Rhineland. Together, these constituted a formidable property—formidable not only in extent but in wealth: no estates were better worth having than those of the Meuse and Moselle valleys, to say nothing of the Rhine. So long as the Carolingians could hold this nucleus together they were safe, if not very safe. They had not the vast landed superiority of the earlier Merovingians but they were better off than anyone else, except the Church. (The Church had been despoiled by Charles Martel and others who needed land quickly for their armed retainers, but it was still richer than any layman.) The first two Carolingian kings succeeded in keeping intact their estates north of the Loire, and indeed added to them by a policy of conquest and clearings. In Alemannia, Thuringia, Frisia and Saxony we read of the estates of defeated kings or magnates *fisci ditionibus redactae*. I do not say that this was the purpose of the foreign expeditions of Pippin III and Charlemagne but only that it was one outcome of them. Constant exertion and vigilance (the hall-mark of the Carolingians) kept these new estates under royal control, but it was a struggle. When we reach Louis the Pious, the struggle is abandoned. Louis adds nothing by conquest to the patrimony, though, on the other hand, he is notoriously generous and willing to grant away property with inadequate safeguards for its return; this is the beginning of the end of Carolingian power, such as it was, and we can watch it happening. Thegan, one of Louis' biographers, writes that the emperor was generous to the point that 'he would give outright to his faithful men royal *villae* that had been his, his father's and his grandfather's'; and, what is more, he actually restored the properties that his father had confiscated from the Frisians and Saxons. Finally, he renounced all claims on Church lands as a means of endowing his vassals. In reversing the domainal policy of his dynasty he was, very largely, following the behests of the Church, and his action should not be condemned outright as a piece of lunacy; his is a difficult reign to understand and nobody has yet written a good book on it or him. Nonetheless, his contemporaries recognized that, from reasons however pressing, Louis the Pious had seri-ously reduced his territorial heritage, had renounced the obvious means of increasing it, and had, at a time of mounting social crisis, increased tension and instability. He had done more: by reducing his means of action, he had reduced his capacity to intervene as a matter of course in the affairs of what may be called provincial France. Stability, the assurance of unbroken control and of unchanging lordship, was the backbone of fidelity, the bond that really held men together; and this the emperor seriously weakened. And so we get back to the problem that worried the lady Dhuoda: why were men less faithful than they had once been?

How to ensure fidelity had been Charlemagne's principal worry, no less vital than the problem of holding together the royal estates; and the same problem of fidelity was becoming the principal worry of all landowners, great and small, throughout the Carolingian world. Uprooted communities, dispossession, insecurity, all tended to make men (armed men and men who could work land) worth more to the landowner than ever before; lordship had to be made attractive; yet a bond that could so easily and so eagerly be entered upon, with whatever public solemnity, could equally be broken by the forces that brought it into being.

The lord whose protection was worth having one day might look less formidable than his neighbour not long after; and there might be better land to work and better terms of service somewhere else. This is the sort of thing that made for social instability and also, increasingly, instability in government. It has often, and rightly, been said that the apex of the Carolingian social structure, the makeshift structure that faced the Vikings and Magyars and Arabs, was the bond of personal service and fidelity, particularly as developed in the *vassi dominici*, the vassals of the lord king and of nobody else, devoted fighting men who looked for a homestead (*casa*) as their pay, and who, if they did not get it, would look elsewhere. More and more reliable fighting men on horseback were needed, and this was the only way of getting them and holding them: they had to be *casati*, given homesteads, settled. Once they were installed and had their land, and knew the terms of their military service, and had expressed their allegiance contractually in the most binding of oaths, the assumption was that the bond so established would never be broken; in fact, of course, it often was. But Charlemagne did more than bind men to himself in this way and use them everywhere on his service; he recognized the existence of the same bond of lord and vassal throughout society, and he encouraged it so long as it made for more obedience to him. The last clause of a famous Capitulary (No. 64) reads: 'Concerning ordinary folk (*de vulgari populo*), let each man so control his dependants that they shall the better obey and accept the imperial orders and decrees.' Once again, in the good Roman tradition, those with actual power over the countryside are being dragooned into responsibility for the public duties and burdens of those who follow them. There is not yet much risk from that infinite shifting-off of responsibility and multiplication of loyalties that marked the advent of subinfeudation. The king knew where power lay and could still, by vigilance, control it reasonably well. Again and again his Capitularies insist on the need for fidelity, especially to him; again and again his *missi* or special agents go out into the countryside to take the oaths of all free men. It is still possible to insist that all free men stand in a personal relationship to their king, and there is no provincial dynasty great enough to prevent this for long; but it is becoming more and more difficult to assert.

I do not propose to attempt a definition of the various terms

49

in which this age expressed its social obligations and rights; they change and shift and will not be pinned down; but one, at least, cannot be avoided—vassalage. Anyone commended to his lord for the purpose of fighting is, by the ninth century, a *vassus* or vassal; the word, originally Celtic, had long since lost its pejorative sense of humble domestic service, but vassalage could still seem very burdensome and unwelcome to some great men. The best way of getting the feel of the word to the Carolingians is to take an example. A good one is provided in a letter from Archbishop Hincmar of Rheims to the future Emperor Louis the German. (Hincmar was an acute and powerful politician with an inventive mind, but in this case there is no cause to suspect him.) The letter is the outcome of Louis' decision to invade France and supplant his brother, Charles the Bald. This was frustrated largely through the resistance of the French bishops, led by Hincmar, and in this masterly letter Hincmar explains why they feel no compulsion to answer his summons; they have, he pleads, too little notice to foregather and anyway it is nearly Christmas-time. Instead of coming personally, however, they will send him some advice. First he should remember that one day he will have to face the Lord's judgement, and in the meantime it would be as well to attack the pagans who are devastating Christian lands (and not, by implication, attack his brother). Then follows some very interesting advice on how a good ruler should act, and how to protect his subjects and the Church; he should only employ God-fearing men, and those who defy law and justice should look to themselves. In particular, there should be good administrators of the royal *villae*. Much of this is general advice that would have suited any ninth-century king. But finally there comes this (Odegaard's translation):

'We ought and wish to believe you such that you would not wish to increase your realm at the cost of your soul, nor to receive us as helpers in ecclesiastical affairs and government if we were dishonoured with the loss of the priesthood, as would be the case if, against God and the authority of reason, we should be zealous in commending ourselves and our churches to you—the churches entrusted to us by God are not benefices or property of the king of a kind that he can give them away out of mere whim and without advice—and we bishops consecrated to God are not men of such a kind that we should commend ourselves into vassalage like secular men—we ought not in any way to swear an oath which evangelical and apostolic and canonical authority forbids.'

In other words, Hincmar will not have it that by oath or by any other means bishops or their churches are compelled to serve their kings like other men, because they cannot be vassals in the ordinary sense. They commend themselves and their churches in order to help govern ecclesiastical affairs, and that is all. In this case, no military help was forthcoming—which is what Louis really wanted. Hincmar seems to have got away with it, though other churchmen, before as well as after, were less lucky, and he himself seemed to withdraw his definition. The point is, that vassalage is seen as the vital relationship in a landed society geared to battle, though it is still fluid enough for a bishop to give a public lesson to a king on what it does and does not imply. Reading between the lines of the letter, it can be seen that royal vassals, whether or not Hincmar was right about the bishops, are important men who may be called on to bring armed help to the king, for they have formidable followings of their own. Military service is mediatized.

It would be wrong to give the impression that the Carolingians (at least to Charles the Bald) were so taken up with the implications of vassalage, to say nothing of worries over their fisc, that they had no time or strength for the traditional public duties of their office. This is a field in which they are less powerful than the Merovingians; but their writ does, so to say, run. The doing of justice is still a main concern of the earlier Carolingians. *Magna* or *alta justitia*, the major pleas or pleas of blood, are still reserved for the count in his court and, under Charlemagne at least, are not granted to the count as a personal reward; nor, as an immunist in his own right, would a count hold these pleas. It is for the immunist, whoever he is, to present persons involved in major pleas to the count in his court, though he will keep the minor pleas for himself. In distinguishing so clearly between major and minor pleas (and indeed in somewhat rearranging local courts to take account of this) the early Carolingians were delimiting what rights of justice the crown must expect to surrender to immunists and what rights were to be retained if at all possible.

The distinction lasts through the Middle Ages. The practical difficulty was, of course, to keep any sort of control over the count himself. Charlemagne leaned heavily on the services of friends and relations from Austrasian Francia, though even these proved hard to handle and harder to replace; an official could not be prevented from identifying himself and his family with the locality where his work lay. This, the control of counts, is the true measure of the power of government under the Carolingians; it is much more important than the high-sounding terms of the Carolingian Capitularies or the antiquarian zest of the age for writing-up and misunderstanding the old barbarian laws. The Carolingians really end with a burst of Byzantine splendour at the court of Charles the Bald in the mid-ninth century; but outside that court circle (which certainly satisfied one of the contemporary requirements of kingship) there was not much left.

Two great partition-treaties in the ninth century, Verdun and Meersen, dealt the final blow to the royal Frankish fisc. Their principal object was to provide a share of fiscal territory for each of the Carolingian brothers with a claim to any. To do such a thing was to carry out a major operation on the great Austrasian nucleus of fiscal lands that still survived; it was necessary but there was no other justification for it. The commissioners entrusted with the division went about their work with very great care and only after much preparation; it was not the extent of the lands (and the dioceses) they were splitting that worried them, but their value. When the partitions had taken place, Austrasia was destroyed and Lorraine artificially created. The brothers had their shares and out of them had to satisfy the demands of their supporters for rewards and restitutions; but the economic power of the Carolingians was split and ruined for ever. Thereafter, the fiscal lands of Lorraine become the chief bone of contention between the East and West Frankish Carolingians, for there lay the only reserve of lands rich enough to solve their problem of how and where to enfeoff their followers and recoup their losses. It was not the *kingdom* or *duchy* of Lorraine that mattered but the *estates* of Lorraine, from which the first Carolingians had drawn strength.

How did society meet this collapse of kingly power? In the first place, it is plain that no one welcomed it. Nobody wanted to smash kingship, though some did want to displace the Carolin-gians, and in course of time succeeded. Too much is written of the 'greed' of magnates whose incessant demands increased Carolingian worries and distracted attention from the Vikings, for the magnates were placed in much the same position as their kings; they, too, had followers clamouring for land, and not enough land to give them. Nor should we be surprised at the great areas of land thought necessary to sustain comparatively few people, when we remember what the fate of that land for several generations had been; as always, it was its actual yield that men had to take into account, not acreage. So, all down the social scale men bargained and fought for land. Probably the most successful bargainers were the men who managed to establish their dynasties in what, in effect, were independent territorial principalities; their growth, and the decline of royal power, are the most obvious features of French society in the late ninth and tenth centuries.

A territorial principality in this sense has been defined as a place where the king intervenes only by permission, or from which, in other words, the immunist has power to exclude the king when he wishes. This may place too much emphasis on the will of the immunist whose first object, after all, was not in-subordination; it might be better to say that the king was generally content, in such cases, to leave the immunist free to run his principality as best he could on his own resources. If the king gained no prestige from this exclusion he clearly gained in several practical ways. But in any case the phenomenon of the practical exclusion of the state from the affairs of a great immunity was not new to the ninth century; it is a commonplace of the Later Empire. More interesting is surely the emergence of new families, sustained by these immunities and destined to run France for generations. Great families do not, on the whole, have much luck in permanently establishing themselves before the late ninth century. Not even the royal families of the Dark Ages succeeded in persuading men that they had an inalienable right to go on ruling because some bogus genealogy linked them with Woden or Julius Caesar. The truth, I suspect, about the Merovingians is that they actually succeeded in doing this for two and a half centuries, because that was as long as their wealth lasted; but they were not unique in the West. In every other case it was strength and wealth, not blood at all, that decided the issue of survival, usually in a matter of two or three generations. There was, it has been said, no aristocracy of blood in the Dark Ages, and hence no ancient families. Written genealogies are a game of a later age. Under Charlemagne and Louis the Pious, in the ninth century, a very few such families do succeed in establishing themselves. As a rule they are Frankish intimates of the king, who are sent off to govern some March of the Empire with viceregal powers, and there establish themselves. The dynasty of St William of Toulouse, surrounded with its colonies of Aquitanian vassals, is a case in point. But these are very rare. By the middle of the ninth century family succession to official appointments, especially that of count, becomes fairly widespread. Even if a son does not succeed his father, the succession may be restricted within a group of local families. This happened at Autun. Charles the Bald lost some ground in this way and had to admit the practical claims of heredity in the matter; but he was still strong enough to displace a comital family on occasion with brutal severity, and would never have admitted that he had no business to interfere in the appointment of counts and bishops. To the end of his life his *missi* continue to inspect and visit his *pagi*. By then, eight great principalities had been established in France through the accumulation of *honores*, though some of these did not last for long. Among those that did last were the dynasties of Robert the Strong, who held the counties of Angers, Blois, Touraine, Autun, Auxerre and Nevers, and Baldwin who was count of Ghent, Waas, Ternois and Flanders. These multiple counties, and a consequent reduction in the total number of counts, worked well so long as the fidelity of the few great families could be relied on. Charles the Bald seemed to have no doubt; he was put under no pressure, other than military need, to establish these principalities and did not consider that the crown lost anything in the process. They were a frank acceptance of his own limitations in skilled manpower and resources and a falling-back upon the ancient divisions of Gaul—Aquitaine, Burgundy and Neustria.

Charles' death altered all this, for with him died stability. For a century at least, it is the great marcher dynasties who settle the affairs of the kingdom and dispose of the crown. The accession of the Robertinian Odo marks the first break in the Carolingian succession. The facts are not in dispute; it has always been clear that tenth-century kingship was a hazardous business. But what does this mean? What is the difference between Charles the Bald, the last effective Carolingian, and his successors? It is not that they are much weaker in a material sense, though it is interesting that the wretched Odo found it necessary to spend most of his time in cities and monasteries since his *villae* could not sustain him. It is rather that men have lost confidence in what the king can do; there is no basis for fidelity, no assurance of continuity. The last Carolingians exercise continuous authority in northern France only, and then not everywhere. Their poverty is seen for what it is; and no king ever commanded fidelity for long without the means of rewarding it. Thus it is something negative, not positive, not, above all, the wicked planning of the territorial magnates, that ruins Carolingian monarchy and the last shreds of public administration. Against this tendency the magnates themselves sometimes try to react. Public instruments are still issued by the last Carolingians in the conventional form, and royal charters of attestation, though rare, continue to look impressive; the reason is that the recipients like and value them. But royal rights are slipping away all the time, more and more royal functions are exercised discontinuously or not at all; and once such functions are discontinued they are nearly impossible to resume. It is fair to add that the trouble was not with the personalities of these last Carolingians: they were really quite impressive people. It took some resolution for them to turn once more, against French advice, and in the teeth of German opposition, to the traditional task of winning back the Lotharingian fisc, though it was too late. Also it took resolution to concentrate attention and resources, as they did, on the control of the key-bishopric of Rheims. Readers of Flodoard's *History of the Church of Rheims* will remember that hardly any king of the ninth and early tenth centuries, Carolingian or Robertinian, failed to grasp the tactical importance of Rheims or failed to do all he could to control it.

That vassalage on which Charlemagne had rested his hopes had long since ceased to hold society to its king. Mixed and rapidly changing loyalties, and the stress now laid on the contractual aspect of kingship, acted together to alienate men from the king; between him and them stood the territorial princes and others who had land to give. By the tenth century it is the feoff, the benefice, that looms large in every sort of contract. In practice, the *petit seigneur* no longer thinks of the king as the war-leader, the law-giver or the enforcer of justice; someone much nearer at hand fills these rôles. The local comital dynasties are as secure as the marcher-princes above them. None of this comes about through anyone's planning it, and few indeed could have seen precisely what was happening. No one would have thought—or should have—that vassalage itself had undermined the state; rather it was all that was left when the state disintegrated for the reasons that have been suggested. Odo of Cluny tells how one royal vassal in Auvergne, Gerald of Aurillac, obstinately refused to become a vassal of the duke of Aquitaine because of the faith he owed the king; but even here, in the end, a compromise had to be reached and Gerald, in effect, surrendered.

The vital strand running through Gallo-Frankish society from the fifth to the tenth centuries is the *seigneurie*, the lordship. We start with the Gallo-Roman *seigneurs* of the age of Sidonius Apollinaris, living on their estates among their *coloni*, some of them great landlords, others very small. These are joined by barbarian landlords, Visigoths, Burgundians and finally Franks. Whatever the fate of the *colonus*, the cultivator, and whatever his mother-tongue, he will generally be the man of a lord. In due course, the lord of the sub-Roman colonate will give place to the lord of the Merovingian and the Carolingian immunity (Marc Bloch has shown how this happened). The *seigneurie* remains the effective world of the peasant-cultivator, free or unfree. The problem is, how does the state—that is, the king—come into contact with the *seigneurie*? He does so, most obviously, through the count and the officials of the *civitas* and the *pagi*. As time passes, the count may find it harder to exercise his judicial and other rights within every *seigneurie* of his area; but that will be nothing to the difficulty of the king in keeping control of the count, especially after the count has ceased to be a mere royal official and has become, instead, the local dynast. It is then that loyalties are strained, and while the crown binds men to itself afresh in vassalage and fidelity, these same men expose themselves daily to the charge made by the lady Dhuoda: fidelity is not easy. All the links of control are weak, but none is weaker than the link between count and king. Royal power disintegrated; that is clear; but paradoxically it did so just when it was most needed. There never was any desire to weaken kingship; usurpations of royal authority are the assumption of what the king himself can no longer manage; acts of insubordination are personal, not institutional. Royal power disintegrates not because it is attacked but because it lacks the material means to continue.

No Englishman will make the mistake of underrating the bigness of France; it is a country at all times impatient of centralized control, and geography has not a little to do with it. When to this is added the absence of any conception of centralization as a political or administrative good to be pursued for its own sake, we begin to see how hard it is to fathom the intentions of those who governed France in the Dark Ages.

Huns, Saxons, Franks, Visigoths, Burgundians, Arabs, Vikings: is it not altogether remarkable that France, when she emerged, could still claim to be in so many ways recognizably Roman? Her rulers could not do much; the rule of a Charlemagne, even, was a fragile, personal thing bearing little resemblance to that of a Caesar or a Napoleon; but by taking account of the Roman shape of Gaul they perpetuated it where it most mattered, at the level of the *civitas* (or bishopric) and the *villa*. Their decisions, as recorded by the narrative writers of their time and enshrined often enough in their diplomas, charters and edicts, reflect their acknowledgement that the life of the *civitas* and the *villa* is the life of Gaul.

BIBLIOGRAPHICAL NOTE

For sources, the reader should consult Joseph Calmette, *Le Monde féodale* (rev. Ch. Higounet, 1951, 'Clio' series) and the earlier volumes of Wattenbach's *Deutschlands Geschichtsquellen im Mittelalter* (rev. Levison, Löwe and Buchner, Weimar, 1952–3). The most convenient edition of *Lex Salica* is by H. F. W. D. Fischer in Vol. I of his *Leges Barbarorum* (Leiden, 1948).

The completest survey of Frankish institutions is still that of Fustel de Coulanges, *Histoire des institutions politiques de l'ancienne France* (6 vols., 1888–91, subsequently revised by Camille Jullian; Vol. III, 3rd edn., 1905, is particularly germane to this lecture, though it needs using with caution). More up-to-date studies will be found in Lot, Pfister and Ganshof, *Les Destinées de l'empire en occident de 395 à 888* (2nd edn., 2 vols., 1940); F. Lot, *La Fin du monde antique et le début du moyen âge* (rev. edn., 1951), of which there is an English translation; and E. Salin, *La Civilisation mérovingienne* (4 vols., 1950–9), the last being specially valuable for its assessment of archaeological work, which has been extensive and methodical in recent years. Vols. 5 and 6 of Fliche and Martin, *Histoire de l'Eglise* (1947) cover, in outline, the history of the Frankish church, though reference should also be made to C. de Clercq, *La Législation réligieuse franque de Clovis à Charlemagne* (1936). Mrs. N. K. Chadwick's *Poetry and Letters in Early Christian Gaul* (1955) is stimulating though I think it over-emphasizes the specifically Celtic element as a force in Gallo-Roman literature.

Sir Samuel Dill's *Roman Society in Gaul in the Merovingian Age* (1926) is a classic. It should be read in conjunction with A. Dopsch, *The Economic and Social Foundations of European Civilization* (1937); F. Lot, *Recherches sur la population et la superficie des cités remontant à la période Gallo-Romaine* (4 vols., 1945–53; to be completed for the north of France by F. L. Ganshof); Ch. Verlinden, *Les Origines de la frontière linguistique en Belgique et la colonisation franque* (Brussels, 1955) and the same writer's 'Frankish colonization, a new approach' (*Transactions, Royal Historical Society*, Fifth Series, Vol. 4, 1954) and F. L. Ganshof, 'Manorial organization in the Low Countries in the 7th, 8th and 9th centuries' (*ibid.*, Fourth Series, Vol. XXXI, 1949). J. Boussard, 'Essai sur le peuplement de la Touraine du Ier au VIIIe siècle' (*Le Moyen Age*, LX, 1954) discusses some instances where Franks made their settlements away from Gallo-Roman estates. See also E. Lesne, *Histoire de la propriété ecclésiastique en France* (6 vols., 1910–43) and, for the survival of Roman law in Gaul, Ernst Levy, *West German Vulgar Law* (Philadelphia, 1951) and E. Volterra 'Western Postclassical Schools' (*Cambridge Law Journal*, X, 1949).

The *Cambridge Economic History*, Vols. I and II, contains valuable chapters, notably those of Marc Bloch and Alfons Dopsch in Vol. I. Marc Bloch is also the author of *Les Caractères originaux de l'histoire rurale française* (2nd edn., 1952–6) and of the one great modern study of early medieval society in its prime, *Feudal Society* (trs. L. A. Manyon, 1961). Some of the same problems are ably discussed in F. L. Ganshof's *Feudalism* (trs. by P. Grierson, 1952) and by C. E. Odegaard, *Vassi and Fideles in the Carolingian Empire* (Harvard, 1945). Important recent work by the Spanish historian, C. Sanchez-Albornoz, is summarized in a valuable review by Gautier-Dalché in *Le Moyen Age*, LVII, 1951. H. Pirenne's epoch-making *Mahommed and Charlemagne* (trs. 1939) is still the subject of fruitful controversy, notably in the pages of *Annales*, but must be read for itself.

For the later part of the period, the safest guides are Louis Halphen, *Charlemagne et l'empire carolingien* (1947) and J. Calmette, *L'Effrondrement d'un empire et la naissance d'une Europe* (1941). From a series of remarkable articles by F. L. Ganshof, one only can be picked out: 'Charlemagne et le serment' (*Mélanges Louis Halphen*, 1951). An outstanding example of local study is L. Auzias, *L'Aquitaine carolingienne* (1937), though attention must also be drawn to the articles on the rise of local French dynasties and offices in the ninth and tenth centuries that have been appearing in *Le Moyen Age*. J. Dhondt, *Études sur la naissance des principautés territoriales en France* (Bruges, 1948) is very valuable, and J. W. Thompson's *The Dissolution of the Carolingian Fisc in the Ninth Century* (Berkeley, Cal., 1935) is indispensable though uneven in value. Mention may finally be made of L. Halphen, 'L'Idée d'état sous les Carolingiens' (*Revue Historique*, 185, 1939) and of M. David, 'Le Serment du sacre du IXe au XVe siècle' (*Revue du Moyen Age Latin*, VI, 1950).

Frankish Gaul is surveyed in two chapters of the present writer's *The Barbarian West*, 400–1000 (3rd rev. ed., 1967) and detailed aspects of its social problems are considered in his 'The work of Gregory of Tours in the light of modern research' (*Transactions, Royal Hist. Soc.,* Fifth Series, Vol. I, 1951) and 'Archbishop Hincmar and the authorship of Lex Salica' (*Revue d'Histoire du Droit,* XX, 1952) (both reprinted, with other matter, in *The Long-Haired Kings,* 1962, together with an expanded version of the present paper).

ADDITIONAL BIBLIOGRAPHY (1970)

An authoritative introduction to Merovingian history is now G. Tessier, *Le Baptême de Clovis* (Paris, 1964); F. L. Ganshof's *Frankish Institutions under Charlemagne* (1968) is indispensable; H. Fichtenau, *The Carolingian Empire* (trs. by P. Munz, 1957), stresses the seamy side of politics; R. Boutruche, *Seigneurie et Féodalité* (1959), sees feudal problems in a refreshingly new light; and J. Lemarignier, 'Les Fidèles du roi de France, 936–987' in *Recueil de travaux offerts à Clovis Brunel,* vol. i (1955), is important. On the intellectual side, we now have: P. Riché, *Éducation et culture dans l'Occident Barbare* (1962); Donald Bullough, *The Age of Charlemagne* (1965), a fine piece of work, and handsomely illustrated; Walter Ullmann, *The Carolingian Renaissance and the Idea of Kingship* (1969), difficult but thought-provoking; Luitpold Wallach, *Alcuin and Charlemagne* (Cornell, 1959)—even more difficult; and the contributions of Peter Lasko and Philip Grierson to *The Dark Ages,* edited by D. Talbot Rice (1965), with beautiful plates. *The Birth of Western Economy* (1961), by Robert Latouche, highlights the role of France in the growth of an 'Atlantic' economy.

BERYL SMALLEY

Capetian France

'Government and Society: Capetian France.' My title as it stands makes nonsense. I shall begin by transposing it into terms that make sense. To start from the end, 'Capetian': Hugh Capet would have been flattered to hear at his election in 987 that he was king of 'Capetian France'. By the time that the house of Valois succeeded to the direct line of Hugh, France could truly be called Capetian. The change is a central problem of the period.

Then we must alter the title by putting 'society' into the plural. Medieval France was divided into provinces or regions. Differences arising from history and geography criss-crossed with political divisions caused by wars or marriage alliances. They survived this artificial fractioning or unification, as indeed they still do. Marc Bloch said of the Capetians in one of his unforgettable phrases: 'They put France together rather than unified her.' In fact they bought political unity at the price of a deep emotional cleavage, which still finds expression in the legends dear to a conquered people. Southerners smart at the memory of the annexation of Languedoc. The northerner, Simon de Montfort (father of the Simon who fell at Evesham), leader of the conquering army, stands for Cromwell in Ireland. His victory at Muret (1213) stands for Drogheda. The Nazi command tried to use this cleavage between north and south when France was divided into the Vichy Government area and the Occupied Zone, just as it tried to play on the separatist tradition of Brittany. It takes a common enemy to bind men together.

Modern research is uncovering the deep roots of French regional divisions. The latest and most readable of these studies is the history of the Mâconnais by Professor Georges Duby. His book recalls a saying of Eileen Power, a pioneer of English economic history: she spent her life in a search for 'the classical

English manor'. Since France is larger than England, it seems that many lives might be spent in such a quest. Even when research is confined to a limited area, customs and institutions seldom fall into a uniform pattern; the rhythm of development varies so much. Marc Bloch's synthesis on French agrarian history serves the purpose of all first attempts to generalize. It makes a starting point for correction and modification.

Modern research has made it even more difficult to generalize on the subject of French urban development. One school of historians regards the rise of privileged towns and communes as marking a new era in history. This 'corporative' school would like to distinguish between the 'feudal period' of the early Middle Ages and the period of 'groups and corporations', which began in the twelfth and thirteenth centuries. France in this later medieval period no longer consisted of a hierarchy of landlords. Instead we see a pattern of communities, towns, universities, guilds, cathedral chapters and so on, each with its rights and customs. The kingdom has become a *communitas communitatum*. This view exaggerates the importance of privileged groups within the kingdom at the expense of the great privileged families. It is easier to think of the French towns as islands of privilege of varying degrees. They were usually too weak and too isolated from one another to unite in leagues to guard against encroachment on their rights from above. Each has its own features and each its own history of inner conflict, depending on its peculiar class structure and economic development. The towns fit into our picture of diverse societies as smaller units within their regions and provinces. We have two general histories of the development of *communes* in Northern France, but no equivalent for Languedoc and Aquitaine. It is agreed that their paths to freedom varied in the early stages. The South French *communes* rose more smoothly than the Northern, which often wrested privileges from the overlord by violence.

The word 'government' in our title must go into the plural, too. France was decentralized, a kaleidoscope of competing, overlapping governments. We simplify English constitutional history, for teaching purposes at least, by presenting it as a history of the growth of royal control. This is probably a simplification rather than a falsification. A similar approach to French history would falsify the process. In 987 the king was only one ruler among many others. These others cannot be ignored.

But the very word 'government' presents difficulties to a medievalist; it sounds anachronistic. Today it conveys an atmosphere of green baize in stuffy rooms and of stupid, interfering, but not exactly savage bureaucrats. Perhaps the feminine 'governess' in our subconscious sheds a faint scent of refinement. A medieval clerk would choose *imperium*, *regnum* or *regimen* as a word to express the ruler's function. *Gubernatio* was sometimes used for 'administration', but more rarely than some equivalent for 'rule'. In the Middle Ages *rule* meant primarily police work, just knocking people on the head. As civilization progressed, and it progressed rapidly from the tenth to the fourteenth centuries, *rule* came more and more to mean getting money out of them. It had little to do with social services. Charity, care for the sick and disabled, and education fell within the sphere of private almsgiving, of voluntary associations and especially of the Church. Medieval thought contrasted rule over men's bodies, exercised by the secular State, with guidance of their souls, which was the Church's business. This difference in function justified the claim put forward by medieval churchmen to superiority over the State, since the Church had the higher vocation. If the argument today strikes us as unreal, we must remember that in fact the gentler and more constructive functions of administration as we know it belonged to ecclesiastics. Rule over men's bodies was accepted as being sordid and brutal, a sad, though necessary consequence of sin. It is true that a new view of political life developed in the later thirteenth century. Government expanded and became more complex, involving an increasing number of educated civil servants. The urban 'patriciate' managed town affairs. Aristotle's *Politics*, translated into Latin about 1260 and studied by the masters of Paris, suggested a more positive conception of government: political activity gives scope to virtue; we should say: 'it is creative'. But this theory, though it had the authority of St Thomas Aquinas, did not supersede the older and more actual view entirely. When we speak of medieval 'government', therefore, we must exclude 'welfare' and all kinds of 'benefit' from our ken. Even so, we shall find a contradiction in medieval teaching on rulership.

It seems a contradiction to us. The medieval clergy saw none.

The repressive character of temporal rule in their eyes sprang from human imperfection and inhered in the very nature of earthly life. Justice was admitted to be a form of rent: *'iustitia est magnum emolumentum'*. This saying applies to France as much as to England. The profits of justice formed part of every lord's budget from the king downwards. Yet the ruler must behave as a Christian. A good lord must judge impartially: *'Recta iudicate, filii hominum'*, as the Psalmist taught. How justice could be both impartial and a form of rent was never explained. The good lord must also protect his subjects against enemies. This duty justified his possession of armed force; a military caste was necessary. The justification ignored the fact that a military caste, unless controlled by a strong superior and diverted to border warfare, spent most of its time and energy in local fighting. The lord was often engaged in defending his people against his enemies, not theirs.

This double current in medieval thought helps us to understand the development of government in those French societies which were subject to the Capetians in name or in fact. Government stood for coercion, income and fun; war was great fun to the knight of our period. Government also drew its sanction from a divine trust, to be executed for the good of the ruled rather than of the ruler. Just rule was contrasted with tyranny. The contrast mattered. It did not become a mere cliché. Any government, to be stable, must take significant public opinion into account. The more effective medieval governments set up public relations departments for propaganda purposes, without calling them by the modern name. Public opinion, when government was decentralized, depended less on subjects, the governed, than on competing governors. Each ruler had to reckon with his opposite numbers, whether peers, overlords or vassals. Their jurisdictions impinged upon his at every turn. If he tried to expand at their cost, they might combine against him. Bishops and barons alike had standards in the matter of just government, though what these standards were very often escapes us. Tyranny, whatever it meant, shocked them without fail. The most admired and most successful ruler, therefore, would be he who combined the maximum exploitation of his subjects from a financial point of view, since this constituted government by definition, with the minimum appearance of tyranny in the eyes of all who had means of resistance. Somehow or other he must profiteer justly.

In practical terms his success depended on his skill in sucking up his subjects' surplus. Every medieval government aimed at this. Tallage, the right to tax unfree subjects at will, mopped up the surplus left by dues and profits of justice. The picture from the subjects' point of view is less gloomy than might appear. The suction was ineffective. To be effective it would have required an incorruptible personnel. Failing this, the suction pipe leaked at all levels. The process of administration produced a ministerial aristocracy at all levels, beginning in the village. An Abbot of Cluny was simply facing facts when he got a written promise from one of his local officials 'not to steal more than twelve pennies a year'. The people at the bottom, moreover, had a dogged determination to resist pressure. A peasant revolt might be quelled easily; it made a hole in the suction pipe for the moment. The proof of this ineffectiveness is that no medieval government has ever been accused by serious historians of 'killing the goose that laid the golden eggs' by over-exaction, with one exception: that is the Angevin government of the kingdom of Naples, and even that accusation has been challenged recently.

The brighter side of the picture is that wise rulers would aim at increasing their revenues by keeping the peace in their territories and by stopping the leak of brigandage. Suger, Abbot of Saint Denis near Paris, a born estate manager, has left an account of his administration of the abbey and its dependencies in the twelfth century. He increased the yield of its lands by careful police work and by capital expenditure. For instance, he rebuilt a ruined chapel. It became an object of pilgrimage and brought custom to the neighbourhood. His account of his stewardship shows vividly how peasant labour might be converted into gems to beautify his abbey church; Suger was a collector and connoisseur. The book ends with a description of the writer meditating on the mystical significance of his gems and raising his soul to heavenly contemplation 'in an anagogical manner'. Not only the gems, but the whole book is charged with symbolism for the historian.

We must now, against this background, consider two changes which transformed France in the period 987–1328. The economic change can be described but not analysed; the demographic curve retains the secret of its movement. We only know that France developed from being a thinly populated country, with stretches of forest and waste separating its local communities, into the most densely populated region in Europe for its size. The urbanized territories of Lombardy and Flanders naturally surpassed France, but she heads the list for predominantly rural areas. It has been calculated that by 1300 her modern geographical boundaries carried in them well over fifteen million inhabitants. The corresponding figure for German imperial territory would be five or six million. Germany remained a country of forest and heath in spite of her flourishing towns. French population had increased everywhere, though its greatest concentration lay in the more fertile areas. These figures give a population as large as that of the eighteenth century. Farming had expanded into marginal land which was abandoned as uneconomic in later times. The heroic period of clearing and colonization fell into the eleventh century, overlapping into the early twelfth. From then onward the growth of trade and industry relieved the pressure of the peasantry on the soil to some extent. France remained largely a food and wine producer. Viticulture played so important a part in her economy that in the early Middle Ages the sites of bishop-rics were sometimes moved into better wine country. But she had the ports of Marseille and Bordeaux. The fairs of Champagne brought in the profits of an international exchange centre. The 'Cahorsins', the men of Cahors, gained as bad a reputation as bankers and usurers on an international scale as the Lombards and Tuscans themselves. All readers of Matthew Paris know his feelings towards them. France also had manufactures of weapons, textiles and luxury goods. Limoges enamel, to mention only one example, was famous throughout Europe. There were flourishing local centres. Everyone who has travelled in France outside Paris knows that she is a country of local capitals, going back to the Middle Ages. And Paris became the intellectual capital of Europe on account of her university.

Most historians who have generalized on French history lay stress on the fertility of French soil as a constant factor, apart from a few highland zones. Given a modicum of political quiet, France could reach the height of prosperity that was attainable in the working conditions of the Middle Ages.

Which of the many governments operating in medieval France gained most from her increased prosperity? Political history will answer the question. Here we come to our second big change.

Hugh Capet controlled a small area in north-east France, centred on Paris, plus a much smaller residue of Carolingian crown lands, lying even farther to the north-east with their capital at Laon. He inherited a more solid asset from the Carolingians in the shape of their extensive ecclesiastical patronage. That was all. Hugh was put in, with the consent of secular magnates, by a group of Rhineland ecclesiastics, strongly imperialist in their sympathies. These men disliked the Carolingian policy of expansion in Lorraine at the expense of the Saxon emperors. There must have been some understanding that Hugh would drop the Carolingian policy and would leave to the Empire this section of the old Middle Kingdom, of whose importance you are already aware. Anyway, the policy was dropped for the time being. The Capetian and his successors gained recognition as kings and overlords from all those powers which had recognized the last Carolingians. In practice, this implied almost no authority south of the Loire. An eleventh-century chronicler, Adémar of Chabannes, shows what Capetian rule looked like to the clergy of Aquitaine. Adémar describes the duke of Aquitaine as acting 'royally'. He distinguishes between the duchy and the Capetian-controlled territory, 'France': 'The duke of the Aquitanians, William, disapproving of the wicked French, refused to be subject to Hugh; so Hugh called out the French army and beseiged the town of Poitiers.' Hugh won a battle eventually and 'the French returned victorious to France'. The count of Toulouse was known to contemporaries as 'an uncrowned king'. It has been argued recently that Gascony, unlike Aquitaine and Toulouse, was not subject to the king of France even in name at this period.

Hugh's successors in the eleventh century could not even keep a windfall when they had one. The duchy of Burgundy, when conquered, did not go to swell the resources of the royal demesne, but was used to buy off a younger brother. The year 1066 brought a crown to the duke of Normandy. This was a black date for the French monarchy. Normandy had been almost as independent as the southern principalities and was more dangerous, because nearer to Paris. A duke with all the resources of the English crown at his disposal made an uncomfortable vassal. The Norman conquest of England opened the door to Plantagenet rule in France. Henry II and Richard I controlled a long strip of seaboard territory stretching northward from the Pyrenees to the Channel.

bulging out to include Anjou and Normandy and possessing an excellent road centre and capital at Tours. Brittany fell under their influence. Other powerful vassals, the counts of Blois and Champagne, enclosed the royal demesne to the west and east, with a capital at Troyes, the centre of great international fairs. So far, the increase in French prosperity had benefited the Capetian monarchy very little.

Then came a dramatic reversal of rôles. Philip Augustus conquered Normandy from John Lackland and incorporated it in the royal demesne. He pursued his advantage by gaining direct over-lordship over the lords of the intervening territory down to Guyenne, which remained under English over-lordship until 1453. Meanwhile the Pope had called a crusade to suppress heresy in Languedoc. Crusade spelled conquest, if not for the rank and file of crusaders, at least for the leaders. Philip Augustus refused the papal invitation to lead the crusade. He had a previous engagement elsewhere. The south must wait while he tidied up his conquests in the north. His son, Louis VIII, both conquered the north French barons, who had conquered Languedoc as crusaders, and incorporated into the royal demesne a large part of the county of Toulouse. Revolts in Languedoc were suppressed and royal administration introduced. The Capetians had reached the English Channel and the Mediterranean. Infiltration or conquest from England, Germany and Spain had been checked.

Not all this vast area remained attached to the royal demesne. Louis IX kept Normandy for himself, but cut out appanages for his younger brothers from the rest. This sounds more dangerous to royal authority than it actually was. The royal government was still too primitive to cope indefinitely with the administration of distant lands, and cadets of the family had to be provided for somehow. Louis IX and his brothers ruled as a kind of fraternal junto. It also happened that the counties of Toulouse and Artois reverted to the crown by natural causes. Philip IV annexed Navarre, Champagne and the city of Lyon with its territory. Lyon had been theoretically subject to the Empire. French influence was seeping back into the Middle Kingdom as the Empire weakened. More immediately repaying than these territorial gains, which were often granted out again, were the great treasure raids of the period. Philip IV exploited the profits of the fairs of Champagne, suppressed the Templars, a military Order whose members had acted as international bankers, and confiscated their goods. He also developed a system of direct taxation through local representative assemblies. It probably came as close to the contemporary English system of direct taxation as the greater size and decentralization of France would allow. The two main differences between the French and English systems in the early fourteenth century are first that the king of France lacked the power to convoke a general representative assembly from all over France each time that he needed to levy a tax. Bargaining with local estates proved more convenient. Secondly, the magnates on whose territory the tax was raised would often agree to it only on condition that they should take a percentage. These limitations reflected the comparative novelty of direct taxation in France. There was no tradition of 'danegeld'. Hugh Capet had no recognized right or means to enforce any claim to raise taxes outside his royal demesne. The experiments of Philip III and Philip IV marked a triumph of centralization against conservatism and local interests.

Treasure raids and taxation fed an ambitious foreign policy. Philip IV reached out to the wealth of Flanders and harassed the English in Gascony. France had risen to be the most powerful state in Europe by the time of Philip's death in 1314. It looked as though she might replace the German Empire in its palmy days as the leading force in Christendom. A modern English historian, writing with the events of Munich fresh in his mind, has made an implied comparison between Philip IV and Hitler. Neville Chamberlain, rather thinly disguised as Edward I, has the role of appeaser; he was too slow in helping his allies to stem Philip's advance. However far-fetched the comparison, it says much for Philip's prestige and aggressive policy that anyone should see him in such a part.

The Capetians had won back the wealth and control in France that the later Carolingians had lost. How did they do it? What enabled them to outpace all their competitors? Why this quick spurt forward after marking time for some two centuries?

We must exclude personality as a long-term factor. It counted for much at a time when all rule was personal, but ability in a line of hereditary kings tends to average out, as it averages out in their great vassals and rivals. Individual gifts or defects will account for curves in the graph, but not for its secular ascent or descent. From the point of view of sheer energy there seems little to choose between the last Carolingians and the early Capetians. Of the later Capetians neither Philip Augustus nor Philip IV had quite the brilliance and cunning of William I or Henry II. None of them displayed the military prowess of Richard Cœur de Lion or Edward I. Their line perhaps owed more to the accident of an unfailing succession of sons which put the throne above dynastic quarrels.

One reason which is rightly stressed to explain their success is the support of the Church. French ecclesiastics rallied to the crown even in the areas outside and only neighbouring upon the royal demesne. The Church, with its vast endowments, needed protection against robber barons and peace to exploit its possessions. Churchmen had a good understanding of the realities of the political scene. We heard last week how the Church tried to keep the Carolingian Empire from disintegrating. In the conditions of the eleventh century with its disorder and localism a universal western empire proved to be negligible as a factor making for peace and security. French ecclesiastics accepted its bankruptcy as a *fait accompli*. They lost interest in it. The French kingdom satisfied them. Recent research on the German side is confirming one's scepticism as to whether the Capetians ever accepted the supremacy of the Empire over their kingdom. Positive claims to sovereignty against imperial over-lordship, put forward in the thirteenth century, have their roots in this early indifference to the Empire. French prelates, therefore, whether in direct contact with the monarchy or in more remote parts of France, gave it moral and material backing. They offered the Capetians all kinds of pretexts for interfering in local matters outside the royal demesne. No serious conflict of loyalty between their duties to the king on the one hand and the Pope on the other arose until the reign of Philip IV, when it was too late. Conflict between Church and State in the Middle Ages always admitted of compromise wherever it was free of external complications. All parties, including the Popes, found compromise to be in their best interests in France. The French Church, having contributed so much to the success of the Capetians, fell helpless into their jaws. Louis IX and his son and grandson drew on the wealth of the French bishoprics and abbeys and infringed clerical privilege. Philip IV humiliated Pope Boniface VIII. He preserved his lion's share of the taxation of the clergy against the Pope's efforts to divert more of it to Rome.

A second explanation is that the Capetians shone in the rôle of *tertium gaudens*. Much of the work of centralization and consolidation was done for them. In the late eleventh and early twelfth centuries the chaotic mass of French fiefs and principalities began to harden into lumps. If we watch the setting process, we see, not a single lump at the centre, which thins outwards, but many, of which the royal demesne was only one. Counts and dukes built up their crude administrations and rounded off their territories at the expense of their vassals and weaker peers. William the Conqueror had stabilized ducal authority in Normandy before he made his venture of 1066. Mr R. W. Southern in his *Making of the Middle Ages* gives a vivid description of the Counts of Anjou doing likewise. A marriage alliance joined Anjou to Normandy. Henry II benefited from the work of his forbears on both sides. The Angevins continued the process of centralization in Normandy. Philip Augustus stepped into their shoes when he won the duchy from John. It provided him with a more developed bureaucracy and financial machine than he had in Paris.

The marriage between Henry II and Eleanor of Aquitaine, the *divorcée* of Louis VII, used to be thought of as a tragedy for the French monarchy. Eleanor insisted on an annulment of her marriage to Louis and brought her inheritance of Aquitaine to swell the English possessions overseas. A modern French view is that she helped rather than hindered the Capetian cause. Louis VII could never have controlled Aquitaine effectively; it was too disorderly and vast. Henry II, having far superior resources, imposed some kind of administrative unity on a stretch of territory which had escaped unification since the collapse of Charlemagne's empire. His descendants failed to hold it together, so that in the long run the Capetians reaped where their chief enemies had sown.

It was the same in the extreme south. Louis VIII came to Languedoc on the heels of a northern army. He gathered the harvest of private crusading enterprise and of papal efforts to suppress heresy. The annexation of Languedoc came at the right time for the Capetians. A royal government had developed by the second quarter of the thirteenth century which could undertake the running of a large and distant area. The south was pacified and made contributory to the Paris budget. Municipal liberties were laced into the royal administration. Alphonse of Poitiers, brother of Louis IX, copied the royal policy of centralization in his appanage.

The absorption of Languedoc proved easier in that France in the twelfth and early thirteenth centuries fell roughly into two areas, which might be classified as regions of hard and soft feudalism. I use *feudalism* here in the restricted sense of tenure by military service. A king, duke or count whose lands belonged to the hard area could muster a force of knights to fight for him, unless he were peculiarly weak or unlucky; he could more or less discipline his vassals. Northern France was organized for war. The northern knight regarded war as his profession. Tenure by military service formed the bond between man and lord, even though the service was less specific in France than in post-Conquest England. Conditions change as one travels south. Here the allod survived from the Roman period more tenaciously. The holder of an allod in his capacity of taxpayer was subject only to the State or to its representative. He owed only public services or what had originated as such, and hence escaped the other burdens laid on a vassal by his overlord. There were allods of all sizes, ranging from peasant acres to great estates. A recent comparative study of these holdings in various parts of Europe has suggested that they tended to survive wherever the central authority (royal or ducal) happened to be weak. Elsewhere the king or great lord would bring his men into closer dependence on himself. Further, in our soft area, tenure by military service was looser than it was in the north. It often went with some kind of food or money rent. The peasantry of Languedoc had defended themselves better than had their northern counterparts. They had either always possessed or had succeeded in winning more freedom. The proportion of serfs to freemen was lower. Peasants lived together, grouped into rural *communes*, often holding charters from the lord which restricted his rights to levy dues and fines. Lastly, the Church in Languedoc had even more wealth and privilege than was usual in the north. All this implied a freer but more chaotic type of society. The southern magnates could neither prevent their vassals from making private war nor mobilize them to fight for the lord in disciplined levies.

The Capetians profited in their forward movement by the

division of France into hard and soft areas. Philip Augustus penetrated the hard area to the west of the demesne as heir and conqueror of the English kings. His father, Louis VII, had already begun to work his way into the softer area to the south-east. The northern barons conquered the softest area of the Midi, which was then taken over by Louis VIII.

Caution, indeed, was the Capetians' middle name. One admires it in the founder of their kingship. Hugh Capet, as the chronicler Richer tells us, 'did all advisedly'. Instead of snatching at the monarchy, he let it fall into his lap like ripe fruit. His children contented themselves for the most part with making piecemeal additions to their demesne. Louis VI made it his lifework to master his own tenants, the petty barons of the Île-de-France. The early Capetians never desisted from attempts to capitalize their over-lordship over the great fiefs, but proceeded realistically. Their forward policy corresponded to their resources. They went out to conquer when the time came. 'Foreign policy', in the sense of excursions outside their kingdom's ill-defined boundaries, was even less venturesome than their policy towards their vassals. An occasional crusade on behalf of what after all was 'France overseas' would exhaust resources for the time; it did not involve a permanent drain. Louis IX has been blamed for timidity towards England: Henry III's weakness and his difficulties with his barons gave Louis a chance to drive the English out of Guyenne. That was a gamble which lacked appeal. Louis preferred to make sure of English recognition of his suzerainty. It is by no means a foregone conclusion that an attempted French conquest of Gascony could have succeeded. It would have run counter to the interest of the Gascon wine-growers and exporters, who depended on the English market. The new drive for expansion under Philip III and Philip IV had been prepared by their slower predecessors.

Perhaps it was less the family character than family circumstances: financial tightness due to small estates imposed caution and also economy. Happy misfortune! It saved the early Capetians from the disease of overspending. Their contemporaries suffered severely. The habit of luxury and extravagance seems to have begun in the south and to have spread northwards in the late eleventh and twelfth centuries; it was both a consequence of and a stimulus to the trade revival of the period. Silks, spices and precious objects, all the amenities of life as they were then understood, became more plentiful and more easily obtainable for those with money to spend. Monsieur Chronos tells his pupil Juliette in the French equivalent to *1066 And All That*: women had lived for so long in barracks as to forget that they were women (the only time in French history that this has happened). Fashions had not changed for two hundred years; so it was time. Changes came. The waistline dropped dramatically. We know how expensive that is. The new standard of living differed from the solid domestic comfort of later centuries, which might take the form of capital investment in household goods intended to last for generations. This was spending for spending's sake. Lavish display became part of the aristocratic way of life. The hero of a courtly romance, *Joufroi*, living incognito in the house of a wealthy burgher, decides to fill his empty purse by marrying his landlord's daughter. The prospective father-in-law promises a rich dowry on condition that Joufroi will be more economical in future, reading him a lecture on thrift. Joufroi soliloquizes on the new power of money as against knightly virtue, and shows his contempt for it as soon as the wedding is over. He meets his best man, another incognito noble, at the church door; they divide the dowry between them and spend it 'in the twinkling of an eye'. One doubts whether French aristocrats were really so light-hearted about money, even other people's; but they were supposed by their own standards to seem so.

Increased demand sent up prices: luxury goods cannot be mass-produced. Warfare remained fashionable in spite of the more civilized surroundings, and the cost of war rose steeply. It became customary to hire mercenaries recruited from those parts of Europe where population had increased the most in proportion to the country's resources, such as Brabant. This custom probably began in the north and spread in the reverse direction from luxurious living. Mr J. O. Prestwich has pointed to the place of mercenary troops in Anglo-Norman warfare from the Conquest onwards. A count of Mâcon hired some Brabançons for one of his wars in the mid-twelfth century. They were a novelty in the district and caused a scandal by killing more of their enemies than was usual.

Credit was available as banking and business techniques advanced, but at what a price! Most students of medieval history realize that the Church forbad usury and that the courts Christian provided for actions against usurers with stiff penalties against the convicted. Hence the Jews are often regarded as the medieval money-lenders *par excellence*. In fact the Christian usurer of the later twelfth century could supply credit on a much larger scale than the Jew. Canon law prohibitions strewed obstacles in the usurer's path to Hell and caused him to charge a higher rate of interest to offset the risks he was running. A bishop of Arras in the early thirteenth century wrote to Pope Innocent III to ask his advice on enforcement of the usury laws. If they were rigorously applied, the Pope answered him, the churches in many districts would have to be closed, the bulk of parishioners having incurred excommunication. He must use his discretion and make an example of the most notorious cases. The poet Henri d'Andeli in a poem about education exclaims at the new popularity of Arithmetic, the science of accounting. 'La conteress', as he personifies her, is loved better than religion:

> 'Usurer and prince and count
> Now prefer the counting lass
> To the singing of High Mass.'

The need to increase one's outlay irrespective of one's income resulted in a slow bankruptcy for large sections of the French nobility. They got into debt and went over the borderline that separates the man with a chronic overdraft from the bankrupt. The lesser nobles had no easy way of raising their incomes to meet their expenditure. They lacked a field of expansion, since France had no border corresponding to the Slav border of Germany or the Celtic fringes of England, inviting to conquest and colonization. Crusades in Spain and the Holy Land provided an outlet in the late eleventh and early twelfth centuries. Then migration ceased on any large scale. 'France overseas' contracted because the Turks were too strong. Hence noble families had to divide up their lands into uneconomic fractions. This happened especially in the south, where primogeniture had not taken root. In Languedoc many small fees were held jointly by one family or members of a family because they had reached an indivisible size. A few wealthy houses or ecclesiastical corporations benefited from the financial straits of their neighbours. They could raise longer credit and could even borrow enough to lend for themselves, so that they acquired land by mortgage. A count, who was often an irresponsible representative of public power, had more purchase on the government racket than had his vassals. It is not surprising to find a few great families thriving amidst a general collapse, though even their budgets would frighten the man of property of today.

The Capetian watchword was 'austerity' in an orgy of spending. A troubadour sings that he'll keep away from the court of 'le roi de Saint Denis', as he calls Louis VII (as though Henry II were to be called 'king of Westminster'). He'll serve the king of England or the count of Blois and Champagne; *they* know how to reward their poets suitably. Compare the behaviour of Richard I and Philip Augustus on the Third Crusade. Richard was a 'show off'; Philip knew that he could not compete with him and hardly tried. We hear of mercenaries in the royal army under Philip Augustus for the first time. If they were used before, it was not in a measure to impress contemporaries. And they were used when Philip had increased his budget enough to afford them. It is sometimes said that the early Capetians had a peasant rather than a noble mentality. They certainly anticipated the advice of the little book, *Proverbs for Vilains*, written by an unfrocked clerk, who suffered from wanderlust, soon after 1174. The author sympathizes with the peasant's hard lot, but offers him tips for bettering himself in a modest way: 'Never attack a man stronger than yourself; lay up for a rainy day; count your pennies; wall your garden; beware of needy relations; he who lends to his relatives never gets rich.' By practising such un-exciting precepts the Capetians avoided the dangers as well as the sweets of noble generosity. They rose with other great families on the backs of the lesser nobility, but their hold was safer. Some of the lesser nobles, moreover, provided them with reliable and devoted, because wholly dependent, servants.

So far I have suggested rather negative reasons for the Capetian success. There is a positive factor, too. This was a general desire for a restoration of public authority. It never disappeared completely, as is proved by the general recognition that the kingship stood apart from as well as immediately over the feudal hierarchy. If the king should acquire land in sub-tenure, as sometimes happened, he was never expected to do homage to the overlord. Mr Wallace-Hadrill explained last week that nobody contrived or welcomed the Carolingian decline, not even the magnates. The trouble was simply that no one could put a stop to the disappearance of the royal fisc which supported the Carolingian monarchy. We have met the Church already as a fighter and pleader for the survival of royal power. We ought to find, if the argument be correct, a welcome from the secular as well as from the ecclesiastical aristocracy for a royal revival. We should look for it in a demand for royal justice, if anywhere. Men dislike paying taxes, even when these are spent for the taxpayers' benefit. On the other hand, men do want speedy and effective justice and will pay for it in moderation. This applies significantly to the Middle Ages. Today, when the average citizen regards a visit to the law courts as an exceptional event in his life, it is difficult to imagine the extent of medieval litigation. In England, in Maitland's phrase, 'the bloodfeud was transferred to the law courts'. Everyone involved in land tenure found himself almost *ipso facto* involved in law suits. The popularity of Henry II's assizes witnesses to the contemporary need for improved methods and firm enforcement. Can we find an equivalent in France?

Here we must distinguish between the peasantry and the upper classes. Justice over the peasantry was easily enforced and was lucrative to the lord. There was seldom too little of it. We hear of a local peasant community buying a grant from its lord that he will not pursue any complaint *before it is made*. Justice for the warrior sections of society, on the other hand, had a scarcity value in the eleventh and early twelfth centuries; it was barely obtainable. The plaintiff had first to find a judge who would be willing and able to compel attendance at his court and to enforce its decision. A powerful judge, if found, would have it his own way. He might choose the court and dictate its verdict. To repeat an often-quoted example: 'The count of Anjou rose and withdrew to a more private place, calling to him the lord bishop and other important men to give judgment.' If the count were friendly, well and good. A defendant who suspected the opposite would ignore the summons and would apply to some other powerful man for protection. Arbitration, therefore, almost superseded judicial proceedings. The parties would meet at an agreed spot with their friends and kinsmen. Arbitrators acting under a president, also agreed to by both sides, would effect a composition of the dispute. This would obviously have to depend more on the relative strength of the opposing groups than on the rights of the case. The judicial combat strikes modern students as a barbarous and unfair mode of proof. It had the advantage of restricting battle to two men, when the alternative was war between their families and their factions. The working of 'The Peace of God', instituted in some parts of France in the eleventh century, illustrates the problems raised by the absence of any strong central authority. Local magnates, led by churchmen, would try to limit private warfare and breaches of the peace to specific times and places. Sworn bands of volunteers undertook to punish offenders. They imposed heavy fines on the poorer freeman, but could only deal with powerful culprits by an adaptation of the arbitration procedure.

Arbitration was simply a *pis aller*, clumsy and unsatisfactory to the litigants themselves. It did not compensate for an ultimate and effective court of appeal. The frequency of appeals to Rome at canon law and of appeals to the royal court at English common law show how men desired a final authority. The Capetians were handicapped by the disappearance of the old public courts in France. These had blended with feudal jurisdiction and had passed out of royal control. Nevertheless, even before the monarchy emerged from its obscurity, the kings began to receive appeals. At first they responded in the only way possible, as arbitrators rather than as judges. They could bring to bear just that extra pressure that made arbitration the end and not merely a stage in the dispute. Then gradually they built up a judicial system centred on Paris with the *parlement* as supreme court of appeal. Feudal courts were not superseded but became inferior to the royal court. The royal officials, provosts and bailiffs (the latter supplementing and checking the former) represented the crown in the now extensive royal demesne. The Capetians could never have imposed their jurisdiction on an unwilling nobility. Intervention was rather imposed on *them*. They could not even have intervened in alliance with the lesser vassals and the Church against the magnates. These might have liquidated the monarchy at its lowest ebb, had they imagined or desired such a course. Far from it, they not only tolerated but promoted the strengthening of royal justice. 'Turbulent?' yes; 'rebellious?' yes; 'consistently anti-royalist?' no: the great vassals saw monarchy as a force to be used in their own quarrels and against invasion. They had no conscious wish for anarchy, any more than they had a concerted plan of action.

Royal justice leads on to the mystique of kingship. We can distinguish two separable though blending layers of thought and sentiment about the crown of France. The Church insisted on the sanctity of royal rule. His anointing at the coronation ceremony set the king apart from other men and gave him special responsibilities to God for his people. On a lower plane we find a complex of primitive superstition and myth. The king's person was sacred. He had power to work miracles of healing. The early Capetians drew strength from both ecclesiastical and popular feeling without showing signs of outstanding personal virtue. They acted as devout, but not always strictly obedient, sons of the Church. The line produced no one comparable to Edward the Confessor. Louis IX did better than any of his predecessors, being one of the very few Christian kings of any country to be canonized. His holiness focused on himself, and hence on the French crown, the medieval respect for and belief in kingship. St Louis' life and policy gave content to previously vague ideas. He wished to uphold the rights of all ranks of society according to their degrees. He carried out his object to the extent of helping the common people against their oppressors by instituting inquiries into the conduct of royal officials. The inquests had to stop at the boundaries of the royal demesne, but this by now covered a significant portion of France. St Louis' was aiming on his own initiative at the same kind of reform that the English barons forced upon Henry III. The complaints against royal officials revealed by these inquests have survived in the records. They are quite hair-raising. How much permanent relief the victims gained we can never know. But the aggrieved had had their say and at least in many cases they were compensated for past wrongs. The king, it must have seemed to the people, was more than a magician, who could cure one's bodily ills; he was also a benevolent, though all too distant force, who favoured the weak against the powerful.

Readers of Proust will remember Françoise, that prop of the household. She came of a solid peasant family whose mentality belonged to the thirteenth century. Her interests and prejudices take us back to the days of St Louis. Françoise was a royalist and conservative and a snob about money; but her face would darken when she heard the name of a noble.

79

The Capetians had it both ways and got the best of two worlds. They profiteered justly, if any medieval government ever did. St Louis was one of the more successful from a temporal point of view, and yet he was canonized. He represented a moral and material victory for the French monarchy. His reign had laid up a capital which his heirs might squander, but which survived in remembrance. The servants of his grandson, Philip IV, civil lawyers and expert pamphleteers, made St Louis' piety seem old-fashioned and too simple. They outlined a secular theory of government and developed the notion of an independent lay state. The early idea of sacred kingship remained rooted in popular tradition. It would prove its worth in time of crisis.

We leave the French kings on the upgrade, extending their authority over a prosperous, civilized country. They have found a *modus vivendi* with the great nobles. An occasional revolt is just part of the pattern of feudalism. They have found a means, only rather less effective than Edward I's use of Parliament, to tap the wealth of the third estate. The appearance of success continues even past the direct Capetian rule into the period of the early Valois.

BIBLIOGRAPHICAL NOTE

General histories of the period relating to France and containing biblio-graphies

Cambridge Medieval History, III–VII; *Cambridge Economic History of Europe*, I–III; A. Fliche and V. Martin, *Histoire de l'Eglise,* VII–X; M. Bloch, *La Société féodale,* I, 1939, II, 1940; R. W. Southern, *The Making of the Middle Ages,* 1953; G. Duby, *Rural and Country Life in the Medieval West,* translated by C. Postan, London, 1968

Basic introductory works on France

CH. PETIT-DUTAILLIS, *La Monarchie féodale en France et en Angleterre, X-XIII siècles,* 1933, translated by E. D. Hunt as *The Feudal Monarchy in France and England,* etc., 1936. As the author gives a full bibliography on political, social and constitutional history, the following list will include only works on these subjects which are omitted by Petit-Dutaillis or which have appeared more recently.

FAWTIER, R. *Les Capétiens et la France*, 1942.

MIROT, L. *Manuel de géographie historique de la France*, 1948.

PERROY, E. *La Guerre de Cent Ans*, 1945 (useful for the opening survey of France at the end of the Capetian period), translated by W. B. Wells as *The Hundred Years War*, 1951; F. Lot et R. Fawtier, *Histoire des institutions Françaises au moyen âge* (3 vols.), 1957–62.

Legal and constitutional history and development of the monarchy

F. Olivier-Martin, *Histoire du droit français des origines à la Révolution*, 1948; G. Péré, *Le Sacre et le couronnement des rois de France*, 1921; Y. Bongert, *Recherches sur les cours laïques du X au XIII siècle*, 1949; L. Halphen, 'La Place de la royauté dans le système féodale', *Revue Historique*, CLXXII, 1933; H. M. Cam, 'Suitors and Scabini' in her *Liberties and Communities in Medieval England*, Cambridge, 1944; J. R. Strayer and C. H. Taylor, *Studies in Early French Taxation*, Cambridge, Mass., 1939; J. R. Strayer, *The Administration of Normandy under St Louis*, Cambridge, Mass., 1932; W. L. Newman, *Le Domaine royal sous les premiers Capétiens (987–1180)*, 1937; F. J. Pegues, *The Lawyers of the Last Capetians*, Princeton, 1962; M. W. Labarge, *Saint Louis*, London, 1968; C. T. Wood, *The French Apanages and the Capetian Monarchy*, Cambridge, Mass., 1966.

Towns and Communes

Ch. Petit-Dutaillis, *Les Communes françaises*, 1947 (gives a bibliography of earlier studies); A. R. Lewis, 'Seigneurial administration in twelfth-century Montpellier', 'The development of town government in twelfth-century Montpellier', *Speculum*, XXII, 1947.

Economic and Social History

H. Sée, *Histoire économique de la France. Le moyen âge et l'ancien régime*, 1948 (should be used for the bibliography); M. Bloch, *Les Caractères originaux de l'histoire rurale française*, 1931; R. Dion, *Histoire de la vin et du vigne en France*, 1959.

Regional Studies

R. Boutruche, *Une société provinciale en lutte contre le régime féodale. L'Alleu en Bordelais et en Bazardais*, Rodez, 1947; G. Rambert, *Histoire du commerce de Marseille*, I, 1949, II, 1951; G. Duby, *La*

Société aux XI et XII siècles dans la région mâconnaise, 1953 (has a bibliography of earlier regional studies of other parts of France).

Albigensian Crusade

P. Belperron, *La Croisade contre les albigeois et l'union du Languedoc à la France, 1209–1249,* 1946 (students interested in the Albigensian heresies should use more recent and specialized studies; see C. Thouzellier, *Catharisme et Valdéisme en Languedoc,* 2nd ed. 1969. M. H. G. A. Jeanroy, *La Poésie lyrique des troubadours,* Toulouse, 1934, gives an introduction to the court life of Languedoc before the crusade.

English Possessions in France and Anglo-French Relations

Y. Renouard, 'Le rôle de l'empire angevin', *Revue historique,* CXCV, 1945; 'Ce que l'Angleterre doit à l'Aquitaine', *Conférences du lundi* (Université de Bordeaux), VII, 1945–6, both reprinted in *Etudes d'histoire médiévale,* 1968; J. O. Prestwich, 'War and Finance in the Anglo-Norman State', *Transactions* of *the Royal Historical Society,* 5th series, IV, 1954; P. Chaplais, 'Le Traité de Paris, 1259', *Le Moyen Age,* LXI, 1955. Bibliographies in A. L. Poole, *Domesday Book to Magna Carta,* Oxford, 1951; Sir Maurice Powicke *The Thirteenth Century,* Oxford, 1953. A. Kelly, *Eleanor of Aquitain and the Four Kings,* Cambridge, Mass., 1950 (a popular biography of Eleanor, with list of original sources).

The Church in France

Apart from Fliche et Martin and Lot et Fawtier, Vol. III (see above), J. Riviere, *Le Problème de l'eglise et de l'état au temps de Philippe le Bel,* 1926; G. Digard, *Philippe le Bel et le Saint-Siège de 1285, à 1304,* 1936; Y. Renouard, *La Papauté à Avignon,* 1954 (selective bibliography).

C. A. J. ARMSTRONG

France of the Hundred Years War and the Renaissance

The Hundred Years War was a disaster without consolation, for the war brought no spiritual or intellectual compensation. The material damage was horrible. Everywhere churches and abbeys were among the worst sufferers; and a great ecclesiastical foundation like La Chaise Dieu (Haute-Loire), endowed by Pope Clement VI, had to be built as a fortress, reverting to the type of fortified church current in the Midi at the period of feudal anarchy. The peasantry, as in all medieval warfare, was hit hardest; and the rising of the *Jacquerie* (1357) was a witness to their desperation. In 1417 the remaining inhabitants of Vignolles (Charente) took refuge in Bordeaux carrying with them the altar cross of their parish church. After the victories of Charles VII attractive leases had to be offered to induce a return to the land, reminiscent of those granted in earlier centuries to colonists who would reclaim the waste.

The destruction and hardship can scarcely be exaggerated, but this is not to say that in themselves they were productive of far-reaching political and economic change. The eclipse of royal power led to some provincial particularism in Languedoc; but the provinces were as much debilitated by the war as was the crown, and no general centrifugal tendency set in. The only fief, which, through diplomatic circumstances directly connected with the English war, moved out of the orbit was Flanders, though it was not until 1529 that the crown could be brought to renounce its feudal suzerainty over Flanders. In the sphere of economics the prosperity of the defensible towns increased relatively to the exposed countryside, and facilitated, when more tranquil conditions returned, the investment of urban wealth, as at Toulouse, in landed property; but this was in keeping with the general European trend towards the conversion of trade profits into land. In France the nobility remained a match for the towns, and they never acquired over the rural area that ascendancy thanks to which the towns of the Netherlands changed the economy of entire territories.

The war, it is said, began as a dynastic and grew into a national struggle; but to say so, is to underrate the maturity which French society had already reached, for in France patriotism, within the limitations of medieval loyalties, certainly antedates the Hundred Years War. To suppose that the tribulations of the fourteenth century engendered French patriotism is to be unfair to the generation of Joinville or even to the contemporaries of Philip Augustus. To a foreigner, French patriotism, in existence before, would seem to have rapidly faced the challenge of the war. The *aide* as an instrument of general taxation was the work of the Three Estates in 1355, who during the reign of Jean 'le Bon' led the way in making the defence of the realm a public burden, accepting the national beyond the feudal concept.

Nevertheless the motive power, which started the conflict and kept it alive, was the quarrel (in the medieval sense of *querela*) between two families and their adherents, the English Angevins and the Valois. Jeanne d'Arc dedicated her vocation to the rescue of the Valois dynasty by securing the unction of the dauphin at Rheims. Her sanctity and heroism are only obscured by denying the singleness of her purpose. She is best understood against the background of such late medieval female saints as Bridgit of Sweden and Catherine of Siena, who however unlike Jeanne in their social origins were like her inspired to disregard the dangers of personal intervention in public affairs.

During the first phase of the war, France was weakened by the misgivings that the first two Valois kings felt about their own title to the crown. Their suspicion of their vassals led them into acts of weakness or violence, as when Philippe VI broke off the attempt to relieve Calais (1347) and Jean 'le Bon' summarily executed the Harcourts (1356). When the intellectual revival of Charles V's time had spent itself, political theory was neglected in France until the end of the fifteenth century. The ideal systems of medieval thought scarcely corresponded with the realities of the period, which, however, made a characteristic contribution by elaborating the theory of the succession to the crown. The result was that the sixteenth century accepted the Salic Law (the exclusion of females) as a fundamental law.

The activity of Charles V both as dauphin and (1364–80) king was probably decisive in preventing the war from causing a complete breach in secular institutions. The Estates in a political sense had burnt themselves out during his father's reign, largely through the mischievous agency of Robert le Coq; and Charles developed in theory and enforced in fact the royal prerogative over the raising and spending of the *aides*. In drawing justice and finance firmly within the prerogative Charles V gave his country a lesson in the burden of absolutism and set the monarchy on a course of estrangement from the Estates. Charles refounded the ideal of wise kingship, but in a sense more academic than St Louis would have approved.

The second phase of the Hundred Years War proved the more corrosive, for the attack of the Lancastrian kings was invited by contending factions. The proto-Renaissance nurtured by Charles V withered away; but institutions were more tenacious. The *aide* was essentially a war tax *aide de guerre* or *aide des gens de guerre;* and even a kingdom at war with itself could not forgo war taxation. To curry favour with the crowd the Burgundian faction might abolish the *aide* (1418); but in practice renunciation of *aides* only meant that the government turned for profits to the mint, in other words to the debasement of the coinage. In its hour of triumph the Lancastrian dynasty restored the *aides* (*ordonnance* of 11 March 1421); and by preserving in the northern area the *aides* and by maintaining the authority of the *parlement* of Paris, the Regent Bedford safeguarded the foundations of the state at a moment when the Valois were incapable of doing so. The failure of Henry VI's double monarchy was tragic for the two constituent realms, but had it proved viable the institutions of France would doubtless have continued to derive from the tradition of Charles V.

In surmounting the military and diplomatic obstacles that delayed the eviction of the English, Charles VII and his advisers showed infinite resource; but as regards civil administration Charles VII mainly relied on refurbishing the principles of his grandfather's government. There is little originality in the *ordonnances* which reformed justice, finance and the army in his reign.

Although the structure of officialdom came through almost unscathed, the break caused by war in the memory of society must have been severe. Some hint of it may be detected in the language. Classical Old French, surviving in literature, was a curiosity when François Villon started writing (1461) his *Grand Testament* which included the *Ballade en vieil langage françoys* with its sprinkling of obsolete flexions and terms, the correct use of which was quite beyond Villon. The most notable grammatical war casualty was the declension system in Old French, of which the nominative had weathered the 'Dark' [*sic*] only to founder in the Later Middle Ages. So late as 1529 Geofroy Tory was complaining that French changed from one half-century to the next; but by his time care of the language had reasserted itself, and the earliest grammars and dictionaries were about to add their weight to the barriers that ever since have protected French against any major linguistic cataclysm.

An indirect legacy of the war was the prominence of the Loire Valley as the seat of the court and therefore of diplomacy until, after his return from captivity at Madrid (1526), François Ier restored to the Île-de-France not only the royal headquarters but pre-eminence in being the scene of great artistic creations. In the meanwhile, the Loire Valley, besides being the cradle of native artists (e.g. Jean Bourdichon) and the resort of foreign masters (e.g. Leonardo da Vinci) during the early stages of the Renaissance, provided the crown with a variety of servants. A curious sequel to the regionalism of the monarchy, when recuperating from the aftermath of the Hundred Years War, was that the lesser nobility and the *bourgeoisie* of the district, by taking royal service, proceeded to the civil, ecclesiastical and military government of France and North Italy. A close parallel to the de Brézé family is offered by the du Bellay. The editors of the *Mémoires* of Martin and Guillaume du Bellay describe their family thus: 'de date ancienne et d'origine angevine elle essaima aux environs, dans le Maine, le Dunois et le Vendomois', and so it might have remained had not the young Guillaume resorted to the court of Louis XII at Blois. Of humbler origin, the Briçonnet family of Tours are another instance of royal service leading to fortune, in their case mainly ecclesiastical.

Between the end of the Hundred Years War (1453) and the outbreak of the Wars of Religion (1562) the monarchy, while never acquiring an absolute power, became all-embracing. In one sense Francois Ier and Henri II were the embodiment of personal rule, but the monarchy had also grown into a system. The loans to the crown of the municipalities of Paris (1522) and Lyon (1536) were met by the subscription of *rentiers*, or holders of bonds, who drew their interest of 8 per cent or 10 per cent on their stock. In the eyes of *rentiers*, it was the continuity of the system to which the personal rule of kings had given rise that mattered. Not that sentimental loyalty was absent, quite the reverse, for the French liked a patriarchal quality in their kings. The spokesman of the notabilities gathered at Tours in May 1506 styled Louis XII 'Father of his People'. Ronsard (ob. 1584) could write 'les roys et les pasteurs ont mesme estat de vivre', while G. Cappello, ambassador of La Serenissima to Henri II in 1554, reported to his government, after noting the relatively good credit of the crown, so that scarcely a soldier was more than two instalments in arrears with his pay, 'che ciascheduno s'obbliga a servirlo (the king) per amore'.

Thomas More and Ulrich von Hütten, who were professèd gallophobes, regarded the king of France as a despot obeyed by servile subjects. Their views were unrealistic, for apart from the emotional loyalty which the king shared in common with other European princes, the crown was the symbol of a social machine which was served by an intelligent ruling class. The energies of innumerable groups were directed towards the public, or rather the royal, service, in which they found their reward. In 1561, on the eve of the Wars of Religion, another Venetian ambassador, M. Suriano, commented on the familiarity existing between the king and his subjects, whom he treated more like companions. The ambassador had in mind those members of society, with whom a diplomat comes in contact. But as a diplomat, he was trained to discern motives, and he was in no doubt that 'what retains . . . the love of these people [*delli populi*] is their own interest and hope of profit [*dell utile*], because the king distributes honours, offices, magistracies, ecclesiastical goods and provisions, pensions and gifts'. The symbiosis of the crown and the governing classes was summed up in the current proverb 'le roi paye tout, le roi prend tout'.

The attitude of the crown towards intellectuals if always self-interested was more often than not enlightened, and the case of François Rabelais is instructive. With forty-four editions to his credit in the twenty years following 1530, Rabelais was admittedly a publicist worth encouraging, moreover he was protected by members of the family of du Bellay, both the cardinal Jean and the king's lieutenant in Piedmont, Guillaume. Satirical allusion to the emperor Charles V is already to be found in *Pantagruel*, published at Lyon in 1532, and condemned the following year by the Sorbonne. Securing a privilege in September 1545 for the *Tiers Livre*, Rabelais showed that in his quarrel with the Sorbonne he had the backing of royalty. The *Tiers Livre* was eminently patriotic with its talk of foreign invasion, referring of course to the imperialists, and on the home front it made propaganda against the clergy over clandestine marriages, which as the crown alleged were being celebrated without regard to the personal and legal position of contracting parties. In 1550 Henri II issued a privilege for the *Quart Livre* with a promise of protection 'contre les calomniateurs'. The 'Decretals' chapters of the book are unmistakably related to the royal policy towards the papacy; and the description of Rabelais as 'collaborateur dévoué du gouvernement royal' (Abel Lefranc) seems borne out by Henri II lifting, on the occasion of his entry into Metz (1552), the ban of the Sorbonne on the *Quart Livre*.

The crown had only the remotest share in the introduction of printing, which was brought to Paris in 1470 by academic private enterprise, and to Lyon in 1473 as a commercial venture. But in 1488 Charles VIII included the printers when he confirmed the privileges of the university of Paris, for already the twenty-four *librarii jurati* of the university were all printers or were employing printers. The first use of the official style *impressor regius* (by Pietre Le Rouge) also dates from the same year; and in 1513 Louis XII exempted printers from the *taille*. In the latter part of the reign of Francois Ier, royal patronage increased the usefulness of printing to learning. Although the printing of Greek had been found to be uneconomic, an entire fount of Greek type was executed by Claude Garamond, modelled on the script of Angelo Vergecio the keeper of the king's Greek manuscripts. It was paid for by the Treasury in 1541 and handed over to Robert Estienne, who held the office of king's printer. The duty of acting as custodian of the royal Greek type 'les grecs du roi' kept alive the office through a succession of subsequent printers.

As the language of administration and of polite society, French, 'lingua gallicana', the speech of the northern provinces, superseded the 'lingua occitana' the vernacular of the south. The language with the stronger literary culture prevailed, for after 1500 literary provençal, in which the troubadours had written, was a dead language; but the process of linguistic unification did not receive, until it was virtually complete, the backing of the state. The *ordonnance* of Moulins (December 1490) permitted evidence in Languedoc to be collected 'en langage françois ou maternel'. Nevertheless, for many generations French had naturalized itself in the south as a second language. Among the magnates the choice was presumably dictated by personal preference, for, while Froissart admired the pure French spoken by the count of Foix, at a later period an ecclesiastical councillor of Jean IV d'Armagnac had to use Latin, not knowing enough French to negotiate with Thomas Bekyngton, the envoy of Henry VI. The administrative and legal usefulness of French proved overwhelming, so that the estates of Languedoc admitted French in 1442, and the *parlements* of Toulouse and Bordeaux (created 1443 and 1462) used it from the start.

The Parisian, who in 1460 won a literary prize at the 'jeux floraux' of Toulouse had written in the 'lengatge de Tholosa', but a prize-winning ballad of 1513 was in French; and at Toulouse the consistory of the 'Gay Saber' kept in step with northern fashion by becoming a college of rhetoric. But, however strong the literary attraction of French the expansion of printing was probably a more powerful agency in hastening its spread. French was already familiar to the book trade of the Midi, for when in 1478 the professional *enlumineurs* of Toulouse protested against printing they couched their petition in French. Latin was retained for academic publications at Toulouse; but French, especially after 1520, was adopted for all but the more homely works, which continued to be printed in 'lingua occitana'.

Calvin, unlike Luther, had no need to evolve a middling idiom in order to be comprehensible to north and south. It is hard to say whether the diffusion of French facilitated the extension of protestantism more than the dissemination of protestant literature in French promoted a wider knowledge of the language in the south. In the Alps, the region in which De Thou refers to the inhabitants reading their Bible in French, a suit of 1533 before the ecclesiastical court of Sisteron (Basses-Alpes) illustrates the connexion between the language, protestant doctrine and the book trade. A notary of Manosque named Aloat, who was a relative of Farel, stood accused of spreading heresy through the agency of a bookseller called Picard, who sold Gospels printed in French.

In common with much royal legislation of the period, the *ordonnance* of Villers-Cotterets (August 1539) which universalized French as the official usage of the realm, was largely sanctioning existing practice. The *ordonnance* declared (art. 111) the need to avoid ambiguities arising from the use of Latin, and directed that the proceedings of the royal courts ('nos cours souveraines') were to take place in 'langage maternel françois et non autrement', which was also to be used for 'registres, enquêtes, contrats, commissions, sentences, testaments'.

The complex legal geography of France was divided between the 'pays de droit coutumier' in the north and the 'pays de droit écrit' to the south. Although Lyon, the banking capital of France in the sixteenth century, lay in the latter, the former was the larger and wealthier area. The 'droit coutumier' was customary law, or rather laws, for there were several hundred regional customs. The 'droit écrit' was in principle civil law; but in practice the distinction between the two areas should not be exaggerated, for in the south Roman Law was administered as the custom of the country, and in the north custom was strongly influenced by civil law.

The prolonged effort to rationalize legal conditions, far from leading to an unqualified triumph of the central power, stimulated (in the 'pays de droit coutumier') the provincial estates, which were concerned with defining local customs and the assemblies of the *bailliages* through which the customs were ascertained. Moreover the States-general in 1484 and 1560 took the lead, the former in demanding the completion of the redaction of local customs, and the latter, as the customs were generally published by 1560, in pressing for the systematization of royal *ordonnances*.

The *ordonnance* of Montils-lès-Tours (1454) required that customs should be ascertained with the object of eventually promulgating a standard custom for every place. But by the end of the century the task of collection was far from complete. Measures by the crown, under Louis XII, proved more efficacious. In 1507 an assembly of the representatives of provincial estates was held to secure their depositions regarding custom; and even the estates of Artois were compelled to send delegates although this province was then politically, if not juridically, a part of the

Hapsburg Netherlands. By 1550 the impetus given to the movement at the opening of the century had achieved the publication of local customs with few exceptions. These collections were printed in innumerable country towns, especially in business centres like Troyes which lay on the confines of several jurisdictions, and did much to perpetuate provincial traditions.

The publication of the great majority of customs did not terminate the process, and before the end of the reign of François Ier certain districts had reached a second stage, that of revision. It is this stage which is closely associated with Christofle de Thou, who in 1555 was charged with presiding over the assemblies of *bailliages* for the revision of customary law. By the time of his death in 1582 he had visited a number of *bailliages* in northern and some in central France. Far more than hitherto it became the practice at these assemblies to convene the peasantry of the neighbourhood; and precisely in those districts (Sens 1555, Vermandois 1556, Touraine 1559) where the peasants had been recently summoned for the revision of custom, evidence is forthcoming to show their participation in electing representatives to the States-general between 1560 and 1614. In so far as it did exist in the late sixteenth century, rural suffrage for choosing representatives to the States-general seems to spring from the presence of peasants at the assemblies of *bailliages*, to which they had been bidden by agents of the crown like Christofle de Thou, as being well qualified to know custom.

The monarchy never issued a complete official code of its edicts and *ordonnances*. Louis XI, if Commynes is to be believed, would like to have gone beyond the scope of the *ordonnance* of Montils-lès-Tours so as to reduce regional variations to one custom and one measure for the whole realm; and in 1517 François Ier thought of appointing experts to prune out some of the dead wood from the royal *ordonnances*. The crown had to share with the *parlement* of Paris, which was the authority that registered them, the right to give permission for published *ordonnances*. Robert (II) Estienne received a royal command from Charles IX 'de recueillir en un volume . . . tous les edicts et ordonnances qui par vous et vos predecesseurs rois . . . ont este faicts'; but he had to contend with the reluctance of the *parlement* to allow him to consult its registers, and with competition of certain printers of Lyon, whom he was preparing to prosecute in 1566 for their infringement of his privilege. Nevertheless he managed to enforce his monopoly to the extent of issuing the collected *ordonnances* of François II and printing up to 1567 all the *ordonnances* of Charles IX.

Perhaps the most valuable contribution came from the scholars, who studied the civil law with the textual methods of the Renaissance. Guillaume Budé (ob. 1540) approached Roman jurisprudence mainly as a classical philologist and Jacques Cujas (ob. 1590) as a lawyer. But the efforts of numerous jurists educated in classical studies amplified civil law into something approaching a general law for France.

There is no longer need to insist that France at the close of the Middle Ages was neither so united nor Germany so disunited. In some respects fifteenth-century France resembled a confederacy of princes, with which the Empire provides an analogy; but competing with the feudal divisions of the nobles and 'appanagists' there existed an official view that France was divided into provinces, not fiefs. The use of the term 'province' occurs under Charles V, is frequently found under Louis XI and becomes regular in the sixteenth century. However, those whom the monarchy raised up to exercise delegated power in the provinces assumed many attributes of the former feudatories.

Pierre (II) de Brézé, who belonged to an ancient but purely local Angevin family, received in return for his services at court and in the field against the English the office of *grand sénéchal de Normandie* in 1451. He built up this office and the captaincy of Rouen into a veritable provincial government embracing finance and justice, ecclesiastical and municipal affairs. Acting like an hereditary duke he even collected an 'aide pour fille marier' from the estates of the duchy. After a temporary disgrace at the hands of Louis XI, he was restored and eventually fell at Montlhéry (1465) on behalf of the royal cause against the coalition of princes. His widow, who kept the citadel of Rouen like a family castle, preferred to hand it over to the coalition in the person of Charles de France. Altogether the offices of *grand sénéchal* and *maréchal* of Normandy stuck, with interruptions, in the de Brézé family for three generations.

Normandy was in a strategic sense a frontier province; and it is another frontier country, Picardy, which enabled Philippe de Crèvecoeur to pursue a virtually independent career as a lieutenant of the crown. Philippe abandoned the Burgundian cause in 1477, some years after Commynes had left Charles the Bold for Louis XI, and until the treaty of Senlis (1493) he dominated the northern frontier of France and acted as the political and financial pleni-potentiary of Charles VIII to the towns of Flanders. The treaty of Senlis recognized him as a local third force between the Valois and Hapsburg dynasties. It was not sufficient that the king of France should undertake to evacuate certain frontier places, but Philippe de Crèvecoeur must also deliver his bond that they would be surrendered under the treaty.

In the sixteenth century the provincial governorships fell less to promoted royal servants and more to the great magnates like Claude de Lorraine in Burgundy (1538). Although the terms of appointment to governorships frequently spoke of their duty towards the 'utilité de la chose publique', confusion still prevailed between the feudal and monarchical concept of office. The *ordonnance* of 6 May 1545 stressed the latter, and declared that governorships were not hereditary dignities, which was un-doubtedly the theoretical position. At the outset of his reign Henri II regrouped and reduced the governorships; but they fell into the hands of the leaders on both sides during the Wars of Religion, causing a recrudescence of the dangers of particularism. To an even greater degree than in other states the domain ought to have been the backbone of royalty throughout the provinces, for in principle the crown and the domain were combined in a sort of public trust. The *parlement* of Paris, in 1556, represented the Salic Law and the inalienability of the domain as the twin mainstays of the realm. Although François Ier used the theory of inalienability to justify his refusal to cede Burgundy to the emperor under the treaty of Madrid (1526), he and his son de-lapidated and neglected the domain, for it was neither so profitable nor so easy to raise loans upon as the direct and indirect taxation, which the crown controlled.

The framework of social structure was rigid, but economic conditions were by no means static, so that individuals were constantly being raised or depressed. There was on the one hand a striving after security by attaining to nobility or officialdom, and on the other Montaigne welcomed adventure:

> 'Sachans gré au sort de nous avoir fait vivre
> dans un siècle non mol languissant ny oisif.'

The purchase of a title of nobility was one way of obtaining social security. There never had been a general theory of nobility, for if the concept of the noble 'vivant noblement' was recognizable, each province had varying customs regarding immunity from *taille* and the privileges resulting from holding a noble fief. The most persistent demand for ennoblement came from Normandy. In 1470 Louis XI, after sending a commission into Normandy to ascertain the names of commoners, who had acquired noble fiefs, ennobled them for a total sum of 47,250 *livres tournois* (November 1470). This enabled aspirants to purchase their nobility, but upset rather than confirmed the view that possession of a noble fief conferred nobility. The ennobled acquired not only dignity but immunity from the *taille*. In exploiting by the sale of nobility the cupidity of its subjects the crown was realizing capital like selling the domain. Besides paying a variable price for obtaining letters of nobility the purchaser had in theory, and usually in practice, to redeem his liability to *taille* by paying to the parish in which he was assessed a sufficient sum to enable the parish to buy a rent the annual income of which would equal the amount of *taille* that was lost to the parish by his ennoblement. As the *taille* was frequently amortized on a 10 per cent basis, the newly ennobled, not to speak of his offspring, enjoyed after ten years a real financial privilege at the expense of other members of society, for resumption by the crown did not occur in the first half of the sixteenth century. The opportunism of François Ier in war expenditure was reflected in sales of patents of nobility. Coinciding with the first war against the emperor, nineteen patents were issued in 1522, the highest total up to then of any year of the reign; but in 1543, with the war against the English and imperialists, the total rose to thirty-two but sank to twenty-seven in 1544. The sale price also varied not only from person to person but from year to year. The early grants of the reign were selling at from 225 to 675 *livres tournois*. Prices rose sharply in 1543, but the large creation of that year brought the prices in 1544 back to those of the start of the reign.

As is well known, the same period witnessed the establishment of the trade in offices. Louis XI's *ordonnance* of 21 October 1467 giving security of tenure to office-holders was devised not only to appease the indignation aroused by his former revocation of officers, but to raise the value of offices so that the crown might profit more by intervening as a broker in transactions concerning them. Following medieval tradition a distinction was drawn between the sale, open or disguised, of finance offices and that of judicial offices. While the former was permissible, the latter was graver than an abuse and approached simony. Louis XII, rather than augment the *taille*, sold finance offices and intervened to levy a fee on the exchange of offices by resignation and survivorship. Although censured by contemporaries, he was moderate compared with François Ier, whose *Trésor de l'Épargne* (1522) was largely fed by the sale of offices. Courts such as the *parlement* of Paris and the *Chambre des Comptes* opposed the trade; and venal resignations are less commonly found among their members. In 1522 François Ier granted the filling of two offices of *conseiller* recently created in the *parlement* to merchants in return for a loan. The *premier président* objected, but the merchants quickly sold the offices to candidates, whom the *parlement* on the king's order had to admit. The crown could over-reach itself and at the death of Henri III offices created in 1573 had found no buyers.

These developments favoured the growth of an official class by no means dependent on the arbitrary will of the king, for as de l'Hôpital declared (June 1561) an officer could only be removed under certain conditions and even then not without a law suit lasting a year. Contemporaries were not blind to the abuse, for as the saying went the official was a gregarious beast, but the abuse was a social convenience, which enabled families to transmit offices, and the practice of resignation was said to provide an opening for the young.

More than to any other single cause, the recovery of the second half of the fifteenth century was due to the pertinacity of the peasants in restoring cultivation. In northern France the peasantry often had the land back into cultivation before their lords had time to reassert seignorial rights. When the work of the peasants had rendered fields productive and profitable, which was scarcely before the later years of Louis XI, there came a spate of law suits between lords and tenants. It was these conditions which made the *arpenteur juré* such an important figure in rural affairs. The *bourgeoisie* continued to invest in land; and of forty *seigneuries* confiscated from the Connêtable de Bourbon all but three were bought by commoners. But investment in the sixteenth century often took the form of profit sharing. The citizens of Paris and religious houses would invest capital by buying flocks and arable land on the basis of receiving a proportion of the annual profits to be remitted in cash or in kind.

In the south of the Île-de-France, and probably elsewhere, agricultural wages remained static during the reign of François Ier; but the purchasing power of money declined. A hectolitre of wheat could be bought under Charles VIII and Louis XII for 2½ days' wages, whereas in the later days of François Ier the same quantity was worth 8 days' wages. Rents remained unpaid; and when the *châtellenies* of the Île-de-France were surveyed in 1529, the crown was found to be receiving under 50 per cent of the total rent due. The price rise played havoc with the numerous fixed rents payable in kind. A measure of wheat contracted for in 1500 to yield an annual rent about equal to 8 per cent on the capital invested would by 1545 represent an approximate yield of 25 per cent. In 1531 the *parlement* of Paris annulled as usurious a contract for a fixed rent in wheat of some twenty years previous. In 1539 the journeymen-printers at Lyon went on strike mainly to obtain an increase in wages commensurate to the rise in the cost of living.

The economic situation, promising at the close of the fifteenth century, appeared bleak in 1550. Although the same might be said in varying degrees of most European countries, the position of France betrayed special weaknesses. The fiscal conduct of the government was deplorable, although here again there was little to choose between the French and other administrations. However, France lacked England's export trade in cloth, or Holland's growing carrying trade, or Germany's mines and metallurgy. State loans and ground rents perhaps attracted an unduly large share of investment. Louis XI keenly promoted mineral prospecting; but by 1550 foreigners recognized that the soil of France hid no great mineral riches. Commynes, originating in Flanders, having acquired (most unjustly) Les Sables d'Olonne (Vendée), began to polder the marshy lands and improve the harbour. The custom of certain towns (e.g. Troyes) and provinces (e.g. Périgord, Limousin) allowed local nobles to engage in a trade or industry without forfeiting their status of nobility. The king also granted the same right to favoured members of the noble class, but on the whole strongly discouraged the nobility from participating in business. The *bourgeoisie* was probably jealous, for the *tiers état* in the Estates of 1560 opposed the petition of the nobles of Touraine to be permitted to enter commerce.

Since their assembly at Tours in 1484 the States-general no longer granted taxation, and no longer were they considered to impart an additional moral strength to the monarchy. In 1468 Louis XI repudiated the treaty of Conflans before a fairly representative gathering of the Estates, but in 1527 François Ier repudiated the treaty of Madrid before a select assembly of notables. In his *Grande Monarchie* Claude de Seyssel only introduces the Estates when speaking of the representatives of towns who may be called to an *'assemblée casuelle'*. Calvin, however, in 1536 requires the three estates of a contemporary kingdom, but only when lawfully assembled, to reprove a king arbitrarily vexing his subjects:

'ut nunc res habent, funguntur in singulis regnis tres ordines, cum primarios conventus peragunt, adeo illos ferocienti regum licentiae, pro officio intercedere non veto, ut si regibus impotenter grassantibus et humili plebeculae insultantibus conniveant, eorum dissimulationem nefaria perfidia non carere affirmem, qua populi libertatem, cuius se Dei ordinatione tutores positos norunt, fraudulenter produnt'. (*Institutio*, cap. VI.)

So long as the Estates remained unsummoned probably few Frenchmen missed them, and when the Estates were summoned in 1560 they aroused disquiet after such a long intermission.

At the death of Henri II (July 1559) Christians in France were divided between the Roman and the Reformed church. Although the former was the church of the monarchy and of the majority, the latter was powerfully organized and had just held in May 1559 a secret synod representing two thousand congregations.

A revival of ecclesiastical discipline and learning, emanating from monastic and academic circles in Paris, had been active for over twenty years when François Ier ascended the throne. The most prominent figure of this Christian humanism was the aged Lefèvre d'Étaples, under whose influence Guillaume Briçonnet, becoming bishop of Meaux in 1516, initiated a programme to raise the standards of clergy and laity in the diocese. Lefèvre produced the first translation into French of the entire Gospels

(Paris 1523) to assist this effort, which based on episcopal authority was in keeping with high medieval tradition.

The provincial councils of Sens and Bourges in 1528 were expressions of the same traditional striving after improved discipline; but the reinvigoration of the church within the medieval framework of secular and regular clergy was hampered because the Concordat of 1516 negotiated between Leo X and François Ier, increased the king's power to nominate to bishoprics and abbeys. When a diocese, an abbey (or several) could be used to finance a servant of the crown like Jean du Bellay on costly diplomatic missions, or to recompense a well-affected poet like Ronsard, the higher clergy continued to be non-resident and pluralist. By the time that the council of Trent started to remedy the situation, many Frenchmen had turned to evangelical pastors.

Protestantism in France before Calvin was mainly disruptive rather than creative. Luther's works and opinions were widely known, despite their condemnation by the Parisian Faculty of Theology (1521); their influence was nevertheless limited. Guillaume Farel, who came from the home of the Vaudois, proved more formative. He was a disciple of Lefèvre. Summoned to work in the diocese of Meaux, Farel was dismissed by Briçonnet in 1523, after which he began to preach and officiate on his own authority in many parts of France, until compelled to take refuge at Basle. From there ('Turin' according to his cautious printer) he published in 1525 the *Summaire et briefve declaration* . . . asserting that the existing church was not only defective but false and must be replaced by a new church with a ministry and liturgy inspired by early Christianity.

Converts to this kind of teaching perpetrated against the Roman church many acts of defiance, of which the *Affaire des Placards* (1533) was the most unreasonable, for it brought on Protestantism the suspicion of being subversive. To dispel this connexion, Jean Calvin, who had contributed to the Olivetan Bible, published an open letter to François Ier defending the loyalty of Protestants, and sought in the *Institutio Christianae Religionis* (Basle 1536) to demonstrate the reasonableness of their doctrine. In 1536 Calvin paused at Geneva on his way to Strasbourg, and was recognized by Farel in a flash of prophetic insight for the intellectual and organizing genius needed by French Protestantism. Calvin finally returned to Geneva in

September 1541 and enforced to the letter his doctrine of a new church as exclusive and universal as the church of Rome. Only by the conversion of the king and governing class could Calvin's reform fully succeed in France, for it required the absolute co-ordination of religion and politics. But François Ier and Henri II had little material advantage to expect from becoming the agents of Calvin, for their control of the ecclesiastical hierarchy and endowments was very nearly complete. Moreover, Catholicism was not altogether devoid of vitality, and counted, particularly in the eastern half of France, enough staunch supporters to prevent a complete landslide to Protestantism. From Geneva, Calvin could only organize within his church system a section of French society. The fact that it was a section which, transcending the boundaries of class included artisans and nobles, only made it a more dangerous element within society.

A revolution in the visual arts transformed the aspect of society in the sixteenth century. Personal and social factors were responsible for many typical creations of the French Renaissance, academic opinion for relatively few. 'Mais je hay par sur tout un sçavoir pedantesque', wrote Joachim du Bellay.

Royal collectors from René d'Anjou to Catherine de Medicis were forming cabinets of small portraits, their passion for which was communicated to the noble and official class. Their mania was ministered to by Jean Clouet of Brussels (ob. 1541), who created the genre of drawing in chalk, and his son François (ob. 1572). The tension, which broke in bloodshed after the death of Henri II, had already found expression before 1559 in pictures of massacre. The source of this dreadful theme is classical, the massacres of the Roman Triumvirate, of which the constable Anne de Montmorency possessed a canvas in 1556. The arch-type of the massacre picture came from foreigners and developed under the influence of humanist ideas, but its compelling success as a subject in the hands of Antoine Caron (1521–99) was due to its immediate relevance to the religious persecutions. In the mid-century, France brought into existence a daring type of social portrait, that of the lady at her toilet in the bath. The best known, and one of the latest (1591) of these pictures, is that of Gabrielle d'Estrée and her sister, in the Louvre. The bath portrait combines an artistic and social contrast, the former depends on the anti-thesis between the unconventional setting on the one hand and on the other the stiff pose of the bather, her coiffure and jewels, the latter relies on the lady in the foreground contrasting with a laborious scene of domestic employment in the background.

Through the provinces taste varied. The painters of Lyon specialized in architectural compositions and ruins, which had an irresistible charm for the wealthy, judging by the analogy of the Antwerp school. The devout spirit, which inspired the many diocesan reforms such as that of Langres, manifested itself in the Apocalypse engravings of Jean Duvet (ob. after 1561), who sacrificed aesthetic rules to a didactic purpose. Gothic feeling was strong and found expression in the forest of gables, pinnacles and chimneys that crowned Chambord, or at the *château* of Fontaine-Henri (Calvados) in the steep slate roof, which in height considerably exceeds the distance from the ground to the eaves. In sculpture Gallic taste found satisfaction in a lanky elegance, that gave the human body a soft slender form and classical features pushed to the verge of caricature.

The elongated style was diffused from Fontainebleau by two Italians, G. B.˙ Rosso (ob. 1540) and F. Primaticcio (ob. 1570), who were responsible for the *Galerie François I*ᵉʳ (1534-37). This was not only the prototype of innumerable long galleries in France and England, but its composite decoration relying on stucco in high relief framing a continuous series of mural paintings, provided an entirely new spectacle technically more advanced and emotionally more appealing than anything in Europe. Better than anyone Primaticcio knew how to handle the elongated style, and his decoration (1540-45) of the *chambre de la duchesse d'Étampes* was a model for figure sculpture in stucco.

The Fontainebleau style in the decorative arts, though an eclectic product of Italians, pleased French patrons and naturalized itself. But, almost contemporaneously, Philibert de l'Orme (ob. 1570) was evolving a native style in engineering, architecture and decoration. His performance in theoretical writing and practical building was prodigious. His most spectacular surviving work is the domed chapel built on the circular principle at the *château* of Anet (Eure-et-Loir). Here, and in the windows of the long gallery across the Cher at Chenonceaux, de l'Orme made the arches cut directly through the surface of a cylinder, so that the outline of the arches' soffit follows a three-dimensional curve.

A high degree of success in adapting classical forms and

ornament to the needs of contemporary life was achieved in towns like Caen and Toulouse. Particularly the latter, thanks to its school of civil law and cosmopolitan merchants, was a centre of enlightened classicism. In the Midi direct observation of Gallo-Roman monuments, like the Temple of Diana at Nîmes and the triumphal arch at Orange, supplied the distinctive design and decoration of the *châteaux* of Bournazel (Aveyron) and Tour d'Aigues (Vaucluse).

The artistic debt to Italy was immeasurable; but Frenchmen were remarkably slow to accept the revived classical style of Italy. In the fifteenth century they admired the hybrid Lombard art, which was not so unlike their own, in examples such as the Certosa of Pavia. The classical monuments for which Italians were responsible before 1480 at Les Baux (Bouches-du-Rhône), Le Mans and Marseille aroused no general imitation in France. Thanks to the Italian artists, whom François Ier assembled at Fontainebleau, the first Renaissance style that was generally received in France was mannerist rather than the classical of Bramante and Raphael. French criticism of Italy was not only jealousy, but reposed on an appreciation of the more delicate native materials. 'Plus que le marbre dur me plaist l'ardoise fine' said Joachim du Bellay; but in fact slate in place of marble was used on the chimney stacks and roof-fantasies of Chambord in conjunction with some very pure Italianate ornamental motives.

BIBLIOGRAPHICAL NOTE

Sources

Les Sources de l'histoire de France: Des origines aux guerres d'Italie, ed., A. Molinier, vols. iv, v (1328–1491), 1904.

Les Sources de l'histoire de France: Le xvie siècle, H. Hauser, 2 vols., 1906–1916.

Narrative and political

BRIDGE, J. S. C. *History of France from the death of Louis XI* (–1515), 5 vols., Oxford, 1921–36. (Useful for Italian wars, vol. v devoted to general conditions at the accession of François Ier.)

CHAMPION, P. *Louis XI*, 2 vols., 1928 (2nd and enlarged edition).

DU FRESNE DE BEAUCOURT, G. *Histoire de Charles VII*, 6 vols., 1881–91. (Standard work with valuable footnotes.)

LEWIS, P. S. *Later Medieval France. The Polity*, 1968.

ROMIER, L. *Les Origines des guerres de religion*, 2 vols., 1913–14. (Important.)

TERRASSE, C. *François Ier*, 2 vols., 1945–8. (Also valuable for the art history of the reign.)

Religious

CRISTIANI, L. *L'Église à l'époque du concile de Trente*, 1948. (Being vol. 17 of *Histoire de l'église*, ed., A. Fliche & V. Martin.) (References and bibliography.)

DOUMERGUE, E. *Jean Calvin, les hommes et les choses de son temps*, 8 vols., Lausanne, 1899–1927. (Most complete and sympathetic study of Calvin.)

FEBVRE, L. *Le Problème de l'incroyance au xvie siècle*, 1942. (Important for the history of ideas.)

KINGDON R. M. *Geneva and the coming of the Wars of Religion in France, 1555–63*, Geneva, 1956.

RENAUDET, A. *Pré-réforme et humanisme (1494–1517)*, 1916. (Valuable and much documented.)

Institutional

BOUCHARD, H. 'Philippe Pot et la démocratie aux états-généraux de 1484', *Annales de Bourgogne*, xxii (1950), 33–40.

CHURCH, W. F. *Constitutional Thought in Sixteenth Century France*, 1941, Cambridge, Mass. (Comprehensive, references and bibliography.)

DOUCET, R. *Étude sur le gouvernement de Francois Ier dans ses rapports avec le Parlement de Paris*, 2 vols., 1921–6.

DOUCET, R. *Les Institutions de la France au xvie siècle*, 2 vols., 1948. (Valuable, with good bibliography.)

DUPONT-FERRIER, G. *Études sur les institutions financières de la France à la fin du moyen âge*, 2 vols., 1930–2.

DUPONT-FERRIER, G. *Nouvelles études sur les institutions financières de la France à la fin du moyen âge*, 1933. (Detailed erudition.)

RUSSEL MAJOR J. *The Estates General of 1560*, Princeton, 1951.

RUSSEL MAJOR, J. 'The Third Estate in the Estates General of Pontoise 1561', *Speculum* (1954).

ZELLER, G. *Les Institutions de la France au xvie siècle*, 1948. (Valuable short survey, references.)

Social

ARMSTRONG, A. E. *Robert Estienne, Royal Printer*, Cambridge, 1954. (Bibliography.)

BEZARD, Y. *La Vie rurale dans le sud de la région parisienne 1450–1560*, 1929.

BLOCH, J. R. *L'Annoblissement en France au temps de François Ier*, 1934.

BOSSUAT, A. 'Le Rétablissement de la paix sociale sous le règne de Charles VII', *Le Moyen Age* (1954), 137–62. (Important.)

BOUTRUCHE, R. *La Crise d'une société, seigneurs et paysans du Bordelais pendant la Guerre de Cent Ans*, 1947.

BRUN, J. E. A. *Recherches historiques sur l'introduction du français dans les provinces du Midi*, 1923.

CHAMPION, P. *Paris au temps de la Renaissance, paganisme et réforme fin du règne de François Ier et règne de Henri II*, 1936. (Suggestive.)

DOUCET, R. *Finances municipales et crédit public à Lyon au xvie siècle*, 1937.

FRANCOIS, M. *Le cardinal de Tournon, homme d'état, mécène et humaniste (Bibliothèque des Écoles françaises d'Athènes et de Rome*, No. 173, 1951).

P.-C. TIMBAL (ed.) et al., *La Guerre de Cent Ans vue à travers les registres du Parlement 1337–69*, C.N.R.S., 1967.

LEFRANC, A. 'Rabelais et le pouvoir royal', *Revue du Seizième Siècle*, xvii (1930), 191–202.

SZLECHTER, E. 'La Monnaie en France au xvie siècle', *Revue historique du droit français et étranger*, 4, xxix (1951), 500–21, 4, xxx (1952), 80–116.

Renaissance Art

ADHÉMAR, J. *French Drawings of the Sixteenth Century*, 1955.

ADHÉMAR, J. 'French Sixteenth Century Genre Paintings', *Journal of the Warburg and Courtauld Institutes*, viii (1945), 190–5.

BLUNT, A. *Art and Architecture in France 1500–1700*, 1953. (Valuable, bibliography.)

DIMIER, L. *Le Primatice*, 1928.

DU COLOMBIER, P. *Jean Goujon*, 1949.

EHRMANN, J. *Antoine Caron*, Genève, 1955.

HAUTECOEUR, L. *Histoire de l'architecture classique en France. Formation de l'idéal classique,* 2nd ed; Vol. I, pt i (1495–1540), 1963; Vol. II, pt ii (1540–89), 1965.

The Making of Absolute Monarchy (1559-1683)

————— ❧❀❀❀❧ —————

The seventeenth century saw France become the dominant nation of Europe. The strength of the French crown and the panoplied splendour in which it was enshrined evoked the envy and emulation of the monarchs and princes of the West. The Bourbon monarchy as it emerged in the reign of Louis XIV became the prototype of absolute monarchy and the classical grandeur of Versailles its incarnation. The Emperor Leopold I, the hereditary enemy of the Bourbons, bowed to the glory of Versailles when he built Schönbrunn in imitation. Each German princeling paid his tribute by following suit, so that from the Rhineland to the Elbe appeared editions of Versailles, indicative of the new climate of absolutism.

Cultural imitation came hand in hand with political imitation. Italian culture now gave way to French. The French language, pruned and stylized by Malherbe, purified and regulated by the authority of the Academy founded by Richelieu in 1635, became the language of diplomacy. French fashions dominated dress. Charles II had French tailors and his coronation robes were made in Paris; he had too his French gardeners and French musicians. An English commentator, acutely sensitive to the problem of the balance of trade, commented sourly in 1668 that: 'the laudable fashions of former times have begun to alter in favour of France. The women's hats are turned into hoods made of French silk whereby every maidservant in England becomes a standing revenue to the French king for the half of her wages.' In the same year, the German mercantilist Becher, economic adviser to the Emperor Leopold, complained hysterically: 'Now no clothes are suitable unless they come from France. French razors shave German beards better than any others. French clocks keep time better, even though they are made by Germans in Paris, all because Paris air is better than Augsburg air. French hats cover German heads, and French wigs suit German skulls better than German hair.'

The Elector of Brandenburg sent to Paris for the uniforms of his pages. French ribbons and laces, French furniture and dresses softened the bleakness of life in the North German plain, while in increasing quantities French wines and brandies mitigated the rigours of northern winters for Prussian junkers and Polish nobles. For his part, John Locke wrote moodily: 'French wine is become a modish drink among us, and a man is ashamed to entertain his friends or almost to drink alone without it.'

Englishmen spent increasingly long periods in France while on the Grand Tour. They visited Paris and then could follow one of the best roads in Europe into perhaps the loveliest valley in Europe, that of the Loire, where at Blois or Saumur they might learn French in a suitably Protestant atmosphere. Indeed it can be pleaded, as Mr J. W. Stoye suggested in his *English Travellers Abroad*, that in the seventeenth century Touraine and Anjou played a greater part in educating the English upper classes than Winchester or Eton. Even before the building of Versailles, the reconstruction of Paris with classical frontages and spacious gardens was making it the outstanding capital of Europe. The feverish tempo of building in the reign of Louis XIII has been compared by M. Tapié to the furious reconstruction of Haussmann and Viollet-le-Duc working under the auspices of Napoleon III. Marie de Medicis had constructed for her the palace of the Luxembourg, while the Cours la Reine beyond the Tuileries became the fashionable meeting-place of society. Richelieu built the Palais-Cardinal, today the Palais-Royal, and the church of the Sorbonne with its massive cupola. In 1665 Le Nôtre redesigned the gardens of the Tuileries, beyond which lay the Champs Elysées and the road to Versailles. In the same year Christopher Wren was in Paris, watching the work upon the Louvre which led him to declare that it was probably the best School of Architecture in Europe. On his return he completed the Sheldonian theatre at Oxford, fronting it with the semicircle of Emperors' stone heads upon their pedestals. His inspiration is said to be that of the semicircle of stone gods at Vaux-le-Vicomte, the most exquisite example of French classical architecture, built during the minority of Louis XIV by Louis Le Vau.

The achievement of the French monarchy stands out in bold relief against the sombre background of the anarchy and civil war which had scarred the reigns of the last Valois. Shielding their ambitions behind the ideology of religion and backed by the military power that the widespread system of clientage gave them, the nobility had then attacked the fabric of authoritarian monarchy built by François I and Henri II. Illustrative of the power of the great nobility at that time was Anne de Montmorency, Constable of France and the greatest landed proprietor. Eight hundred clients accompanied him to a meeting of the royal council at Fontainebleau in 1560; some months later the road to Orléans, where the States-general was meeting, was so thronged with his followers that the Queen-Mother was alarmed. The Constable's eldest son was Governor of the Île-de-France, where he ruled less as the King's representative than as his Protector. Obtaining from Henri II the office of Admiral of France for his nephew, Coligny, the Constable added Normandy to the number of provinces his family controlled, which now stretched from the Channel to Languedoc. In the east of France the Guises ruled from Champagne to Dauphiné; the family owned wide lands in Champagne, the Cardinal of Guise was Archbishop of Rheims, while the Duke of Guise was Governor of Dauphiné. They seemed to have reconstituted the middle Kingdom of Lotharingia, an historical memory which they carefully fostered. In the west of France flourished the power of the Bourbons; thousands of gentlemen in the area from the Pyrenees to the Loire jostled to be clients of Antony of Navarre and the Prince of Condé.

Deprived of the profits of war by the Peace of Cateau-Cambrésis in 1559, the nobility now fought for the pensions and offices at the disposal of the crown. The Italian wars had infected the nobility with a taste for extravagant living which bordered on frenzy. Their gains had often been potential rather than actual; they now felt the pinch of poverty and land-sales were frequent in a period of rising prices. But the social climate demanded conspicuous expenditure on building, entertainment and clothes which fashion dictated should be as richly jewelled as chalices. Subsidizing by the state was a necessity. The rival families fought not only for the favour but even the control of the crown, at the same time consolidating their local power and independence. French institutions were manipulated by the nobility who mounted constitutional opposition through the States-general, the *parlement* of Paris and the local *parlements*, and again through the Provincial Estates. Theoretical justification for the programmes of both the Huguenots and the League was provided from the armouries of the political theorists who postulated doctrines of resistance, invoking the contract, natural law and pleasing conventions of the Merovingian age. As the reign of Henri III drew to its violent close, victory seemed to be within the grasp of the House of Guise, had not that victory so palpably meant France becoming a dependency of Spain or involved a dangerous alliance with the urban proletariat and connexions with the disaffected peasantry. Henry of Guise alone was prepared to play the demagogue, a dangerous rôle when the ambitions of the lower classes 'to live after the manner of the Swiss, to be exempt from taxation, to pay no rents, and perform no services for their lords' were being articulated. On these rocks, after the murder of Henry of Guise, the League foundered. Concern for the social order gave Henri IV the allegiance of the propertied classes, while his conversion re-established the union of Crown and Church.

The Bourbon monarchy went from strength to strength. 1614 saw the last summoning of the States-general before 1789. Provincial governorships ceased to be hereditary fiefs, thus breaking the stranglehold upon local government of the nobility. By the Peace of Alais in 1629 the *imperium in imperio* of the Huguenots was destroyed and the danger of a resistance movement with foreign connexions disappeared. The nobility were tamed; they no longer led marauding bands around a pillaged countryside. Duels in the early decades of the century still disturbed the public peace, but increasingly the nobility crowded to court to spend their energies genteelly intriguing for the offices and perquisites which the kings lavishly bestowed. In the reign of Louis XIV, Mme. de Sévigné wrote with uninhibited gaiety: 'Le roi fait des libéralités immenses: en vérité il ne faut point désespérer; il peut qu'en faisant sa cour, on se trouvera sous ce qu'il jette.'

The political pretensions of the *parlement* of Paris, the main organ of potential constitutional resistance, were curbed. In 1641 the *parlement* was forced to accept a draconian edict by which the Sovereign Courts were forbidden to consider affairs of state, finance or administration without special command of the king.

The edict began with a preamble which might stand as a definition of absolute monarchy: 'A monarchical state cannot suffer any hand to be laid upon the sceptre of the sovereign or to share his authority.'

The right of remonstrance was whittled down; the formula 'we neither can nor should' was disqualified as injurious to the authority of the crown. The Edict of 1641 set the seal upon the fiscal powers of the monarchy already implicit in the steady increase of taxation during the reign of Louis XIII. Although the monarchy in the preambles to fiscal ordinances paid lip-service to the theory that the king should live of his own and maintained that the *taille* and *gabelle* were only emergency taxes, such apologies hardly concealed the real strength of the monarchy or the magnitude of its exactions. The *taille* was doubled between 1626 and 1636, rising again by an average of another four million *livres* as the war still proceeded. Similarly, the *gabelle* was more than doubled, while indirect taxes upon consumption added additional burdens.

The Edict of 1641 in effect relegated the powers of the *parlement* to the judicial sphere, but here already the crown had made encroachments. The authority of the *parlement* of Paris and of the local *parlements* had been undermined by the royal council and its agents, the *maîtres de requêtes* and the *intendants*. The transformation of the king's council to which the princes of the blood had technical access, into a smaller effective unit composed of the king's ministers revolutionized the central government. Administration was departmentalized, while the whole was supervised by a supreme committee, the *Conseil d'en Haut* which took all aspects of policy and government within its purview. The *parlement* of Paris jealously disputed the powers of the council, contemptuously referring to the king's ministers as 'clerks' and refusing to recognize its orders unless the king himself had been present at the session. But the council won; in 1654 it was recognized as *première compagnie du royaume*, a title to which the *parlement* had once aspired.

The *maîtres de requêtes* and the *intendants* had been used on occasion since the middle of the sixteenth century; increasingly utilized by Henri IV, their powers and services were systematically extended by Richelieu. Although they were not yet given permanent appointments in any one area, they more and more encroached upon the administrative authority of the local *parlements* and curtailed the judicial work of these by either judging cases themselves or referring them to the royal council. By the ordinance of 1629 which Richelieu forced through the Paris *parlement* by resorting to a *lit de justice*, the existence of the *intendants* was covertly legalized, their right to by-pass local authorities by direct communication with the royal council recognized and their supervision of local taxation accepted. The older officials of the crown were left complaining that all that remained to them was the 'useless name of magistrate'. The pressure of war led to increased reliance upon the *intendants*. From 1637 they appeared in all the provinces. In 1636 the need to screw extra taxes out of the towns led to a new extension of their influence. The attack upon the autonomy of the towns had begun, to be completed by Louis XIV. By 1680 the last vestiges of urban independence had disappeared. The *intendants* ruled everywhere supreme, no longer with their terms of office restricted to temporary appointments, and enjoying in Colbert's memorandum of 1664 the classic exposition of their powers and duties. Now the *parlement* of Paris lost even its attenuated right of remonstrance. In 1673 letters patent of Louis XIV declared that representations by the *parlement* of Paris should take place only after edicts had been registered. Even the simulacrum of power had gone.

Political theory echoed the facts of political power. In 1611 Louis Turquet de Mayerne had published a work of political theory, originally written in 1591, redolent of the revolutionary theories of the sixteenth century, postulating sovereignty of the people, the contract, natural law and advocating power for the States-general. He wrote: 'The King is the heart of the State which gives him life . . . the States-general should be the brain.' His book had a sympathetic reception in Paris until understandably the government suppressed it. The theme was that of the preceding age: now the divinity that hedges a king was sonorously expounded. In 1625 at the instance of Richelieu, the Assembly of the Clergy declared that: 'It should be recognized that over and above the universal consent given by peoples and nations, the Prophets announce, the Apostles confirm and the Martyrs declare that Kings are ordained of God, and not only that, but that they are indeed Gods.' Bossuet played majestic chords on the same notes: 'The royal throne is not the throne of a man, but the throne of God himself.' On Palm Sunday in 1662 he told the king 'Vous êtes Dieu'. The sanctity of the person of the king was manifest in the power of the French kings to touch for the King's Evil, which brought to France pilgrims from all parts of Europe, causing annoyance to other monarchs.

The divinity of the king equated resistance to royal commands with sacrilege. Passive obedience to the crown was as firmly emphasized by secular writers in the context of *raison d'état*. Le Bret, a member of the *parlement* of Paris first and later of the royal council, wrote in 1632: 'Should commands be obeyed, which, although they seem unjust, have nevertheless as their object the good of the State? ... My opinion is, that on such occasions, one should obey and without scruple ... *Necessitas omnem legem frangit.*'

Although French theorists drew a distinction between despotism which they deplored and absolutism which they applauded, this involved some hair-splitting. Thus secret trials before specially constituted tribunals and *lettres de cachet* were interpreted as acts of justice by the king in the name of public safety. The guarantee of the rights of citizens and of good government lay in the simple fact that the king would eventually have to render his account to God. For those who preferred rational justification for absolute monarchy there were the works of Hobbes, particularly apt in view of the disquietude felt at the excesses of the English Revolution. By 1660 five translations of the *Leviathan* had appeared and even Bossuet found Hobbes useful as a change from theological mysticism.

Finally, the justification for absolute monarchy lay in the facts of foreign policy and war. Dictatorship as a concomitant of war was an argument that Le Bret respected. Danger of encirclement and absorption by the Hapsburgs was the French nightmare not exorcized till the middle of the century. In the reign of Louis XIII, cold war gave way to exhausting campaigns in Italy and on the eastern frontiers. At Westphalia, the French finally secured Alsace, thrusting the frontier forward a hundred and twenty-five miles beyond the Vosges on to the Rhine. The grant of two fortresses on the right bank of the Rhine, Breisach and Philipsburg, meant that the road to Germany was open, while that to France was closed. The acquisition of Artois by the Peace of the

Pyrenees gave a strategic frontier in the North, sealing the valley of the Sambre, the most dangerous invasion route in the North-East, thus protecting the capital. Twenty years later by the Peace of Nimuegen, the French acquired Franche-Comté: Burgundy was no longer a frontier province and its vineyards were secure from the marauding bands of guerillas descending from the Jura, owning allegiance to Spain. In the North-East the frontier now reached the Meuse. Vauban had secured what he called the 'pré carré', an easily fortifiable frontier unimpeded by enclaves of enemy territory. His contented comment that the new frontier 'closes the entry into our country by the enemy while facilitating our entry into his' is symptomatic of the new offensive temper.

Yet although the authority and achievements of the French monarchy appear so effective and successful, the reality was much less splendid. Although rebellion was identified with sacrilege, the century was scarred by conspiracy and revolt. It is difficult to name a year between 1620 and 1660 when there did not occur a peasant revolt. In 1636 a revolt beginning in Angoulême, spreading into Poitou and Gascony, affected a third of France and troops, at a particularly dangerous crisis, had to be recalled from the front. In 1639 came a revolt in Normandy against the *gabelle*. The *Surintendant des Finances* wrote fearfully to his son: 'I am afraid that our foreign war will degenerate into a civil war.' The next decade saw the war still continue, taking a particularly heavy toll in the east of France subjected to troop movements. Outbreaks of *jacquerie* were a constant feature of the last decades of the war against the Hapsburgs. Nor did the reign of Louis XIV see the disappearance of such revolts, understandable in view of Colbert's testimony in 1672: 'The reports from the provinces all say that the people are in a state of great misery'. And there is La Bruyère's description of the French peasant: 'One sees certain savage animals in the countryside, blackened, livid and burned by the sun; they seem to be able to articulate, and when they stand on their feet they show human faces; and in effect, they are indeed men. They retire at night into caves where they live on black bread, water and roots.' This reads like the language of literary hyperbole, but the reports of the *intendants* are not very different.

Flickering consciousness of the great causes of the sixteenth century often glimmered in the earlier revolts. In Avranches in 1639 there were memories of the League; in Bordeaux and

Guienne the Huguenot cause was remembered. Irresponsible utilization of endemic discontent in all strata of society by the nobility had in the sixteenth century nearly engulfed the monarchy. The seventeenth century did not see the disappearance of similar dangers. Splits inside the royal house gave opportunities in both periods to ambitious factions. The reversionary interest, represented in the reign of Henri III by Alençon and in that of Louis XIII by Gaston d'Orléans, successfully fomented rebellion. In both periods, but with far more success in the sixteenth century, the nobility tried to draw into dependence the local *parlements* and the discontented bureaucracy. In 1632 Gaston d'Orléans intrigued with the dissident Governor of Languedoc, who in his turn utilized the discontent of the Provincial Estates. Already before this, Marillac, the Keeper of the Seals, had opposed Richelieu's plans for war as dangerous in the light of internal unrest, detecting the *parlements* showing dangerous complicity in their handling of the urban and rural revolts. In 1630 he wrote: 'There is sedition everywhere in France; the *parlements* punish nobody. The king has appointed judges for these trials and the *parlement* refuses to ratify their judgements. As a result, sedition is authorized.'

Marillac's nervousness and opposition cost him his office, but his warnings found justification in the Fronde when, from 1648 to 1653, France, in the middle of war, was faced with internal unrest almost reaching the dimensions of a civil war. The simultaneous disaffection of the nobility and the *parlement* of Paris now meant that the French monarchy faced its most dangerous crisis before the French Revolution. The *parlement* of Paris nearly strangled the conduct of the war when, in their efforts to assume moral leadership of the kingdom, they advertised their concern for the under-privileged by demanding a 25 per cent reduction in the *taille*. But their real interest was the recovery of their lost power, apparent in their political programme which attacked the whole framework of absolute monarchy as it had been established by Richelieu. They attempted to reverse the edict of 1641, claiming the right of examining all aspects of internal administration and foreign policy. They claimed that the presence of the king violated their freedom and demanded that they should consider edicts and ordinances uninhibited by his presence. Further, they asserted their right to convoke the princes of the blood, the ecclesiastical peers, the vassals of the crown, the ministers of the crown, and to unite with them in a great assembly to consider the affairs of the kingdom and the reform of the state. They protested against the way in which the royal council had dispossessed the *parlements* of judicial cases and demanded the suppression of the *intendants*; they asked for a scrutiny of accounts and that all fiscal edicts should be submitted to them. In spite of their declarations of loyalty to the king and absolute monarchy, they were, in effect, demanding constitutional monarchy, if not a republic. The pamphleteers echoed these revolutionary doctrines and once again the themes of the contract and natural law appeared. General revolt and anarchy infected the whole of France. At Aix there were cries of 'Long live Spain' and at Dijon of 'Long live the Emperor'. Had it not been for the opportune victory of Lens, the absolute monarchy of France might have been wrecked.

The building of absolutism was therefore neither swift nor sure. The slowness of achievement in foreign policy tells the same tale. The war lasted from 1635 to 1659. The result was one province gained, Alsace, and then not on conditions of complete sovereignty, and rectifications on the North-East frontier which still left the defences weak. Often France had seemed to be on the verge of defeat. In 1636 a double attack was mounted from Franche-Comté and the Netherlands; Spanish troops penetrated to the Somme and there was fear that the enemy might reach Paris. And this against the background of a peasant revolt affecting southern France. In the years following the Fronde, the North-East frontier was constantly menaced by invasion. Even in the reign of Louis XIV the ministers of the crown realized the necessity for limiting objectives in foreign policy, particularly in the context of internal unrest. The French ambassador at Cologne in 1673 wrote back: 'Is it not possible that the new burdens which the king is considering placing upon a people already impoverished, will provoke resistance? The power of the king attacked internally is bound to be enfeebled externally.'

In 1674 there came revolt in Bordeaux. In 1675, revolt in Brittany forced the government to detach six thousand troops from the front. Colbert wrote crisply to the *intendant* at Limoges: 'You can be reassured and make the fact public that the king keeps prepared twenty leagues from Paris an army of twenty thousand men ready to march into any province where there is suspicion of a rising, in order to inflict exemplary punishment and to illustrate to the whole people the obedience they owe to His Majesty.' Like an echo from the days of Richelieu, Vauban wrote: 'Truly, I fear for the monarchy.'

In spite of its apparent powers, the French monarchy suffered from profound weaknesses. Considerable claims can be made for the modernity of the seventeenth century, but they become less confident once the sphere of ambitions and aspirations is abandoned for the concrete ground of methods and techniques. The mobilization of wealth was a problem which no government in this period solved successfully. The financial characteristic of the governments of Europe was chronic insolvency. The era of the religious wars opened with a declaration of bankruptcy; from then on the French crown struggled with deficits, reaching a climax with the crisis of 1648. Efficient taxation of personal income was beyond the administrative resources and the political strength of the French absolute monarchy. In France, as in the rest of Europe, a land-tax was the easiest and the most effective method of raising revenue, but the existence of class and provincial privilege not only curtailed the yield but warped the economy of the country and resulted in acute social strain. Immunity was given by feudal custom to the nobility, by ecclesiastical tradition to the Church, and by Roman Law to the civil servants and crown officials. The loss was the greater since exemption extended to those who rented land from those exempt. The heavy incidence of taxation led to a flight to escape from the burden, and, in spite of government efforts, the reign of Louis XIII saw an increase in exemptions. In 1641 tenants on church land secured exemption; the *don gratuit* voted by the clergy to the crown was insufficient compensation for the fiscal immunity they enjoyed. The privileges of the *Pays d'Etat* meant that a third of France carried a lighter burden. The Provincial Estates keenly combated crown demands: in 1662 the Estates of Languedoc succeeded in reducing crown demands by a million *livres*. In the reign of Louis XIV the area around Tours paid five times as much as Burgundy. The *gabelle* again varied in its incidence. A third of the country bought at a low price, while Brittany, Béarn, and Navarre were exempt altogether. Rationalization of taxation was mooted not only by theorists. Even that monument of orthodoxy, Bossuet, said that the whole state ought to contribute to the needs of the state. Colbert projected radical reform of the *taille*, but like so much of his endeavour, in the face of vested interests, this remained mere aspiration.

Corruption and inefficiency of administration were as much a cause of the perpetual imminence of bankruptcy in France as the ineffective incidence of taxation. In the early seventeenth century the leprosy of corruption attacked European governments with peculiar virulence. The government of Philip III was more corrupt than that of Philip II; that of James I far more venal than that of Elizabeth. Corruption was part of the social climate of the age. Official salaries were low, but profits and perquisites high, since accounting was lax. No government employed double entry as a check upon fraud, while the habit of conflating private and public money led not only to financial chaos, but to losses on a disastrous scale.

The gains of office created the great fortunes of the century. Sully, that pillar of integrity, left great estates and a fortune. Richelieu lived extravagantly and built magnificently, not only in Paris, but in the country. His palace at Richelieu, just south of the Loire, was one of the few buildings to excite John Locke: 'the most complete building in France, where in the outside is an exact symmetry, in the inside convenience and beauty, the richest gilding and best statues that are to be seen anywhere, the avenues on all sides exceeding handsome and magnificence on all sides'.

Richelieu enjoyed lavish grants from the king, but without the perquisites of office and the mingling of his private accounts with those of the Treasury he could hardly have left at his death a fortune of sixteen million *livres*. Mazarin's corruption and rapacity created a spectacular fortune. He was master at the manipulation of army contracts, loaning back his gains to a bankrupt government at high interest rates. Richelieu also lent to the government, but, a measure of difference, charged no interest. The *Surintendants des Finances* occupied key positions. All were corrupt, but Fouquet was pre-eminent. His appointment by Mazarin led to great gains for both, especially since Fouquet's purchase of the office of *procureur-général* to the *parlement* meant that he could smother judicial inquiries. Fouquet's palace at Vaux-le-Vicomte where the gardens were planned by Le Nôtre and the interior decorated by Le Brun, was so spectacular in its splendour that Louis XIV was led to emulate Fouquet and to build Versailles. In return for his fortune, Fouquet's services to the government were the organization on the basis of his own credit, sounder than that of the government, of loans to keep alive a war endangered by the threat of bankruptcy.

Under Colbert's more stringent scrutiny the gains of office were more restrained at the court of Louis XIV. But the great posts were open to purchase and the perquisites keenly calculated. Although in charge of foreign affairs and a Minister of State from 1661, Lionne took six years to negotiate the purchase of the office of Secretary for Foreign Affairs from Brienne, who had bought the reversion for his son. Lionne's qualifications were unquestioned, while Brienne's son was so eccentric that eventually he had to retire to a luxurious monastery, but the million *livres* demanded were beyond Lionne's resources, even with the proffered assistance of the king. Lionne's personal letters abound in eager calculations of the perquisites of office and the court, reaching a climax of joy in 1668. He then acquired for his son supervision of some *départements* which would give him the perquisites arising from three *parlements* and thirty bishoprics. Colbert and Le Tellier made fortunes, but discreetly; they were said to have left ten million *livres* each and again they acquired reversions for their sons. At the end of this period the attitude of the French court towards loss of office is illustrated by the lamentations of Mme de Sévigné on the dismissal of Pomponne in 1679: 'Oh God! What a change! What retrenchment! What economies now in his family! Eight small children!'

All those employed in or by the Treasury made fortunes commensurate with their opportunities, which were at their peak in the first half of the century. The local receivers in the provinces were in a happy position since they accounted always a couple of years in arrears. Failure to employ an efficient civil service led to tax-farming, a practice of all European governments. This meant immediate revenue but long-term losses. A good deal of the yield of indirect taxation never reached the Treasury and the flaunted wealth of the tax-farmers was bitterly resented. Every government contract gave opportunities for fraud and war gave greater opportunities than peace. Richelieu calculated that the siege of Montauban, which in fact cost fifteen million *livres*, should not have cost more than two million; and every military operation in the Thirty Years War saw wastage on a similar scale. Towards the end of his life, having totally failed to bring any order into the Treasury, Richelieu wrote: 'The reform of the finances must begin by suppressing the principal ways by which money is illegally drawn from the coffers of the king. Of them all, there is no more dangerous point than that controlled by the accountants in the Treasury whose abuses have reached a stage at which not to remedy them and to lose the State are one and the same thing.' But the failure to reform meant that the government continued to pledge its credit and to borrow at exorbitant rates. The lenders were those who as revenue-collectors or as tax-farmers were rich enough to afford to plough back their gains at a further profit. The result was the emergence of a small class of moneyed men who excited public rancour. The hatred they aroused helped to cause the Fronde, thus justifying Richelieu's foreboding.

The opportunities for corruption led to the sale of office in the reign of Louis XIII on a scale surpassing anything seen in the sixteenth century.[1] Every post at court or in the government was open to purchase: all the ranks of the administration and the law-courts were affected. Sale of office had been systematized in the reign of François Ier in 1522 when he established the *Bureau des Parties Casuelles* to act, as Loyseau wrote, 'as a sort of shop for the new kind of merchandise'. Attempts were made to confine sale to financial offices, but judicial offices were quickly involved. Reversion was permitted, provided that the transaction took place within not less than forty days of the seller's death. Since the legal formalities took time, in fact three or four months were needed to make the transaction valid. If the gamble against death was not successful, the office returned to the crown which stood to gain considerably. Families therefore frequently resorted to subterfuges to conceal death, sometimes pickling the corpse 'like a young pig' while they waited for the transaction to go through. By the Edict of 1604, office-holders were allowed to dispense with the forty days rule, provided that the holder agreed to pay annually to the crown a sixtieth of the value of the office. If the holder died before making over the office, then it could be sold by his heirs, the new incumbent paying the crown an eighth of the value. The office-holders had complained that the old terms

[1] For most of the details and all of the figures concerning the sale of offices, I am greatly indebted to the authoritative work of R. Mousnier, *La Vénalité des offices sous Henri IV et Louis XIII*, Rouen, 1945.

of reversion were exorbitant; the new terms were ludicrously cheap, particularly since the crown valuation was low. But the crown could now look forward to a steady annual revenue instead of the windfall payments hitherto received.

The business of sale was immediately let out to farm to Charles Paulet, whose name became attached to the new system. The easier terms were immensely popular and office-holding became the characteristic feature of French society. Office was desirable not so much for the salary attached, as for the perquisites carried and the exemption from taxation. In 1550 Nicholas d'Ormesson borrowed to purchase his office of *trésorier de l'extraordinaire des guerres*; in a year he had recovered the purchase-price. The wealth arising from office was the greater since accumulation of office was the rule: thus in 1622 seventeen commissioners for the *taille* in Normandy shared nine hundred and sixty-nine offices between them. Social climbing in France was done by the rungs of office; those who climbed highest could enter the ranks of the nobility. A fourth estate of the realm was thus created, wealthy and ambitious, closely linked by the ties of family, and into which the nobility often married.

Even before the edict of 1604, Le Bret had in 1593 commented sourly: 'This kingdom has for some years suffered from a monstrous growth of office-holders who are prodigiously multiplied . . . to such an extent that of five hundred citizens a half are office-holders.' In 1608 Loyseau decided to write a book about this aspect of French society, and went to seek information from the farmer of the *paulette*. His account of the scene there vividly depicts the eagerness to acquire office:

'In the beginning of the month of January last, 1608, during the icy weather, I decided, being in Paris, to go one evening to the farmer in charge of the annual payment for offices, to consult with him about some of the questions for this chapter. But he was too rushed. I had chosen the time badly. I found inside the office a great troop of office-holders pushing and jostling to be the first to press the money into his hands. Some of them were still booted, not having given themselves time to take their boots off. I noticed that as soon as their business had been dispatched they went straight away to the Notary who lived quite near, to get their certificates of reversion passed and they appeared to me to be walking on ice, for fear of making a false step, so afraid were they of dying on the way. Then, when closing time had come and the farmer closed his register, I heard a great murmuring from those who still had to get their business attended to, demanding that their money should be taken, in case they should die in the night. Contemplating this state of affairs, I came to a point at which I said to myself: "Merciful God, I would we were as anxious to save our souls as our offices." '

The popularity of office meant that the king sold in a seller's market. In response to the demand, the price of office rose sharply, even allowing for the general price-rise. Richelieu in his *Testament Politique* referred to the extraordinary rise in the price of judicial offices, while in 1628 an ordinance of Louis XIII spoke of the 'dearness of office so prejudicial to our subjects'. Offices attached to the *parlement* of Rouen rose nearly sixfold in price between 1593 and 1622. Henri IV had seen the *paulette* in terms of a steady annual revenue, but for Louis XIII it was a main source of royal finance. In war it was invaluable. Henri IV appreciated this in the last year of his reign when war became imminent. He then put a new block of offices upon the market. In 1620 the revolt of the Queen-Mother led to the same expedient. In 1625 when Richelieu's foreign policy took on more ambitious perspectives, involving subsidies to allies and interference in the Valtelline, the bill was footed by more creations, and again in 1627 when the armies were mobilized for the siege of La Rochelle. The year 1635, when open war with Spain began, saw a climacteric and the following years repeated the pattern.

The income from offices could be inflated not only because new offices could be created, but because existing office-holders could be squeezed. The threat of withdrawing the *paulette* was guaranteed to extract, in spite of protests, new capital charges and forced loans. Often the office-holders had to borrow to pay, so that the crown at moments of crisis was drawing upon dormant capital. The importance of the extraordinary revenue drawn from new creations and capital charges is tellingly revealed by an analysis of the accounts of the *Bureau des Parties Casuelles*. Throughout the 1630's it provided the great bulk of the returns. In 1630, 72 per cent of the receipts came from these sources, rising to

92 per cent in 1636 and 98 per cent in 1642. The snowballing of the returns meant that from 1620 to 1632 a third of the total revenue of the state was drawn from the profits of office. In 1633 the returns from the *Bureau des Parties Casuelles* came to rather more than half the total revenue, in contrast to the reign of Henri IV when they averaged only about 8 per cent. If the Hapsburgs financed the Thirty Years War from the returns of their silver fleets, if Gustavus Adolphus launched his armies on the profits of a European monopoly of copper, the Bourbons anchored their war-budgets to the sale of offices.

Sale of office not only brought revenue to the crown, but also, through the new system of hereditary transmission, political security. It can be argued that the creation of absolute monarchy in France was not so much the result of the power of the crown as of its weakness. Henri IV said that he had liquidated the great nobles of the League not so much by the exercise of power as by bribery. He did indeed use the bait of crown patronage astutely. Similarly, by the device of the annual payment, he bought the support of the middle class. Absolute monarchy was therefore in this aspect no more than a gigantic system of bribery of those whom the crown found it worth while to bribe. In the sixteenth century, before the annual payment had given security to heredi-tary holding, sale of office had been causal to the weakness of the crown, for without certainty of reversion, office became part of the system of clientage. The Guises not only had the support of their gentlemen followers and their tenants, they had within their gift the offices which fell within their orbit of influence. Richelieu thought that this more than any other factor had contributed to the power of the Guises and to the anarchy of the days of the League. He wrote: 'Nothing enabled the Duke of Guise to make himself powerful in the League against the king and the state more than the great number of office-holders, who had been introduced by his influence into the principal posts of the kingdom.' Indeed in 1588 the revolt of the towns against Henri III was engineered by the local office-holders, who, elected to the provincial Estates and the States-general, demanded provincial and urban autonomy.

Charles IX had tried to combat the spread of this aspect of clientage by issuing edicts permitting reversion. But the immediate effect was to enable the office-holders to form a closed caste, creating a large body of discontent upon which Guise and Mayenne drew. In the seventeenth century the annual payment, combined with the mass of new offices created, solved the problem. Richelieu, in retrospect, considered that recognition of this aspect of the power of the Duke of Guise had been Henri IV's main motive in establishing the annual payment. He explained: 'I learned from the Duc de Sully that this consideration was the most powerful motive which the late king had in establishing the annual payment; this great king was less concerned with the revenue which he would draw, than with wishing to prevent inconveniences of this nature. . . . *Raison d'Etat* was the most powerful argument on this occasion.' The new dependence upon the crown paid political dividends. The *parlements* in 1615 refused to back the revolt of Condé who bid for popularity by misguidedly demanding the cleansing of the kingdom by the destruction of venality. The Queen-Mother in 1620 found that a regrant of the annual payment robbed her of support. Attempts by Gaston d'Orléans to play the part of Henry of Guise foundered on the rock of office-holding.

But at the same time there was bitter criticism of the system, leading to much unrest. Complaints were voiced that justice had become venal, that excessive fees were being extorted by the office-holders. The office-holders themselves objected to the flood of new creations which, if they themselves refused to buy, reduced the profits of existing offices; and they fulminated against the capital charges to which they were constantly subjected. Richelieu, when he first became minister, optimistically wrote: 'Your Majesty should not continue the annual payment, should banish the sale of offices, two sources of evil, prejudicial to your authority and to the purity of the administration of justice.'

The succeeding years underlined his argument. There was constant friction with the *parlements*. In 1630 when the *parlement* of Dauphiné threw open the corn-stores collected by the *intendants* for the use of the army, Marillac's suspicions that the *parlements* were actively conniving at the popular revolts seemed justified. In 1639 the *parlement* of Normandy came under the same suspicion. The corruption and inefficiency which sale of office engendered could be and was partially offset by reliance upon the *intendants*. But this inevitably aroused the suspicion of the *parlements*. The crisis of 1630 had the makings of a general revolt.

The reckoning came in 1648 with the outbreak of the Fronde, brought on by the overcreation of office and the systematic bleeding of the office-holders. But each crisis was overcome, even that of the Fronde, by adroitly threatening the withdrawal of the annual payment. Resistance always crumbled, since profits weighed more than principles. The importance of the annual payment is thus clear; its small financial return in these years bears no relation to its political implications. Richelieu himself renounced his young man's dream of abolishing sale of office. Instead he praised the prescience of Henri IV. At the end of his life, in the *Testament Politique*, he wrote that in a newly founded state things were different, but that 'prudence does not permit action of this kind in an ancient monarchy whose imperfections have passed into custom, and whose disorder forms part of the order of the state'.

He wrote against the painful background of deficits and anticipated revenue, for political security was bought at the price of unsound finance. The king tapped windfall revenue from offices in moments of crisis, but at the same time the dues claimed by the office-holders absorbed a dangerous proportion of the revenue. In 1639 Richelieu calculated that payments to them came to almost thirty-four and a half million *livres*, a million more than was coming in from payments by them to the *Bureau des Parties Casuelles*. Not surprisingly, the crown had declared a species of bankruptcy and was paying the office-holders only three-quarters of what was due to them. Even so, this absorbed 78·7 per cent of the yield from direct taxation. If full payment had been made, not only would the whole of this have been absorbed, but also part of the proceeds from indirect taxation. But Richelieu was calculating the returns from the annual payment only; new creations and charges in fact meant that 20 per cent of the budget only was being soaked up in payments to officers. The danger lay in the saturation of the market, already marked by 1639. In 1643 offices created and offered for sale since 1637 were still unsold. The returns from the *Bureau des Parties Casuelles* fell sharply from 1639. In 1643 the percentage of the revenue from this source had dropped to what it had been in the time of Henri IV, a mere 8 per cent. The Hapsburg war effort was crippled when at this time the bullion cargoes dwindled; the French capacity to mount campaigns was maimed by the failure to raise capital from the sale of offices. Refusal to pay interest rates on the *rentes*, a direct result of the diminished revenue, led to the Fronde.

The sale of office was ruinous to sound finance and destructive of efficient administration; the economy of the country suffered severely from the strain. New taxes were created to support new offices. The office-holders exploited those beneath them to compensate for the unpaid salaries and the capital charges. The reason for the century being punctuated by peasant revolts becomes clear. Taxation combined with other stresses of war, of which the multiplication of offices was one, made life intolerable. The years from 1635 to 1660 saw the cumulative effect of these strains. In Burgundy, perhaps more affected since it lay on the route-march of armies, the independent peasant proprietor disappeared. Villages were deserted never to be repeopled. The reports of the tax-collectors bear the sombre refrain: 'There are here only those who are useless to the community.' The number of beggars increased frighteningly. In the village of Talent in 1650 there were sixty-four inhabited houses, but only forty-five persons were scheduled for taxation. The others were the destitute. St Vincent de Paul preached charity; the state preferred whipping and the galleys.

The poverty of the peasantry was increased by the demands of the landowners. Patronage and the *paulette* bought the loyalty of the nobles and the office-holders, but they required also a free hand on their estates. In the reign of Louis XIV the *intendants* complained that seigneurial dues were as heavy again as the *taille*. The office-holders who bought land were peculiarly exacting, wishing to run their estates as profitably as their offices. The *taille* itself stunted agricultural development, since it was raised according as the yield increased. Land therefore was left unimproved and farming methods were inefficient. The consequent poverty of the countryside was responsible for the famines, which, like the revolts, punctuated the century. The peak famine years were 1629 to 1630, 1648 to 1651, and 1660 to 1661. Famines brought with them epidemics, and deaths increased four- and five-fold. Between 1648 and 1700 the population of France fell by a million.

Industry and commerce too were stunted. A bad harvest reduced purchasing power, restricted investment and led to unemployment. Besides, the constant deterrent to business investment was sale of office. The general investment pattern of the office-holders was a third in land, a third in office and a third in government bonds. If money was made in business it was invested in office, so that trade and industry suffered from a constant haemorrhage. The office-holders in control of town government refused to be interested in new industries, preferring to invest in land which raised their social status. The *parlement* of Dijon gave Colbert's plans a chilly reception, saying that: 'His Highness the Prince has proposed the establishment of commerce and manufactures; this has been considered, but it has been found that the province is more suited to the cultivation of the ground and to the vine and that it is more useful to have plenty of labourers and vineyard workers than artisans.' In the same spirit, the *parlement* in 1654 had applied for a royal writ to stop the building of iron works in the neighbourhood. That same *parlement* spent its time issuing savage edicts against the unemployed and beggars who infested the town.

Government plans for commercial expansion were frustrated by the office-holders of France. Richelieu's ambitious commercial programme remained a blue-print. The Levant trade declined catastrophically and the linen and canvas trade to Spain, the greatest single export there and a vital bullion-earner, was halved. French ships ceased to appear in the Baltic and overseas trade languished. Money was so scarce in the provinces of France in the later stages of the war against the Hapsburgs that there almost reigned a natural economy. The lack of consumer demand acted as a powerful brake upon economic development. The good coin was scooped up by the tax-collectors for return to Paris; in the provinces there was little but inferior copper coin. The situation seems to have been hardly better in the reign of Louis XIV, which helps to explain Colbert's desperate preoccupation with bullion imports. Mme de Sévigné is witness to the shortage of good coin in the provinces. In 1680 she wrote from Brittany: 'This morning there arrived a peasant hung round with bags; he had some under his arms, some in his pockets, others on his back. . . . The good abbé, who goes straight to the point, believed that now we were rich for ever. "My poor fellow, you are well loaded. How much do you bring?" . . . "Monsieur," he replied, breathing with difficulty, "I believe there are here a good thirty francs." '

In 1660 money was to be found only in the rapacious hands of those who had access to the revenues of the state: courtiers and Treasury officials, tax-farmers and contractors, and the thousands of office-holders. For five years France had been near to civil war and the menace of peasant revolts had not receded. The administrative and economic programme of the monarchy had been thwarted by the office-holders and its revenues filched by its servants. Is therefore absolute monarchy a myth imposed upon this period just as the myth of feudalism has been imposed upon the medieval period? But after all, Charles I of England found himself upon the scaffold on a January morning outside Whitehall, while Louis XIV reigned proudly in Versailles, envied and admired by the kings of Europe. Any interpretation of English government and society in the early seventeenth century which ignores the causation of the civil war avoids the central issue of the period. Similarly, it is equally important to account for the emergence of strong monarchy in France.

The French monarchy enjoyed some obvious advantages. Freedom to tax without recourse to a representative assembly told heavily in favour of the French monarchy, though it must be remembered that financial edicts had to be submitted to the *parlement* and the provincial Estates, who were by no means submissive. The failure of the Huguenots and the League spelt the disappearance of the ideology of resistance, while the Catholic Church was the fervent defender of the cause of monarchy. But since social strains produce political effects, it is important to notice that both monarchies were subjected to similar social pressures, while both suffered from the corroding effects of administrative weakness. Professor Tawney, invoking Harrington, has argued that the sale of crown land in England and the impoverishment of the English nobility so changed the social landscape that political revolution was made inevitable.[1] But in France, the crown was also forced to sell land, a constant source of complaint and grievance, since the sales were equated with rising taxation. It is perhaps significant that the land-sales of the sixteenth century coincided with the crisis of the religious wars, but the French monarchy survived this ordeal to emerge absolved from the rule of law and sanctioned by theories of divine right. The indebtedness of the English nobility and the extent to which

[1] 'Harrington's Interpretation of his Age', *Proc. Brit. Acad.* xxvii, 1941; 'The Rise of the Gentry', *Econ. Hist. Rev.*, vol. XI, 1941.

it was forced to sell land, have been subjected to searching criticism, weakening the argument that social changes were so great that political change had to follow.[1] Paradoxically, the economic predicament of the French nobility, their struggles with rising prices, their extravagant tastes and their failure to run their estates with business efficiency have been emphasized both for the sixteenth and seventeenth centuries. In Burgundy in the late sixteenth century the urban patriciate was the beneficiary of the alienation of crown lands and of the land-sales of the nobility, and Burgundy is not an isolated example. Moreover, in Burgundy the acquisition of land normally preceded the purchase of office.[2] On Professor Tawney's argument the new owners of property should have taken over political power. Up to a point they did so, in so far as the *parlements* came to control administration and combated the authority of the *intendants*. But that conflict ended in the victory of the monarchy, presiding over a civilization essentially aristocratic in tone.

Corruption, sapping both financial stability and administrative efficiency, was a problem facing both governments. Sir John Neale has called attention to the spread of corruption in the last years of Elizabeth I, seeing in it a cause of the downfall of the monarchy, for 'under James I, the scandal and discontent caused by a putrefying political system helped to provoke the Civil War'.[3] There is much to be said for this view. Corruption at the court of James I spread with cancerous rapidity. Like Louis XIII, James was lavish in his rewards to favourites; apart from one brief period, peculation went unchecked and accounting was chaotic. Sale of office was openly practised; prices rose and offices often descended within the family. Resentment embittered Parliament. In 1625 a member of the Commons angrily said that: 'the price of a serjeant-at-law is as well known as the price of a calf; and they which buy dear must sell dear'. Corruption swelled the crown deficits. It was the gravamen of the charge against Buckingham at his impeachment, which was an attack upon the scandalously corrupt administration of the Early Stuarts.

[1] H. R. Trevor-Roper, 'The Elizabethan Aristocracy: An Anatomy Anatomised', *Econ. Hist. Rev.* vol. XI, 1941.

[2] H. Drouot, *Mayenne et la Bourgogne, 1587–1596*, 1937, vol. I, pp. 45 *et seq.*; G. Roupnel, *La Ville et la campagne au xviiᵉ siècle: étude sur les populations du pays dijonnais*, 1922 (pp. 187 *et seq.*).

[3] 'The Elizabethan Political Scene', *Proc. Brit. Acad.* 1948, p. 23.

Corruption brought wealth to those who enjoyed the good fortune to partake of its benefits. The present controversy concerning the part played by the gentry in causing the fall of the Stuart monarchy has a relevance for this analysis of French government and society. Not only the decline of the English aristocracy but the rise of the gentry has been questioned. The mere gentry, it has been said, felt themselves to be a depressed class, aspiring to the tastes of the aristocracy but unable to gratify them, since the patronage of the court was open to only a restricted circle.[1] Again, the privileges and wealth of the capitalists of the City of London, the gains of the monopolists and the customs-farmers, provoked the same jealousy as in France enflamed feeling against tax-farmers and contractors. Not all the aristocracy in England enjoyed the perquisites of the court; as a result, alliances were formed with the discontented gentry, ultimately destroying, through their control of Parliament, the system and the monarchy of the Stuarts. But in France corruption played a different rôle. The monarchy dispensed its favours to the aristo-cracy with a liberal hand, while sale of office spread beyond the court into every province and rung of the administration. Aristocratic factions led by nobles, who considered themselves excluded from a fair share of the golden rewards of patronage, collapsed ignominiously, for they found that their potential allies, the *parlements*, caught in the toils of venality, were prepared to compromise and surrender. The English gentry in Parliament with no stake in the system, since the *paulette* did not exist, had no reason to come to terms. Besides, sale of office provided machinery by which the French monarchy could always raise credit. The English monarchy resorted to forced loans, or bor-rowed from individuals, or, with some difficulty, from the City of London. Again, in the *rentes*, government bonds backed by the corporation of the City of Paris, the French monarchy had an additional source of credit, which was far in advance of anything the English government had at its disposal till the foundation of the Bank in 1694. Investment in Bank stock played an important part in ensuring the stability of the Whig Revolution, just as office-holding and the *rentes* gave security to the Bourbon monarchy.

[1] H. R. Trevor-Roper, 'The Gentry, 1540–1640', *Econ. Hist. Rev.* Supple-ments, I.

Yet the dangerous crisis of the Fronde, when office-holders and government bond-holders flirted with revolution, suggests that to attribute the success of French absolutism solely to the sale of office is an oversimple and overcynical explanation. That success was largely the work of Colbert, who saw that a monarchy maimed by deficits and a crippled economy would one day have to pay the reckoning. The situation in 1661, when Louis XIV began his personal rule, was, as Colbert correctly saw, critical. The frauds of the local receivers of taxes, protected by the hereditary tenure of their offices, meant that only a third of the returns from taxation was reaching the Treasury, to be submitted to further pillaging on arrival. Revenue was anticipated, crown land sold, while the interest charges on crown borrowing were a heavy burden. The long war had increased taxation, while causing a shrinkage in foreign trade. Monetary stocks had therefore fallen. The poverty of the country was such that even though the nominal returns from the *taille* were high, the actual yield was dangerously low. Exaggerating somewhat, Colbert claimed that the *taille* in the last years of Mazarin's rule was fixed at fifty-six million *livres*, but only sixteen million were being screwed out of a starving peasantry, and arrears were mounting. The magnitude of the problem was urgently revealed by the famine of 1661–2, for famine years spelt terrible mortality, unemployment in the towns, and a fall in the returns from taxation.

Colbert urged administrative and fiscal revolution. The *taille* and sale of offices he saw as together responsible for the paralysis of the economy and the penury of the monarchy. Reduction in taxation was as urgently necessary as an increase in royal revenue. Both could be achieved if corruption was ruthlessly attacked by radical reform of the Treasury and a surgical operation upon the whole system of office-holding. As a means of raising revenue, sale of office had played its part. The inordinate increase in offices had brought down the price, while payments to office-holders ate into the revenue, quite apart from the reduction of the revenue by the corrupt practices of those who held office. The figures from the generality of Rouen lend point to Colbert's dislike of office-holding. There 41·66 per cent of the revenue from the locality was absorbed in payments to the office-holders. But these were in 1660 receiving less than a third of what was due to them; had they been paid in full, more than a million *livres* more than the taxation of the area yielded would have been necessary. In 1659 Colbert had already advised Mazarin to reduce the number of financial offices by twenty thousand and judicial offices by rather more. As a result, illicit charges by judicial officers would cease, royal revenue would both be lightened and at the same time increased since fraud would be prevented, while the numbers of those exempt from taxation would be diminished. Further, the *taille* could be reduced, and the threat of deserted villages and peasant risings would disappear. The *intendants* who held their appointments by virtue of their efficiency, would be the executive agents of the new policy. Lastly, those dispossessed of office would turn to industry and agriculture, working for the 'welfare of the kingdom, instead of as at present for its destruction'.

Colbert was therefore as radical as the young Richelieu. But now the crown was stronger, while the threat of encirclement and invasion had disappeared. Colbert was therefore able to effect a high-handed conversion of the *rentes* and to begin his attack upon office-holding. The *parlement* of Paris was too weak to protest effectively. Simultaneously, peculation in the Treasury and profiteering by the tax-farmers were investigated. Ledgers for receipt and expenditure were introduced, and monthly statements drawn up. In the provinces, the *intendants* checked the corruption of the office-holders, taking over more power and, in particular, supervising the collection of the *taille*. Illustrative of the success of the new administrative drive was a sixty-nine fold increase in the returns from crown land, where, Colbert said, the peculations, particularly in the royal forests, were 'convincing proof against the officers in general'. By 1662 Colbert had balanced the budget, and, moreover, reduced the *taille*. He was aided by reform in the expenditure departments. Richelieu had been defeated by the fraud of the army contractors; now Le Tellier and Louvois, depending like Colbert upon the *intendants*, waged war upon corruption in this sphere.

But the vested interests of an absolutist state, together with war, were too strong for Colbert as they had been for Richelieu. Buying out the office-holders was too expensive an operation for a government intent upon war, and involved, now as earlier, political risks. Colbert therefore, like Richelieu, was forced to become an empiricist, but, a measure of the strength of the monarchy and his own forcefulness, while renouncing revolution, he continued to back reform. His initial reduction in the numbers of offices was followed by a diminution in the perquisites, combined with heavy capital charges. Office became much less attractive, but political disaffection was guarded against. The *intendants* were warned to use tact, while Colbert went so far as to refuse to allow permanent appointments to the *sub-délégués*. Sale of office remained part of the political foundations of the Bourbon monarchy.

Empiricism put a brake upon Colbert's original programme. Although he had projected rationalization of the *taille*, the ordinance was never completed. Corruption was by no means obliterated, though lessened. Nevertheless the administrative reform he did achieve, enabled him to inject enough vitality into the economy of France to win considerable success for his export drive. French luxury goods now began to earn much needed foreign exchange, vitally important given the internal monetary famine and the depreciation of the *livre* on the Amsterdam exchange. Silks from Tours went to Spain, the French flag penetrated the Baltic, the Levant market saw a successful revival of French trade. John Locke and the Whigs grew worried. Yet the resistance which Colbert encountered, the agrarian poverty he never solved, the failure of the *livre* ever to reach par, justified his hatred of office-holding as restricting the flow of productive investment. It is significant that he found some of his most willing allies in the Huguenots. Excluded from office, the Huguenots had turned to business, a more concrete reason for their connexions with capitalism than the mystique of Calvinism which is sometimes invoked. At La Rochelle, among the firms of Pagès, Lagny and Raulé, Colbert found support, in contrast to the dusty answer he received from Dijon, where the office-holders so shackled business incentive that a town which had once been a flourishing cloth-centre now concentrated on the hotel business.

With corruption curbed and office-holding curtailed, with administrative efficiency secured and a reviving economy, the absolute monarchy of Louis XIV achieved the building of Versailles and the frontier of the Rhine. Revolutionaries like John Pym and Cromwell did not arise in France, and here the accident of personality plays its part in accounting for the success of the Bourbons and the failure of the Stuarts. James I and Charles I had Buckingham, Louis XIII had Richelieu. The triumphant exponent of absolute monarchy in France was the king, who, as a young man, had the ability to recognize and back the administrative and financial talent of Jean-Baptiste Colbert.

BIBLIOGRAPHICAL NOTE

(The bibliography has been reconstructed to include some of the many relevant publications which have appeared since the essay was first printed in 1957.)

1. Sources

Le Testament politique du Cardinal de Richelieu, ed. L. ANDRÉ, 1947.

Lettres et mémoires adressés au Chancellier Séguier (1633–1649), 2 vols., ed. R. MOUSNIER, 1964 (invaluable as an administrative and social source and the basis for the controversy over the nature of the popular revolts; see below under 4).

Lettres, instructions et mémoires de Colbert, 7 vols., ed. P. CLÉMENT, 1862–82.

Correspondence administrative sous le règne de Louis XIV, 4 vols., ed. G. P. DEPPING, 1850–55.

2. Sixteenth- and Seventeenth-Century France

ARMSTRONG, E. *The French Wars of Religion,* 1892.

DROUOT, H. *Mayenne et la Bourgogne (1587–1596),* 2 vols., 1925 (a very detailed provincial study throwing light on the national scene).

LIVET, G. *Les Guerres de Religion 1559–1598* (Que Sais-Je series, No. 1016), 1962.

ROMIER, L. *Le royaume de Cathérine de Médicis,* 2 vols., 1925.

LOUGH, J. H. *An Introduction to Seventeenth Century France,* 1954 (uses literary material effectively).

PAGÈS, G. *Naissance du Grand Siècle: la France de Henri IV à Louis XIV, 1598–1661,* 1948 (the most concise and illuminating introduction).

MOUSNIER, R. *Les xvie et xviie siècles (Histoire générale des civilisations,* tome 4, 5th ed.), 1964.

TAPIÉ, V. L. *La France de Louis XIII et de Richelieu,* 1952 (a stimulating and elegant study of politics, foreign affairs, social and religious tensions).

LAVISSE, E. *Histoire de France,* vol. vii (i), *1643–1685,* 1906 (still standard).

GOUBERT, P. *Louis XIV et vingt millions de français,* 1966 (translated *Louis XIV and Twenty Million Frenchmen,* 1970).

METHIVIER, H. *Le Siècle de Louis XIV* (Que Sais-Je series, No. 126), 1962.

RANUM, O., *Paris in the Age of Absolutism*, New York, 1968.

3. *Constitutional, administrative and social aspects*

MOUSNIER, R. *La vénalité des offices sous Henri IV et Louis XIII*, Rouen, 1945 (a classic work based on massive research).

PAGÈS, G. 'La vénalité des offices dans l'ancienne France', *Revue historique*, 1932.

MÉTHIVIER, H. *L'Ancien Régime* (Que Sais-Je series, No. 925), 1961.

HAUSER, H. *La pensée et l'action économiques du Cardinal de Richelieu*, 1944.

ESMONIN, E. *La Taille en Normandie au temps de Colbert (1661–1683)* (a classic work not confined to Normandy and covering the seventeenth century).

ROUPNEL, G. *La ville et la campagne au xviie siècle: étude sur les populations du pays Dijonnais*, 2nd edn., 1955.

4. *Current controversies*

MOUSNIER, R. *La Plume, la Faucille et le Marteau: Institutions et Société en France du Moyen Age à la Revolution*, 1970 (an invaluable collection of essays hitherto scattered; especially important for the intendants (1634–48), for the Fronde, and for the challenge offered to the Marxist interpretation advanced by B. PORCHNEV, *Les soulèvements populaires en France de 1623 à 1648*, (French translation, 1963). For an assessment of the controversy, see M. PRESTWICH, *English Historical Review*, vol. 81, 1966.

MOUSNIER, R. *Fureurs paysannes*, 1967 (in process of translation; the first section analyses French risings).

GLASS, D. V. and EVERSLEY, D. E. C., *Population in History: Essays in Historical Demography*, 1965 (contains essays by J. MEUVRET and P. GOUBERT on French population problems).

5. *Political thought*

ARMSTRONG, E. 'The Political Theory of the Huguenots', *English Historical Review*, 1889.

MOUSNIER, R. *L'Assassinat d'Henri IV*, 1964 (also surveys the reign).

MOUSNIER, R. *La Plume, la Faucille et le Marteau*, op. cit. (includes essays on political and social ideas, notably 'Comment les français du xviie siècle voyaient la constitution'.).

XVIIe Siècle, Nos. 25–26, 1955, 'Comment les français voyaient la France au xviie siècle'; includes essay cited by R. MOUSNIER, together with V. L. TAPIÉ, 'Comment les français voyaient' la patrie' and J. MEUVRET, 'Comment les français voyaient l'impôt'.

SÉE, H. *Les Idées politiques au xviie siècle*, 1923.

J. S. BROMLEY

The Decline of Absolute Monarchy
(1683-1774)

—————◄►🔷◄►———————

Were it not for one very important proviso, it might be said that princely absolutism absorbed the idea of society in that of the state. It was content to define a nation simply as people living under the same rule. Rousseau, as we know, found it wholly incompatible with the existence of any society worth the name. Its vocation, as we have often been told, was to exalt state power against any particularist force which might fracture the unity and endanger the preservation of the state in a competitive world, in effect identifying the interests of society with its own. In the century of the Thirty Years War and in the situation of France during the Fronde the general will of society could be construed as favourable to it. On the other hand, its proponents meant something when they distinguished it from despotism or mere arbitrariness. The assumption was that in France, if not in Persia, the monarch would recognize the inheritance of an ancient constitution, those fundamental laws of the realm which enshrined its most cherished memories and what might be called the moral norms of its existence.

It is easy to make nonsense of limits so general and vague, but we may take it that they possessed a concrete meaning for the contemporary apologists of Louis XIV, if not necessarily for the king himself. We are reminded of these deeply felt realities when, for example, after his death, the *parlements* demanded renewal of their power of remonstrance, Brittany the removal of its *intendant*, and members of the nobility a return to conciliar government from the 'despotism' of ministers responsible to the king alone. What is more significant still is that even Louis XIV paid lip-service, if not more, to the historic institutions or practices with which French absolutism was supposed to be compatible. Some, like the liberties of the Gallican Church and the industrial gilds, were, it is true, of direct use to government: the gilds, for example, could be turned into money, by holding up their offices to ransom and even forcing them to buy new ones. But we should note that Louis had never done more than suspend the power of remonstrance—on the plea of an emergency that lasted for the duration of his reign; that Brittany got its first *intendant* only on the eve of naval war in 1689; and that when, in 1695 and 1710, it was found necessary to apply direct taxation to the privileged orders, it was excused as a temporary measure. We shall greatly misjudge the inwardness of absolute monarchy if we forget that its practitioners were nearer to the Middle Ages than to ourselves. Louis XIV took a seigneurial, not a totalitarian, view of his realm; and Colbert, the antithesis of all that is 'gothic' in human intelligence, did no more than apply the outlook of a medieval trading town to a state in the making. Even the philosophy, then, of absolute monarchy in France should not be interpreted as pure system. Far less should it be equated with the megalomania of Louis XIV and the egoism of his successor. Though it permitted self-will in effect, it contained implicit restraints from the very beginning. Some of them were to prove the seeds of its undoing.

In spite of these qualifications, however, the gulf between theory and practice remained extraordinarily wide, as the greater part of this lecture may perhaps suggest. Thus, in its primary task of building up military strength the monarchy's success was notoriously partial. After 1684 its wars brought nothing about, except the independence of the United States and national bankruptcy. Lorraine and Corsica, the sole territorial acquisitions in this period, were the fruit of passing diplomatic revivals. On the whole, in the eighteenth century, French diplomatic influence counted for less than it had done before Louis XIV; for a time it was harnessed to English leadership, later to Austrian. As an instrument of national unification, secondly, the monarchy poured out a stream of ordinances, edicts, *arrêts*, and *règlements*, but it was left to Napoleon to abolish the frontier between a northern region of common law (itself a rich variety of local customary laws) and a southern region of predominantly, but not exclusively, Roman law: it is significant that Colbert's genius for codification spent itself on the relatively malleable law of commerce, admiralty, and colonies. The tariff legislation of Louis XIV superimposed duties which applied to the whole kingdom while failing to remove, and indeed reaffirming, the customs boundary of the Five Great Farms—the central region roughly corresponding with the Capetian kingdom. The newly acquired territories in Alsace and Lorraine could trade more freely with Germany than with France. The intricacies of the toll map remained such that in every generation there were perhaps only one or two who understood it, although in this field government had an opportunity to co-operate with the general wish of society as expressed, for example, by the States-general of 1614. The whole fiscal scene down to the Revolution, indeed, is rich in material for antiquarian inquiry. It reflects not only the tenderness of the monarchy for the forms of historic franchises, which were respected even in the territories newly acquired in the seventeenth century, but also the limitations of its strength when it chose to disregard prescriptive liberties. Whole communities and corporations, towns as well as provinces, exploited their archives to retain the practice of self-taxation like the clergy: the term 'don gratuit' was a polite euphemism, much as 'contribution' is today, but in practice it did result in substantial reduction of the tax burden; there were times when the Estates of Brittany escaped it altogether, though this is an extreme case—the one province which is known to have protested, when Louis XIV died, against the presence of an *intendant* and, later, to have ousted much of his jurisdiction. The ramifications of fiscal privilege, finally, are the most obvious comment on the function of absolute monarchy in the procurement of social welfare and justice—a notion by no means foreign to the outlook of the *intendants* and the Colbertian codes, which at least aimed to protect negro slaves and French seamen. We should appreciate that gross fiscal inequalities resulted not only from formal exemptions and local variations in the incidence of taxation, as with the salt-tax, but also from differences in the mode of assessment and levy, as was notoriously the case with the *taille*, which could work injustice even when it was based on real property. Reform of the *taille* was repeatedly on the agenda of absolute government: that it achieved so little, even when supported by the mass of public opinion, is a remarkable testimony to the weight of the past upon it and to the pressure which privileged minorities were able to exert.

This selection of examples might dispose us to conclude that French absolutism never really existed. That would be an exaggerated conclusion, of course. It is nearer the truth to say that the emancipation of government from historic restraints was a slow process, often interrupted and never complete, but one which advanced considerably under the pressure of local administrative action. From this standpoint royal sovereignty became more of a reality in the eighteenth century. Critics of Louis XIV have even gone so far as to describe his government as a 'mere façade'—rather like the Place Vendôme perhaps, the front of which was dictated by the king but erected by the City of Paris and the plots behind it sold off to individuals to build on as they pleased. Most of them were taken up by high finance.

This was not a new power in the state, but by 1700 a class large, wealthy, and ingenious enough to become in some sense its masters. The almost uninterrupted phase of large-scale war from 1688 to 1714 presented new opportunities, especially in the absence of a state bank, to bankers and wealthy contractors whose credit was so far superior to that of the state that it became a matter of state policy to protect them. This was not, unlike later years, a profitable period for the farmers-general, who indeed offered less and less for the rent of the indirect taxes; but immense profits were made in the equipment and movement of troops, transactions in specie and foreign exchange, speculations in paper money and currency revaluation, naval business, privateering, and (after 1700) trade with the Spanish Indies. In many of these activities the same names reappear: Crozat, Hogguer, Pâris, Bourvalais, and many others. The wealthiest of them, Samuel Bernard, had interests in many parts of Europe. Very often their interests are difficult to detect because they acted through borrowed names and a horde of agents. But it is certain that the financiers owed some of their opportunities to friends at court and that the expenses of court life forced many courtiers into dependence upon them. In fact, one of the major phenomena we have to reckon with in this lecture is the growing interdependence between the moneyed interest and the court and parliamentary nobility, consecrated by intermarriage. At this level the distance from Versailles to Paris was easily travelled. When, during the regency of Orléans, the fountains ran dry and trees withered at Versailles, the centre of government is more obviously to be found in the centre of pleasure and plutocracy, which set the pace of eighteenth-century luxury. Paris, which at this time supplanted Lyon as the financial capital of France, was henceforward to count for more in politics, in an age when private finance was able to buy its way into the bureaux of the Controllers-general, and even to make and unmake the successors of Colbert in the department which he had made the headquarters of administration.

These tendencies were not, of course, peculiar to France. Very close links were developed by the moneyed interest of London with the British Treasury. But in Britain public credit was based on a parliamentary guarantee. The absence of any such security under an absolutist system of government was its chief weakness and in the end fatal to it. One consequence was that it was forced back on the credit of institutions which could offer such a guarantee—the Assembly of Clergy and some of the provincial Estates—and which could therefore borrow more cheaply than the state. This fact alone placed the crown at a disadvantage in any attempt to overcome separatism and clerical privilege. Still more so did the sale of offices. At no time, I think, was this form of state borrowing practised on a larger scale than in the later years of Louis XIV, when a floating debt of unprecedented size drove government to create new offices, exemptions, and patents of nobility by the score. It was then that the new financial power perhaps made its most rapid turnover. Not only did it undertake to place this business, buying up groups of offices in order to resell them at a profit; it was also fertile in suggesting entirely new ones. At no time under the old régime was France afflicted with a greater number of inspectors and controllers, receivers and registrars, accountants and brokers, checkers and weighers, sinecurists of every description. We need not suppose that all of these necessarily encumbered the machinery of government for long, since offices could be converted into *rentes* ultimately and in any case it was especially the practice just then to hold the patentee to ransom by forcing him to 'augment' the original purchase price or even to repurchase his office or title altogether. But this was the dry rot of absolutism at its most insidious. It could hardly fail to demoralize society and lower the efficiency of administration. I know of naval administrators, for example, with years of useful service behind them, who were dropped because they could not raise the capital to buy back their places. One favourite object of exploitation was the craft gild; there the market in licences certainly encouraged an oligarchy of the highest bidders. This very large expenditure on what were often compulsory purchases and useless employments did serious damage to the economy too, since it acted both as a capital levy and a tax on the already overburdened consumer. It is probably the main reason why the financiers earned the reputation of being 'bloodsuckers of the people'. After 1715 government tried to make them its scapegoat. The public inquiry then undertaken into war profiteering, however, showed that the more powerful could still buy themselves out and further wounded the good name of the monarchy.

These events made monarchy prosaic. With the Regency, as we know, moral corruption in high places was there for all to see. It brought down to earth that vision of kingship which had made the old king so cleverly insist on the exact observance of a quasi-byzantine ceremonial. It is the difference between baroque and rococo, Mignard's Romans and Watteau's picnic-parties, the sarabande and the morris dance—a craze for English *contredanses* and Dutch paintings mirrored the failure of a foreign policy and a return to naturalism. We may take it as a symbol of the revolution in manners that women were now free to appear on the public stage and that the ballet moved from the court to the theatre: it was left to Camargo, who died in 1770, to shorten the skirt and develop the *entrechat*. The eighteenth century was the great age of feminine influence on taste, as of petticoat government. As the century went on, the memoirists commented on fractures in one of the toughest units in French society, the very foundation of paternal government—the family. In the higher and middle reaches of society also, there occurred an elusive but profound shift of sensibility—a cult of simplicity and a diffuse humanitarianism linked with a new faith in the critical method of science and the spread of religious scepticism: in other words, 'philosophy'.

All monarchy is rooted in religious belief and absolutist systems are anchored to it. Once that has gone, they are apt to be judged in the harsh light of utility. In essence, of course, the virtues and sentiments fostered by religion have in themselves an obvious utility value for all government; but they lose it if they are seen as such. The old French monarchy relied on the emotion as well as the law of allegiance, on the spirit of devotion as much as on obedience, as the correspondence of the *intendants* makes clear. A merchant, for example, might be expected to suffer a loss gladly if it were in the king's service. In the end, we know, absolute monarchy, by its breaches of faith and its dilution of the principle of 'honour' in the sale of titles and so forth, played this card too often and so assisted in bankrupting the rationale of privilege. At the same time it saw itself genuinely as custodian of a moral order. We can see this quite clearly in its almost intimate concern with moral welfare in its colonies, where it had a comparatively free hand to create: New France, in particular, almost to the end an economic liability, was as much the fruit of religious idealism as New England. This was never more true than when Colbert was in charge—a warning not to interpret his creative effort solely in terms of mercantilist economics and Cartesian rationality. Catholicism gave to absolute monarchy the 'soul' that it could not have derived from Descartes or Hobbes. May we not find pointed if ironical testimony to its value in the attempts of Rousseau and Robespierre to devise a substitute?

It is from this standpoint that the motives and consequences of Louis XIV's religious policies need to be seen. In itself, though not in the brutality of its enforcement, the revocation of the Edict of Nantes was not unpopular and so fine a mind as Bossuet's could celebrate it as the king's chief claim on the gratitude of posterity. It is unintelligible unless we allow that the drive of French society towards external strength and internal coherence was felt to require some positive spiritual unity, in an age when to love religion was still to hate heresy. There were diplomatic and other influences at work as well, but this is its underlying meaning. It had been preceded by an expensive official effort to convert the Huguenots by kindness, in the correct belief that Calvinism was now in decay. It was not expected that persecution would revive it, still less that the *dragonnades* would breed cynicism among good Catholics—though government did not dare use the dragoons in Paris. The real victors, it has been said, were the Deists, but it would have been curious if deism and unitarianism had not invaded France in any event. So far as these were natural fruits of the critical principle in Protestantism, however, it was logical, if sanguine, to try to get rid of Protestantism. Bossuet had already suppressed Simon's *Histoire critique du Vieux Testament*, even though written by an Oratorian to weaken Protestant confidence in the Bible. He was soon to take issue with Pierre Bayle, the Calvinist sceptic, whose *Dictionnaire historique et critique*, offering a determinist explanation of belief and freeing morality to pass judgement on religion, ran through eleven editions between 1697 and 1743. By 1743 dogma may be said to have lost its hold on an influential section of educated France and the ferocious laws against the Huguenots looked barbarous indeed. They were most ruthlessly enforced in Languedoc and it was the death by torture at Toulouse of Jean Calas in 1762 that started the Voltairian war-cry: 'Écrasez l'infâme.' Given the close partnership between monarchy and the Gallican Church, one may regard that philosophic attack as a higher price to pay for religious uniformity than the emigration of thousands of good citizens— partly compensated as it was by the arrival of Jacobite refugees— or the bloody Camisard risings in the Cevennes, or even the stimulus given to contractualist political thinking by the English revolution of 1688. Absolutism, however, can hardly be held responsible for the long-term corrosiveness of scientific and historical method.

What broadcast most widely the seeds of disrespect for authority, without question, was the Jansenist furore, which divided the Church against itself and manœuvred absolutism into an ultramontane position, contrary to its tradition, against the popular Gallicanism of its noisiest enemy, the *parlements*. We need not here decide whether the Jesuits were making a liberal point in giving priority to the free human will over the gratuitous character of saving grace. This was the question at the heart of theological controversy everywhere at the time. But read Pascal on the inescapable self-love in human nature and you are near to the moral pessimism, the spiritual perfectionism, the cosmic determinism of the Calvinists. In the lives of the poor Jansenism was known to excite a morbid enthusiasm, an extravagant hope in miracles; in the professional classes, a somewhat puritanical code of behaviour. By its light the great of this world risked implicit condemnation; it would have no demi-gods. Thus we may try to understand why Louis XIV destroyed Port-Royal and, conversely, discern an attitude of belief deeper than political opportunism in the Jansenism of the parliamentary magistrates. And yet, if eighteenth-century Jansenism was not merely a fabrication of the Jesuits to discredit all opponents, it became above all else a political movement. It created the opening through which the *parlements* could double their historic rôle as the guardians of Gallican liberty with a false championship of the poor and oppressed. It enabled them to exploit the currents of anti-clericalism which flowed strongly when the wealthiest Estate in the land resisted the attempt of the great Controller-general, Machault, in 1749, to increase its share of taxation, and when the archbishop of Paris chose this very moment to refuse the sacrament to dying persons who could not produce evidence that they accepted the Bull *Unigenitus* of 1713. The Bull, I may remind you, had condemned what had been a popular manual of piety for many years. Thus, what had begun as a theological move of Jesuit against Jansenist finally brought into focus a heap of unrelated mass resentments, until the very name of Jansenism could be used by authority as a loose description of anti-absolutist tendencies—what, in fact, was then loosely styled 'republicanism'. Its leading organ, the *Nouvelles Ecclésiastiques*, a clandestine weekly which maintained publication from 1728 to 1803, reached levels of society untouched by, and often hostile to, 'philosophy'. Further, the output of Jansenist pamphlets, together with the illegal circulation of parliamentary remonstrances against 'fanaticism', accustomed quite humble people to the discussion of fundamentals. The diarist Barbier, who knew the people of Paris well, prophesied that the dispute would destroy the spirit of submission and obedience to the Church—qualities 'which are the offspring of ignorance, but necessary to the well-being of a great state'. Not for nothing did Brunetière call this 'the century of Unigenitus'. Unhappily for the fortunes of the monarchy, Louis XIV had both instigated the Bull and made its acceptance a law of state.

How was absolutist philosophy then called in question by the *parlements*? In restoring the power of remonstrance, the crown implicitly conceded, of course, a right to discuss legislation and to object to legal flaws in it. Given a conflict of laws there could even be advantage in that. Far too much, also, can be made of the judicial incompetence of the robe. Not ignorance but pedantry was the vice of these as of other lawyers. There was plenty of genuine learning, ability, eloquence, and culture among them. D'Argenson, who knew their failings, calls them 'the most estimable section of the nation, morally speaking'. From their ranks came not only Montesquieu and Hénault but many of the crown's most distinguished servants: the direct confrontation between crown and *parlements* was, indeed, complicated by the ambition of some magistrates for high administrative office. But if the king paid his sovereign courts the compliment of seeking their advice, it was of course on the understanding that he was not obliged to take it. The sole legislative power confided to his person was simply one consequence of that sacred authority which identified him with the common good. In answer to this, as high priests of the 'temple' of legislation, the magistrates could argue that it was up to them to guarantee the integrity of the laws. Between 1750 and 1760 the constitutional theory implied by the act of registration was elaborated. The courts were there to attest that the king's will was *really* his will and not some momentary aberration: 'votre autorité devenue inaccessible aux surprises'. It was their business to consummate the act of law-making by some process of concurrence which must logically involve free deliberation and the rights of amendment and even of veto. Only in this way, the argument ran, could justice be certified to the people and their obedience guaranteed. Here, in effect, was a new mystique of sovereignty. Agreed that the royal authority was absolute, what, all the same, was meant by the royal authority? Did it not embrace the sovereign courts as the eyes and conscience of the prince? Did not an appeal to history prove as much if the development of princely power was traced back to the *Curia regis* and beyond? The *parlement* of Paris claimed direct descent from that early undifferentiated council which met about the king's person, the provincial *parlements* deriving their authority immediately from the parent court in Paris and so ultimately from the same source. Together, it was urged, the *parlements* of France constituted a single, indivisible body which, in the absence of the States-general, represented the nation.

It was this last stage in the argument, the so-called doctrine of the *union des classes*, popularized after 1755, which made the worst history and the best politics. In the first place, it was the sophistical justification of an ominous new strategy. Without the growth of organized collaboration between the *parlements* it is doubtful whether Choiseul could have destroyed the French Jesuits between 1760 and 1764. Some *parlements* nevertheless expelled the hereditary foe with reluctance and a few not at all. A far more impressive demonstration of unity occurred in 1766. In that year the majority rallied to the side of their brethren in Rennes, then doing battle with the Governor of Brittany, the duc d'Aiguillon, over his prosecution of Caradeuc de la Chalotais, champion of Breton resistance to the government's new roads policy. But the theoretical cover for these inter-parliamentary combinations was in itself significant. It contained, however crudely and perversely, in a new and challenging form, the idea of national sovereignty.

National sovereignty was the most dynamic concept that was crystallized out of the parliamentary struggle. It pointed, clearly enough, to some other principle of unity than the king's person. It suggested at least the possibility, fatal to the principle of absolutism, of a contingency more serious than some failure of synchronization between the king's interests and those of his subjects. Supposing there was an outright disjunction between them? The mere popularization of the word 'nation', quickened by the losses of the Seven Years War and by the attack on the Jesuits as a body 'foreign' to the nation, helped prepare soil for this seed. In the year of the ignominious peace of Paris, which cost France one empire in North America and the hope of another in India, the parliamentary hero, La Chalotais, issued an *Essai d'éducation nationale* in which the word 'citoyen' occurs. A year earlier, Rousseau's *Du Contrat social* carried forward the idea of 'society' as Montesquieu had bequeathed it—as an entity, that is, susceptible of its own laws of development—to a point where society exists independently of all government, where it becomes indeed the rationale and sole source of any legitimate government.

The influence of Rousseau's notion of popular sovereignty is not to be discerned for another generation, however, and the stuffy parliamentarians had even less use for him than for the writers of the *Encyclopédie*, who were poles apart from Rousseau in their disdain for the common man. The fact remains that parliamentary Jansenism, and with it what d'Argenson called Jansenist nationalism, did more to shake the fabric of French absolutism, in its theory and its practice, than the philosophers. In the long run, no doubt, philosophic sociology was more dangerous to absolutist institutions than the rhetoric of a legal caste far more oligarchical in its structure and outlook than it had ever been in the past. The high robe, after four generations of ennoblement, was now sufficiently fused with the older nobility to have become the arch-defender of privilege: as lawyers, the upholders of every property right in the seigneurial régime, of every freak in customary laws and overlapping jurisdictions which could promote litigation; as politicians, the enemies of fiscal equity and economic reform. Philosophic criticism, by comparison, exempted nothing from the scope of free analysis, desired the moral regeneration of society, and believed that the unprejudiced human intelligence could transform its environment, abolish the past, and open the way for the progressive march of mankind towards the fulfilment of unrealized possibilities in human nature. By these lights a great deal in the old France was to be found wanting. And yet, with very few exceptions, the philosophers not only accepted the monarchy but hoped to make it the instrument of benevolent reform, in the spirit of the best *intendants*. They wanted a better educated people as the necessary foundation of strong government. Their ideal was the enlightened despot and the enlightened *bourgeois*, not the man in the street. 'All is lost', said Voltaire, 'once the populace entangles itself in reasoning.' Yet this is precisely what the parliamentarians taught the populace to do. The philosophers reached, and perhaps aimed only to reach, an educated minority. The magistrates could be demagogues. As the defenders of Gallican liberties popularity can be said to have been forced on them; it really dates from their hostility to John Law, the fall of whose credit system brought tributes to the 'amazing disinterestedness' of the *parlement* of Paris. But they fancied themselves in the role of 'fathers of the people', rather like English whigs, quick to cry tyranny whenever bread or fuel went up in price. Like good whigs too, they changed their tune after entering royal service. In method, as in motive, it might be instructive to compare them with the opposition to Walpole, or even with the Wilkites. Perhaps they were the real educators of the *sans-culottes*. At all events it was their influence with the Parisians, through the circulation of their remonstrances and otherwise, which explains why the mid-century diarists have so much to say about republicanism and revolution. Before he died Louis XV talked of it too. The abolition of the *parlements* in 1771 was his answer. But by now the propagandist damage had been done.

The action then taken by the reforming chancellor, Maupeou, one of the strongest if least likeable characters ever to serve the monarchy, was regarded at the time as a real revolution.

This was different from the spirit of opposition to Louis XIV. His principal critics were either disgruntled aristocrats, who wanted a return to the good old days before the *intendants* and 'the reign of the vile *bourgeoisie*', or else the king's own servants who desired to impress on him the misery of his subjects and improve the efficiency of administration. They were mindful of the price of the two great wars which occupied twenty-two out of the last thirty years of his reign. These were years when pressure of circumstances forced the crown to tax both privileged orders and when the *tutelle administrative* of the *intendants* increasingly extruded from real power office-holders who had still had work to do in Colbert's time. There was more even to the resentments of Saint-Simon and Boulainvilliers than injured pride of caste, however. They were not blind to the hardships of the population at large—to the kind of situation which occurred, for example, at Brest in 1708, when a just and humane naval *intendant* was attacked by the king's own workmen—starving, not as yet from a true shortage of bread, but because, with wages years in arrear, they had long since parted with all they had to buy it. Authority underwent a real moral besides material crisis in the later years of Louis XIV—so much so that it furnished a departure point for the criticism of absolute monarchy. But none of the critics—neither Saint-Simon nor Fénelon nor Vauban—cultivated the popular followings which placed laurels on the brows of magistrates in the later, more prosperous, years of Louis' great-grandson.

An unquiet spirit, as these lectures have shown, had been a commonplace of French history. The French of the eighteenth century remained a difficult people to govern at any level. As Bossuet was not ashamed to admit, even government by divine right rested on force and the absolutist state commanded a great deal of that. The reorganization of the French army by Louvois was perhaps its least qualified and most characteristic success. The maintenance of civil order was certainly a military function and one reason why the military budget remained high even during peace. And there were the galleys, the *lettres de cachet*, imprisonment without trial, and not least the Lieutenants of Police.

The Lieutenant-General of the Paris police, one of Louis XIV's creations, virtually took rank with the Secretaries of State and it is hardly too much to say that the absolutist state owed much of its stability to the force at his disposal and still more to the information in his possession. This key post was normally entrusted to men of good intelligence, however, who did not rely on mere repression: thus, it was René d'Argenson, one of the ablest of them and father of two Ministers, who dissuaded Seignelay from suppressing the first coffee houses for fear of seditious gossip. Nothing, in fact, could repress the Parisian love of gossip, the sociability of its congested streets, its satirical songs and squibs and comedies. Highly characteristic of the Jansenist period was the rapid spread of news by uncensored manuscript news sheets, which even the intimate details of Louis XV's private life did not escape. Signs of this liveliness were already plentiful enough by the time Louis XIV made his first formal visit to the Hôtel de Ville, in 1687, to 'forgive' the City for its share in the Fronde. As significant in their way as the removal of the court to Versailles in 1682 were his attempts to impose his will on Paris by his buildings there—the dome of the Invalides, the Observatory, the colonnade of the Louvre, the Place des Victoires, the Place Vendôme. They were a world removed from the simplicity of the original Louvre or the Place des Vosges of Henri IV and their propaganda value is still evident. To a very large extent the 'greatness' of Louis XIV is nothing more than the greatness of his architectural vocabulary. Psychologically, it was a principal instrument of absolutism. Here alone was the policy of uniformity successful throughout the country.

In the provinces too the *frondeur* mentality lived on, at any rate in the parliamentary centres, and habits of violence died hard. It was a normal function of the *intendants* to put down riots, still more to prevent them. Rioting was frequently, as we know, set off by tax collection, the militia draw, forced labour service on the roads, salt-smuggling, cattle-stealing, quarrels between gilds, the enclosure of waste, above all by corn scarcities. Turgot once said: 'One sees a famine every two years in France.' Nothing in later French history, it is true, approached the starvation years of 1693–4 and 1709–10, which took a painful toll of the population; but there was widespread famine again in 1725, 1740, 1759, 1766–8 and 1772–6, often accompanied, especially in the country, by epidemics of smallpox and typhoid. Moreover, local scarcities were liable to occur even in a relatively good year. For violent fluctuations in local market prices and extraordinary variations between the prices ruling in different areas were the natural result of official restrictions on the movement of grain, combined with the prevailing low standards of crop and animal husbandry, the high cost of transport, and the safety-first policy of town and police authorities. The abbé Galiani spoke for average opinion, though not for the new natural law economists (the Physiocrats), when he wrote that bread 'belongs to police and not to commerce'. Because of this attitude a famine could always be ascribed to some malevolent human agency—very often, with the encouragement of magistrates, to the king or his ministers. Such suspicions were of sinister import. Nothing did more harm to the popular faith in monarchy than the belief that Louis XV and Louis XVI made money out of grain monopolies.

We cannot appreciate the connexion between public order and food supply, nor understand why the *intendants* became increasingly important as agricultural advisers, if we overlook the existence of a considerable itinerant population in France. Skilled journeymen, assisted by the quasi-masonic associations known as the *compagnonnages*, were still common on the roads; there was always a fringe of floating population in the towns, varying with the cycle of employment, especially in the building trades. This is why it is difficult to place confidence in estimates of the population of Paris at any time: de Tocqueville tells us of the influx but not of the efflux. In addition, there was a not insignificant amount of outright emigration, not all of it to the colonies. Some thousands who were not Huguenots are known to have crossed the frontiers during the later years of Louis XIV. Throughout the eighteenth century an under-populated Spain was absorbing unwanted Frenchmen. Behind this lay the mass of pauperism which also produced the 'brigands' who occasionally terrorized the countryside. Mendicity, in fact, so far surpassed the resources of private charity and a rudimentary poor law as to create the impression that a major line of social cleavage was the one which ran between the sedentary and the vagrant classes. What is equally striking is the thinness of the margin between farming and vagabondage. The loss of a poorly sown crop after shallow ploughing, a pestilence among the pigs or sheep, could so easily force a peasant to default in his taxes, sell out, and take to the roads. The *métayers*, still so numerous, were particularly vulnerable in the eighteenth century—liable to be turned off at short notice by a new type of farming middleman to whom their rents were leased: Turgot classified them with the growing number of wage-earners in the towns. Still worse off was the growing number of landless agricultural labourers.

It is worth notice that only a minority of the landed peasantry were able to make ends meet without subsidiary earnings in rural industry or as hired farm labour, publicans, and so on. Land was parcelled out in lots frequently too small to support a family, even in those few regions—Normandy, Picardy, the Paris region—where the merger of farms, the practice of leasehold and horse-ploughing, reflected the application of capital to land. It is said that small-scale culture characterized some four-sevenths of the country. Here it was that taxation drained off agrarian capital most perniciously, since it was a feature of tithe, seigneurial dues, and the personal *taille* alike that they were levied, not on net profit, but as a proportion of gross production; tithe might be only a twelfth part of gross product but that could amount to two-thirds of net profit. Furthermore, small capital could be frightened away by the government's preference for taxation by means of the collective assessment. Understandably the fisc found it more efficacious to levy lump sums on communities, and hold them answerable for collection, than to obtain returns from individuals who, then as now, were skilled in evasion. But to act thus meant loading the solvent with the failings of their neighbours. Few features of the old régime more tellingly illustrate the mutual hostility of government and society. Much social injustice was, and is, simply a by-product of this type.

It is not surprising, therefore, that what might be called the peasant question dominated French social thought, on its practical side, from Vauban to Turgot. Bourbon France made a backward agriculture support its claim to the cultural and diplomatic leadership of Europe and it may be significant that a Ministry of Agriculture was first created after the defeats of the Seven Years War. This was the period when agri ultural societies multiplied all over the country, though in most cases they seem soon to have lost themselves in the national vice of academicism. Yet English examination candidates still need to be warned against too sombre a picture of peasant woes. The absence of risings comparable with the *jacqueries* of earlier times is not simply to be traced to the beneficent activity of the *intendants* and the greater capacity of government to maintain order, though there is something in that—obedience to law is a different matter. There is also the fact that a rise in commodity prices between 1733 and 1770 increased the purchasing power of most land-owners, small as well as large. The 'feudal reaction' which turned the screw on manorial dues and rents was yet to come. Meanwhile, the successive augmentations in the bids negotiated for the general tax farm between these dates were based on the reality of an overall agricultural expansion. Gone were the days of Louis XIV when, according to Boisguillebert, half the soil of France was waste and when real property lost nearly a third of its value in half a century.

It is in these facts that we must look for an explanation of the characteristic emphasis of French economic thinking in the eighteenth century: its naïve belief in wealth as essentially the gift of nature, its emphasis on production rather than exchange and on the land as the only branch of production which can create more useful goods than its consumes, its failure to draw a clear distinction (as Adam Smith did) between value in use and value in exchange. We may notice two criticisms of Colbertian mercantilism entailed by this 'physiocratic' point of view: first, the regulation of exchange cannot add to the wealth of the community but instead raises the cost of producing it; and second, the taxation of industry, which creates no values but only transforms them, is in effect transferred to the land. The analysis is important because it captured the minds of enlightened men within the administration; indeed it was a body of ideas worked out almost exclusively by them and the key to most of what government then understood by reform. It resulted in the liberation of the inter-provincial corn trade in 1754 (though not in simplifying the much abused chaos of tolls) and soon afterwards removed restrictions on the movement of raw materials and skilled labour, as well as weakening the industrial monopolies of the towns.

The climax of economic reform came in 1776, with Turgot's Six Edicts, notably in the forthright dismantling of the historic gild régime—as revolutionary a change as Maupeou's abolition of the *parlements* and shorter-lived even than that. Why? Essentially because the gild corporations were felt to be organic cells in the body politic, both as the framework of town life and as the solid core of the whole industrial structure. Much as time had done to change their spirit into oligarchy, the gilds had roots in French society as deep as the monarchy itself. As with so many other institutions, absolute monarchy had grown up with them. It might come to terms with them; it might slowly sap their independence, as it did that of municipal government and most of the provincial Estates, by influencing election procedure and otherwise; but it was not strong enough to destroy them in one fell blow. That Turgot thought he could do so is some indication of the fatal flaw in the fashion for benevolent despotism. It had reason and economic wisdom on its side, but not history, not the human animal. If we remember this, we may be slower to condemn the cowardice and vacillations of the monarchy in the making and pursuit of a policy—its habitual sacrifice of long-term interests to the needs of the moment. Absolutism could never afford to act up to the Cartesian spirit of system implied in its theory. The case of the gilds very well illustrates, moreover, how this type of government could tie itself up in knots which it could not easily loosen when it would. Acting on the economic assumptions of an earlier age, Colbert had made the craft gilds crown agents, supplemented but not supplanted by his Inspectors of Manufactures, for the enforcement of a comprehensive and highly detailed system of industrial regulation; he had indeed extended gild organization for this purpose, trying to fill gaps in it left by the Middle Ages. When economic ideas changed, therefore, it was not easy for government, however enlightened, to practise what its best servants might preach. It encountered the opposition of a huge vested interest which it had itself strengthened. The machine had become the master.

This had some consequences for the progress of the industrial revolution in France. The state which had most extensively applied mercantilist principles to industry was in some ways badly placed for the speedy adoption of new techniques and new forms of organization. Not until 1759, for instance, was the seventy-years rearguard action against calico-printing, which is said to have cost 16,000 lives in the defence of traditional textiles, called off. What is striking, however, is not the late appearance of the industrial revolution, but the slow pace of its spread. English inventions soon crossed the Channel, as did some of the inventors themselves, like John Kay in 1747. The government itself actively encouraged the immigration of English artisans—not all of them Jacobites—and in its factory inspectorate, headed in 1755 by the enterprising and critical mind of John Holker, it possessed a splendid instrument for the propagation of new techniques. It had also done much to favour the concentration of industrial capital. The putting-out merchant and the factory alike existed in Colbert's time and had been extended since, partly because the government liked to encourage rural industry and because control of it was seldom more than nominal. Above all, from Colbert onwards, the crown made free use of the system of privilege in 'royal' manufactures, which were often large-scale undertakings, distinct from state manufactures proper in being privately financed though protected by some form of premium or monopoly—perhaps for production in a given area, perhaps in the purchase of fuel or raw material. It was this system which did much to give French luxury goods a reputation unrivalled in Europe, thanks also to a jealously exercised control of quality and to that exacting sense of elegance in all that concerns appearance which makes it impossible to buy even a box of chocolates in France today without having to await its formal presentation in successive wrappings of decorated paper and coloured thread. When all this is said, however, the emphasis on old types of skilled handicraft and the ultimately sterilizing action of monopolies worked against the rapid diffusion of invention and capital, even in those few industries, notably cotton and iron, for which a mass demand, if only in the shape of military and naval requirements, could be said to exist. So did the state of communications, a relative deficiency of coal and iron ore, and the age-old preference of most investors for public loans and offices—at the expense of agricultural and commercial investment also. Furthermore, with a domestic market of about eighteen million people in 1715, rising to perhaps twenty-six millions in 1789, of whom less than a sixth lived in towns (and a sixth of these in Paris), the pace of economic development in general was bound to depend very largely on rural demand, and the rise of that was slow.

The expansion of maritime trade was far more dynamic and

began much earlier. Between 1715 and 1789 its annual turnover quadrupled in value. But here, as in the world of finance, signs of new growth are to be found long before the Regency and John Law's credit stimulus. It was during the war of the Spanish Succession itself that Chambers of Commerce were established in many of the ports and began, through the admirable machinery of the new Council of Commerce, to turn government policy away from its traditional reliance on state trading companies. In Africa and America these bodies had done their work of forcing opportunities for private enterprise, though the foundling Louisiana long needed nursing at a loss. It was the South Seas trade of those years which made the fortune of Saint-Malo—whose richest shipowners negotiated with the crown rather as if they were the senate of a free city—and it was then that the aggressive capitalism of Nantes began to forge that dominant position in the slave trade which turned downwards only in 1774. The most brilliant transformation of the century, however, was witnessed at Bordeaux, whose population nearly trebled between 1698 and 1790 and which, like Nantes, contains some of the loveliest architecture of eighteenth-century France.

Yet the enlarged prosperity of the ports—and with it an enlargement of the *bourgeoisie* and of leisure—should not deceive us. As late as 1784, when it was running into a silk crisis, Lyon was the only provincial city larger than modern Oxford. France indeed attained rank as the second commercial power in Europe under Louis XV, but she owed it primarily to a world-wide expansion of the colonial trades; and these were extremely vulnerable for a country whose government continued to sacrifice maritime strength to a continental foreign policy—even when London merchants had succeeded the House of Habsburg as the mortal enemy. War could deal catastrophically with her trade statistics. During the Seven Years War shipping insurances at Bordeaux rose to 60 per cent and the value of its West Indian imports fell to one-eighth the figure for 1753. It is true that overseas trade picked up quickly after eighteenth-century wars; but the colonial cycle of French trade was open to the further weakness that French exporters could not meet all the demands of French colonists at prices which would compete with the contraband trader from Boston, Philadelphia, or New York. As early as 1767 this fact had to be recognized by the creation of two free ports in the West Indies. The French carrying trade, moreover, was never much developed on the long-haul routes outside the colonial and Mediterranean orbits. Foreign shipping still predominated at Bordeaux as late as 1740. Between 1713 and 1780 France sent only ten vessels a year, on average, through the Baltic Sound. Dear timber, large crews, and the high wages paid to them were among the factors which weakened her competitive power whenever there was competition to meet. The bulk of French tonnage, in fact, considerable as it was in the aggregate, was employed in a coastal trade whose attractions need no underlining, given the geography of France and the high cost of overland communications. It is significant that 'free trade' in the mouths of the *économistes* meant the removal of barriers to internal movement. Imports as a whole were hampered by duties often prohibitively high and remained small in volume.

Government was by no means insensitive to the demands of the economy so far as it understood them. It certainly had ample information on which to found its economic policies, thanks not least to the reports and statistics of the *intendants*, who were as much its consultants as its representatives. Government could also adapt its policies to business opinion. If anything, it was too responsive to such opinion. But clearly it could not please everybody. Thus, though the wine exporters favoured liberal trading, the colonial merchants were wedded to monopoly. The silk interests of Lyon and Marseille were not to be reconciled with the importation of Indian cotton goods. Protection of domestic coal mining was a drag on industrial growth. Nevertheless, state paternalism was by no means barren. Without it France would have had no colonies, for example, nor some of her industries. It placed French company law far in advance of English and displayed wisdom in the regulation of the stock market. From 1726 to 1785 it even maintained a stable currency—though this achievement also reflects the closeness of trading links with Spain. It did much by its diplomacy to preserve a strong trading position in the Levant and elsewhere. But perhaps the most enduring monument to the creative power of absolutism at its best was the *Ponts et Chaussées*, which by 1789 had given France 25,000 miles of the best highways in Europe, largely because the state jealously protected its standards of professional competence

—as it did the navy but not the army—from encroachments by birth and wealth. Private enterprise in waterways made nothing like this progress. Together with the development of credit and of the instruments of credit which brought the rate of interest down to 5 per cent, in spite of a popular fixation against paper money, this line of advance was beginning to make of France a single economic area in which capital could circulate more freely and the division of labour accelerate. The day was passing when an *intendant* could not buy hemp or sailcloth for the arsenal at Brest for lack of a centre of good commercial credit nearer than Nantes, or when small, unspecialized cotton-mills and glass-houses must be scattered throughout the country.

It is hard to resist the conclusion that in many respects French absolutism was capable of a reforming energy which, however fitful, showed that it understood better than most sections of society the needs and possibilities of a more scientific and wealthier age, except only that it should think itself out of privilege or abolish the theological foundation on which, so unsteadily, it rested. Had it been otherwise, the philosophers as a whole would hardly have claimed stronger powers for it. They were more practical and, at bottom, perhaps more pessimistic than their Romantic critics have allowed us to recognize. Is not the stress laid by the Enlightenment on citizen virtue, education, and philanthropy some indication of the low standards of public morality with which government had to compromise? And did de Tocqueville altogether see truly in blaming the monarchy for the distances that divided social classes and for destroying insti-tutions from which a society draws vitality? French society was at war with itself long before the Bourbons. In practice, the first loyalty of the king's subjects was still to the social, functional, or local group to which they belonged. So far from levelling them, absolute monarchy respected vested interests, local habit, and the spirit of close corporations nearly as much as the unreformed British Parliament and, in effect, betrayed much of its trust to eighteenth-century conceptions of liberty. It was not absolutist enough. It relied on the *intendants* to defeat in detail what it would not itself destroy *en bloc* and to bring some sort of harmony out of a chaos of prescriptive jurisdictions and franchises, so that it might almost be said that the *intendants*, with their expanding staffs, were more substitutes for central government than its agents. For this very reason, therefore, we cannot well judge it until the history of the intendancies has been written.

When that has proceeded further we may well find ourselves more respectful of the good which absolute monarchy accomplished. It is, after all, chiefly the evil that lives after a fallen system. We shall do best to think of it meanwhile as an instrument for the achievement of certain limited ends, far short of those required in a new utilitarian age. Its essential limitation, indeed, was that it was constructed largely for tasks which were obsolescent in the dawn of *laissez-faire*. Hence much of the inconsistency in its record. But the contradictions within French society were tougher than the monarchy which set out to resolve them and found itself their prisoner. One reason why relations between government and society in this period remain so rich in instruction for ourselves is surely that liberty and justice were then in conflict as they are now.

More than we realize, many of our own assumptions were worked out by French intelligence at odds with a society that lived so largely in the past. In some ways the past might seem to matter little enough: the amphitheatres of Arles and Nîmes were now cluttered with mean tenements, the abbey of Mont Saint-Michel showed cracks, and the *château* of Blois, overgrown with ivy, was tending to decay; Figaro and the Vicaire Savoyard had arrived. Indifference to the past, disrespect for Church and King? Yet in reality the memories, emotions, and allegiances of the past were the strongest force in eighteenth-century France. In Brittany and the Cévennes peasants still worshipped saints older than Christianity and farmed with medieval implements, paid *censives*, *champart*, *terrage* and so on. The common green glass of the Gauls was still blown by half-savage workers in the forests. Godefroi de Bouillon could still fire a noble in battle; 'noblesse' still symbolized wisdom, grace, and courage. The most famous of French tolls, the *trépas de Loire*, was a monument to the campaigns of Bertrand du Guesclin. The centuries of territorial aggregation had not expunged all traces of English rule in Gascony and Normandy, and the brigandage of the Thirty Years War could vibrate in the memory at the approach of rogues and beggars in Alsace-Lorraine. If the *parlements* evoked the memory of Charlemagne, Henri Quatre was idealized as the philosopher on the throne. And people wept for rejoicing when the doors of

Rheims cathedral swung open on the figures of Louis XVI and his Queen, the oil on his head fresh from the sacred phial of Clovis.

BIBLIOGRAPHICAL NOTE

1. General

SAGNAC, P. *La Formation de la société française moderne, 1661–1788* (2 vols., 1945–6; orthodox but masterly synthesis).

TOCQUEVILLE, A. DE. *L'Ancien Régime et la Révolution* (1856; new ed. by J.-P. Mayer and A. Jardin, 2 vols., 1952–3; the classic work, whiggish in attitude and based largely on the study of a single *généralité*).

MARION, M. *Dictionnaire des institutions de la France aux XVIIe et XVIIIe siècles* (1923).

ESMONIN, E. *Études sur la France du XVIIe et XVIIIe siècles* (1964; the collected articles of a leading authority on institutional aspects).

LECLERCQ, H. *Histoire de la Régence* (3 vols., 1921).

'Clio' series (largely bibliographical), vol. VII; Part I: E. PRECLIN et V. L. TAPIÉ, *Le XVIIe siècle* (2nd edn., 1949); Part 2: E. PRECLIN et V. L. TAPIÉ, *Le XVIIIe siècle* (2 vols., 1952).

GOUBERT, P. *L'Ancien Régime*, vol. i, *La Société* (1969; brief but authoritative textbook of which vol. II will deal with government).

LOUGH, J. *An Introduction to Eighteenth Century France* (1960; informed, attractive).

2. Public Finance and Society

SAINT-GERMAIN, J. *Les Financiers sous Louis XIV: Paul Poisson de Bourvalais* (1950) and *Samuel Bernard, le banquier des rois* (1960).

MARION, M. (1) *Histoire financière de la France depuis 1715*, vol. i (1914); (2) *Machault d'Arnouville: étude sur l'histoire du Contrôle Général des finances de 1749 à 1754* (1891; strongly anti-clerical but important).

LÜTHY, H. *La Banque Protestante en France, de la Révocation de l'Édit de Nantes à la Révolution* (2 vols., 1959–61).

MATTHEWS, G. T. *The Royal General Farms in the Eighteenth Century* (New York, 1958).

3. Other Aspects of Administration

DAKIN, D. *Turgot and the Ancien Régime in France* (1939; touches almost every aspect; the best work in English on the eighteenth-century monarchy).

GIRAUD, M. *Histoire de la Louisiane* (3 vols., 1953–66; in progress; vol. III deals with the period of John Law).

GIRARD, G. *Racolage et Milice 1701–1715* (1921).

LÉONARD, É. G. *L'Armée et ses problèmes au XVIIIᵉ siècle* (1958; stimulating lectures, with an eye on public opinion).

ALISON, J. M. S. *Malesherbes: Defender and Reformer of the French Monarchy, 1721–1794* (New Haven, Conn., 1938).

FRÉVILLE, H. *L'Intendance de Bretagne, 1689–1790* (3 vols., Rennes, 1953; studies an intendancy in retreat, with emphasis on subdélégués).

BOSHER, J. F. *The Single Duty Project: a study of the movement for a French Customs Union in the 18th century* (1964).

BACQUIÉ, F. *Les Inspecteurs de manufactures sous l'Ancien Régime, 1669–1791* (1930).

MCCLOY, S. T. *Government Assistance in 18th-century France* (Durham, N.C., 1946).

CARRIÈRE, C., et al. *Marseille ville morte: la peste de 1720* (n.d. (1968)).

4. The Economy

SÉE, H. *Histoire économique de la France,* vol. i (ed. R. Schnerb, 1948).

POITRINEAU, A. *La Vie rurale en Basse-Auvergne au XVIIIᵉ siècle, 1726–1789* (2 vols., 1965).

HECKSCHER, E. F. *Mercantilism* (transl. M. Shapiro, 2 vols., 1935).

COLE, C. W. *French Mercantilism, 1683–1700* (New York, 1953).

BAMFORD, P. W. *Forests and French Sea Power, 1660–1789* (Toronto, 1956).

DELUMEAU, J. *Le Mouvement du port de Saint Malo, 1681–1720: bilan statistique* (n.d. (1966)).

RAMBERT, G., et al. *Histoire du commerce de Marseille,* vols. iv-vii (1660–1789) (1954–1966).

GASTON MARTIN. *Nantes au XVIIIe siècle: l'ère des négriers, 1714–1774* (1931).

DARDEL, P. *Navires et marchandises dans les ports de Rouen et du Havre au XVIIIᵉ siècle* (1963)

PARISET, F. G. (ed.), *Bordeaux au XVIIIᵉ siècle* (1968): vol. v in *Histoire de Bordeaux,* ed. C. Higounet).

GILLE, B. *Les Forges françaises en 1772* (1960).

SCOVILLE, W. C. *The Persecution of the Huguenots and French Economic Development, 1680-1720* (Berkeley, L.A., 1960).

RÉMOND, A. *John Holker, manufacturier et grand fonctionnaire en France au XVIIIᵉ siècle* (1946).

5. Social Groups

MONGRÉDIEN, G. *La Vie quotidienne sous Louis XIV* (1948; slight but attractive and useful, with bibliography).

SÉE, H. *La France économique et sociale au XVIIIe siècle* (4th edn., 1946).

CARRÉ, H. *La Noblesse de France et l'opinion publique au XVIIIe siècle* (1920).

MCMANNERS, J. 'France' in A. Goodwin (ed.), *The European Nobility in the Eighteenth Century* (1953).

MEYER, J. *La Noblesse bretonne au XVIIIe siècle* (2 vols., 1966).

BLUCHE, J. F. *Les Magistrats du Parlement de Paris au XVIIIe siècle, 1715–1771* (1960).

FORD, F. L. *Robe and Sword: the Regrouping of the French Aristocracy after Louis XIV* (Cambridge, Mass., 1953).

LEVASSEUR, E. *Histoire des classes ouvrières et de l'industrie en France avant 1789* (2nd edn., 2 vols., 1901).

COORNAERT, E. *Les Corporations en France avant 1789* (2nd edn., 1968).

CORVISIER, A. *L'Armée française, de la fin du XVIIe siècle au ministère de Choiseul: le soldat* (2 vols., 1964).

6. Religion and the State

MCMANNERS, J. *French Ecclesiastical Society under the Ancien Régime: a Study of Angers* (1960).

PRÉCLIN, E. and JARRY, E. *Les Luttes politiques et doctrinales aux XVIIe et XVIIIe siècles* (1955; vol. XIX of the now standard *Histoire de l'Eglise*, ed., A. Fliche).

ORCIBAL, J. *Louis XIV et les Protestants* (1951; sensitive and fair-minded).

GAZIER, A. *Histoire générale du mouvement Janséniste* (2 vols., 1922; hostile to the Jesuits).

CAHEN, L. *Les Querelles religieuses et parlementaires sous Louis XV* (1913).

LEPOINTE, G. *L'Organisation et la politique financière du clergé de France sous le règne de Louis XV* (1923).

7. The Critics

SÉE, H. (1) *Les Idées politiques en France en XVIIe siècle* (1920); (2) *L'Evolution de la pensée politique en France au XVIIIe siècle* (1925).

ROTHKRUG, L. *Opposition to Louis XIV* (Princeton, N.J., 1956).

WADE, I. O. *The Clandestine Organization and Diffusion of Philosophic Ideas in France from 1700 to 1750* (Princeton, N.J., 1938).

ROCQUAIN, F. *L'Esprit révolutionnaire avant la Révolution* (1878; valuable on political Jansenism).

MORNET, D. *Les Origines intellectuelles de la Révolution française, 1715–1787* (rev. edn., 1954; important but controversial thesis).

HIGGS, H. *The Physiocrats* (1897, reprinted 1963 by Archon Books).

WEULERSSE, G. *La Mouvement physiocratique en France de 1756 à 1770* (1910) and *Le Physiocratie à la fin du règne de Louis XV, 1770–1774* (1959).

LEROY, M. *Histoire des idées sociales en France,* vol. i (1946; often profound).

HAMPSON, N. *The Enlightenment* (Pelican History of European Thought, 4: 1968).

DIBON, P. (ed.) *Pierre Bayle* (1959).

SHACKLETON, R. *Montesquieu: a Biography* (Oxford, 1962).

BRUMFITT, J. H. *Voltaire Historian* (Oxford, 1958).

POMEAU, R. *La Religion de Voltaire* (1956).

SOBOUL, A. (ed.) *Textes choisis de l'Encyclopédie* (Éditions Sociales, 1962).

DERATHÉ, R. *J. J. Rousseau et la science politique de son temps* (1950).

GAY, P. *The Party of Humanity* (New York, 1964).

BICKART, R. *Les Parlements et la notion de souveraineté nationale au XVIIIe siècle* (1932; quotes freely from the Remonstrances).

GLASSON, E. *Le Parlement de Paris,* vol. ii (1901).

MOY, A. LE. *Le Parlement de Bretagne et le pouvoir royal au XVIIIe siècle* (1909).

RÉBILLON, A. *Les États de Bretagne, 1667–1789* (1932; studies a vulnerable sector of the monarchical system).

FLAMMERMONT, J. *Le Chancelier Maupeou et les parlements* (1883).

LOUGH, J. *Paris Theatre Audiences in the Seventeenth and Eighteenth Centuries* (1957).

BOLLÊME, G. (ed.) *Livre et société dans la France du dix-huitième siècle* (1965).

JOHN McMANNERS

The Revolution and its Antecedents
(1774-94)

————◆◆◆◆◆◆————

W hat would have happened if Mirabeau had lived to rule and Bonaparte had died uncrowned? The examples chosen are not perfect: Mirabeau was almost as bankrupt politically as he was financially when overwork and excesses removed him, and it might be argued that some lesser genius than Napoleon would have trimmed off the loose anarchical ends of revolutionary achievement. Even so, Sainte-Beuve's famous question retains searching force, and is calculated to discomfort determinists. The Revolution is not a simple pattern of logical happenings. It is not, as Clemenceau once said, a *bloc*, a monolithic unity, which must be accepted as a whole—equality, democracy, wars, cruelty, irreligion—all together and undifferentiated. 'Far from being a *bloc*', said Vandal, 'the Revolution is possibly the most complex phenomenon that has ever existed. It is an essentially multiple phenomenon, diverse in its causes, in its elements, in its development, in its consequences.' There was in fact, not one Revolution, but many revolutions. Men who willed certain changes found that their errors and crimes—or those of other people—were driving them on into new and unpredictable courses, culminating in an hysterical struggle for survival. Whatever recent theorists on 'totalitarian democracy' may say, Rousseau's writings had very little to do with Jacobin dictatorship and Terror; poor Rousseau, who said so many things so brilliantly, who could have perished in a *fournée* with aristocrats or Girondins as easily as with Hébert or Robespierre! Right-wing historians of Taine's school, who believe with Malouet that the Terror began with the fall of the Bastille are unjust to Robespierre's circle when they talk of cruel fanatics who foresaw government by execution and used it for doctrinaire ends. A left-wing historian like Mathiez is being equally unjust when he condemns Danton's

161

peace negotiations as the work of a contemptible adventurer, aping the aristocratic diplomacy of salons and green carpets, and blind to that ideological abstraction, the 'totality of revolutionary war'. Men cannot be judged by their complicity in, or loyalty to, such a chaos of events. In what follows, we will be primarily concerned with causes, with describing how the Revolution arose from the society of the old régime, and to do this, we should first move upstream through the furious torrent, looking for the fatal moments of miscalculation, when sluice-gates were opened which might have remained closed, and powerful forces were unleashed which swept away the inhibitions and ideals and sanity of the men who thought they were directing history.

Dictatorship and Terror came into the Revolution as a result of total war against foreign kings and internal rebels. On 10 October 1793 it was decreed that 'the provisional government of France will remain revolutionary until the peace'. Exactly a month before this, David's *Fête de la Nature* had celebrated the acceptance of a new Jacobin constitution which summarized the ultimate implications of revolutionary ideals— freedom to work and worship, a right to public assistance and educational opportunity, and universal suffrage. This blurted confession of the nation's half formulated aspirations was a propaganda document which had served its purpose once the Girondins were executed. Thereafter it reposed in a cedar box in the Convention, while the Committee of Public Safety, the Committee of General Security, representatives on mission and the network of popular societies ruled. 'The Revolution', said Robespierre, 'is the war of liberty against its enemies; the Constitution is the rule of liberty victorious and at peace.' For more than twenty years there was no peace, and, considering the ideals of '89, no constitution.

On the home front, the weapon of 'liberty' was Terror, and Terror, once started, achieved a sinister momentum of its own, for the survival of the men at the head of the revolutionary dictatorship came to depend upon their mastery of the guillotine. Haunted by fears of assassination, Robespierre, once the prim opponent of capital punishment, became the promoter of the atrocious law of 22 Prairial. Outside his immediate entourage, ideals were not only debased, they were dead. That is why his fall is so confused and cruel a business. 'In the strife of Thermidor', said Marc Antoine Baudot, 'it was not a question of principles, but of killing.' Means had triumphed over ends. The Revolution had lost its soul.

Yet the *dénouement* of the Terror and rivalries among the men who were directing it should not divert our attention from its beginnings and justification. The pathological and spontaneous butchery of the September massacres—when Paris heard the news that Prussian troops were at Verdun—is our clue to understanding the Terror once it became an institution. It proceeded in a feverish delirium which is better studied in *Les Dieux ont soif* than in conventional historical records; it arose from a surcharged atmosphere of crisis which inevitably accompanies a war for survival. That a statistical peak of executions was reached just after the worst danger was over only serves to give us a sombre insight into the psychology of ferocity. Cruelty was born from both fear and revenge. It was used punitively as well as preventively. Most victims came from areas of actual warfare, and were condemned by military tribunals, while only sixteen out of every hundred were nobles or clergy. War brought corruption, cowardice and conspiracy, and that fear of conspiracy which corroded sincerity. Terror was the reply.

Why, in April 1792, had the original peaceful ideals of France been betrayed? There were fears of an 'aristocratic plot', of spies and saboteurs directed from counter-revolutionary headquarters at Brussels, Turin and Coblentz, and of *émigré* officers with long swords and empty purses drilling beyond the Rhine. Refugee patriots from Holland, Belgium and Switzerland stirred up a febrile enthusiasm for a crusade. Village mayors and Oratorian schoolmasters proclaimed that a people in arms against foreign despots would be invincible. Yet a strictly diplomatic appraisal would have recognized that an attack of coalized despots was a distant possibility. It is hard to resist the conviction that a shooting war, as distinct from a cold war, started because those who were directing French policy used national enthusiasm to help them play the wicked old game of using war as an instrument of domestic faction fights. The Brissotins wanted to force themselves into power, Narbonne meant to use his armies to fortify the throne, Marie Antoinette meant to compel that foreign military intervention which she had been unable to negotiate, Louis said that his country could not last half a campaign, and that 'in defeat the nation will have no alternative but to throw itself into my arms'. It was Robespierre, whose name is inseparably linked with the Terror, who opposed the war which made Terror inevitable.

Second only in importance to this fateful decision of April 1792 was the divorce between Church and nation which had been crudely brought about a year before. Half the clergy of France refused to accept the Civil Constitution, a schism which created a potential fifth column and supplied the emigration with a conscience. When war came, orthodox opposition to the Constitutional Church became treason. A tragic history of executions and deportations ensued, an attack on Catholicism began, and a morbid rash of artificially invented substitute religions arose which would have appalled conventional anti-clericals like Voltaire and romantic deists like Rousseau. 'Dechristizaniation' (it began in September '93 when Fouché consoled the inhabitants of Nevers by revealing that death was 'an eternal sleep') was, as Aulard said, 'an expedient of national defence'. It was an outburst of patriotic fanaticism, directed by Chaumette and the Paris *Commune* and individual representatives on mission rather than the Convention, against the Catholicism which was now in league with the armies of the kings of Europe. Without the outbreak of war, without the Civil Constitution of the clergy, all this would have been unthinkable. In 1790, no one could have predicted a festival of Reason in the cathedral of Notre-Dame.

It is true that the first two years of the Revolution saw the origins of a new 'religion' of patriotism, drawing its symbolism from masonry, science and classical antiquity, and that along with it went a few extreme suggestions from publicists—Cloots proposing a purely 'natural' religion, Naigeon recommending the separation of Church and state to benefit atheism, Sylvain Maréchal painting idyllic pictures of insufferable grandfathers beating the bounds of their farms at Rogationtide, 'with a venerable beard serving them in place of sacerdotal ornaments'. But suggestions like these were confined to the lunatic fringe of journalism. At the great Federation ceremonies of 14 July 1790, the rites of patriotism and Catholicism were allied. No sane supporter of the Revolution wished to separate them. The Constituent Assembly was not a crew of *philosophes*, still less of Jansenists or Protestants; most of its members were nominal adherents of the Gallican church. There was no intention of subverting religion: on the contrary, Catholicism, which had been a prop of the old monarchy, was to be nationalized and put at the service of the new order. The new legislation was intemperate, and bears a stamp of ideological affinities which the clergy could not welcome—the arid Gallicanism of lawyers, the *philosophes'* bland inclination to regard religion as an adjunct of social cohesion, the Erastianism of the old régime magnified to suit the new dignity of national sovereignty, and the startling introduction of lay election in place of 'richerist' rule by the community of pastors which was the ideal of so many *curés*. However, the question is, not whether there was general clerical approval of the Civil Constitution (and there was much that was good in it, including economic justice for parish priests and the breaking of the aristocratic monopoly of higher promotions), but whether, in the last resort, a substantial majority could be found which did not dislike it enough to risk rejecting it. Archbishop Boisgelin had a majority, even of bishops, with him in wanting to 'baptize' the Civil Constitution and avoid schism. We have not time to consider why the Constituents blundered—the belief that Avignon could be used as blackmail against the Papacy, and a desire for a firm settlement before sales of ecclesiastical property began, go a long way towards explaining their haste and over-confidence. It is enough to say that on 27 November 1790 the Assembly imposed an oath to the Constitution and was thunderstruck when, in the beginning of 1791, half the clergy refused it. Most priests, both those who swore and those who did not, were bewildered men who simply kept on hoping that someone would engineer a compromise. But, as Montlosier said, 'the oath of 27 November cut all the bridges'. It is hard to believe that statecraft could not have found a solution, and a church-state compromise, however illogical, might have developed and grown and woven itself into the fabric of a new society.

27 November 1790, when the possibility of a *modus vivendi* with the church slipped like water through the clumsy fingers of inexperienced legislators, 20 April 1792, when the gambler's throw of war set the nation on the path to Terror—these dates are milestones in a journey whose course could have been shaped in other directions by honesty and ingenuity. De Tocqueville concludes his study of the *ancien régime* with a chapter entitled 'Comment la Révolution est sortie d'elle même de ce qui précède'.

It did, of course, but when we turn to the tensions, hopes and hatreds within the social structure of the old order, we must remember that there were other possible emphases, other possible combinations of action, other impulses and motives, which, for better or for worse, were either not recognized or not chosen. Human miscalculation released forces and created potentialities which might otherwise have remained obscure and marginal. When Louis XVI came to his throne, *a* revolution was inevitable; *the* Revolution, as we know it, never was, and to the king himself, goodhearted, unimaginative and very ordinary, was left in the first place that choice of alternatives which makes potential history real.

A revolutionary situation is born from a paradoxical marriage of hope and despair. Booming prosperity (which de Tocqueville and Jaurès emphasize) and desperate hunger (which dominates Michelet's picture) combined to produce the critical economic tensions of 1789. From the second quarter of the century, a sudden upward movement of population gave momentum to a long steady price rise. Landowners with agricultural surpluses for sale grew rich from this profit inflation and their spending primed industrial production, more particularly in textile, building and luxury trades, as well as stimulating activity in colonial and Levant markets. Here then is a suitable economic background for Jaurès' theme of a rising *bourgeoisie*, convinced of its 'right to and its almost infinite chances of development', claiming a voice in national affairs, and trembling lest a spendthrift government repudiate its enormous borrowings. Free institutions, it was believed, would be a guarantee of continued economic expansion. 'Liberty alone', said the *Encyclopédie*, re-echoing Montesquieu, 'allows men to multiply', an axiom which was generally accepted during the revolutionary years, until Chateaubriand and J. B. Say began to insinuate Malthusian doubts. In 1770 a regression began which was prolonged by debt and disruption resulting from French participation in the American War of Independence, by the unfavourable commercial treaty of 1786 with England, and by Spanish restrictions on the export of precious metals. An already weakened economy, whose basis was still agricultural, faced a disastrous crop failure in 1788 and the harvest of '89 was known to be a poor one. As the price of cheaper grains shot up and poor folk had to spend all their income on bread, a crisis of underconsumption narrowed manufacturers' markets and brought the textile industry to ruin. Commercial men resented the end of the boom. The urban proletariat was starving. Poorer peasants, who did not till land enough to feed their families, were in as bad a case, and rural France throughout the 'seventies and 'eighties had been feeling the pressure of a feudal reaction as landlords screwed the last *sol* out of obsolete dues to compensate for the falling value of leases. For some there was a dashing of hopes which had been growing for a generation, for many more there was a brutal threat of starvation. Developments which in other times might have appeared as factors working towards prosperity now took on a sinister air. Financial capitalism had never been so active in Paris as in the 'eighties. Troubles in Geneva and Belgium brought foreign bankers to France, the *Cie des Indes* was re-established in 1785, and there was a wave of speculation on tontines, insurance projects, companies for running street lighting and cabs and for extracting odourless dividends from the latrines of the capital. The government was making fitful. though intelligent attempts to enrich the nation and moved steadily towards economic liberalism, suppressing gilds, making commercial treaties, freeing (when it dared) the internal and external corn trade in accordance with Physiocratic principles. As conditions deteriorated, the people, whose concept of crisis was, says M. Labrousse, 'anthropomorphic rather than economic', looked for the authors of their ills and saw combinations of speculators on one hand and criminal inaction by their rulers on the other. When the government allowed grain to move freely it was in league with profiteers, when it turned again to control supplies the odious legend of a *pacte de famine* revived: 'On a faim de par le Roi.'

Social discontents conform to this pattern of economic tension. Everywhere there were signs of progress and hopes were rising, yet everywhere progress was retarded and hope deferred. Peasants were becoming landowners, the more degrading forms of personal service were obsolescent, and inflation had mitigated those dues which were not paid in kind. Towns, theoretically in tutelage to *intendants*, in practice bought off royal taxes for those of their own imposing, and were ruled by oligarchies of *bourgeois* office-holders. Wealth was increasing and urban life became more civilized. There was talk of new public squares and buildings, promenades, street lighting and paving, botanical gardens, musical societies and coffee-houses. Never had the Gallican church appeared in such outward splendour and dignity. In its cathedrals, newly adorned with marbles, gilt, and panelling, a pageantry of stately ritual and lavishly endowed music mocked the criticisms of sceptics and anti-clericals. Oratorians, Benedictines and *Frères des Écoles Chrétiennes* were giving a progressive education to a rising generation. With the exception of boorish parish priests in backward rural areas and a few scandalous high ecclesiastics, the moral standards and reputation of the clergy stood high, and the historical researches of Benedictines of Saint-Maur and the work of religious sisterhoods in caring for the sick and educating children did something to offset the mellow decadence of monastic ideals. In Louis XVI's reign the army regained its status as the finest force in Europe. Experts of other nations studied Guibert's tactical theories, Gribeauval's improved artillery and de Ségur's disciplinary regulations—new ideas of the old régime which were to serve French ambitions well under the Revolution and Empire.

There was promise everywhere: but everywhere, as a barrier to fulfilment, stood privilege. Peasants resented feudal dues, hunting rights, monopolies of mill and oven, and ecclesiastical tithe more bitterly now that feudal dependence had lost its meaning and usefulness. The *bourgeoisie* hated having to render sycophantic homage to great nobles, prelates, military governors and *intendants*, and envied the shady enclosures of monasteries and the urban fiefs of chapters which constricted every avenue of municipal improvement. *Avocats* resented the pride of magistrates of sovereign courts, and the lesser *bourgeoisie* generally reacted against middle class families which bought high office or noble status. The lower clergy detested a system of patronage which reserved all episcopal sees and most well-endowed ecclesiastical sinecures for youthful aristocrats scarce out of their seminaries, and complained of tithes and honorific precedences which chapters and monasteries exacted within their parishes. And what could army officers, commoners or country nobles, think of hordes of colonels of the court, secure above them in unearned promotions and decorations, despite all the reforms of Saint-Germain and de Ségur? Then, of all privileges, the most odious and most obvious was exemption from taxation. In 1788, total government expenditure was 630 millions, and of this 318 millions were payments of interest on public debt. As the economic crisis deepened, it became manifest that, without reform, existing schedules of taxation could not bear the load. Yet privileged exemptions remained intact, more scandalous among nobles in areas of *taille réelle*, but significant also in the case of *bourgeois* office-holders, *pays d'état*, and towns paying by composition, and in the church's independent votes of benevolences. To control a changing social and economic situation, indeed, merely to rescue itself from bankruptcy, the Bourbon monarchy must break the network of privilege which bound down the nation.

'Lorsqu'on veut empêcher une Révolution, il faut la vouloir et la faire soi-même', said Rivarol. True, but there were enormous difficulties in the way of an officially sponsored revolution. Abuses and anachronisms were complex and interdependent. France was not a united nation, it was not even three Estates: it was a labyrinth of vested interests which could swallow up the most ingenious reformers. And kings were only absolute in theory. In practice, they were trapped in a whole system of pensions, intrigue and etiquette which constituted Versailles. Edicts and *lettres de cachet* were never an end; with *parlements*, the Church or provincial Estates one always ended by negotiating. Even *intendants*, supreme agents of centralized power, were members of a caste of families which had bought their way to the summit of the judicial hierarchy, men of wealth and independent spirit, not pliant and expendable bureaucrats. Louis XV had been a spectator of his own reign like a gallant at a play, and his successor lacked those dynamic qualities which alone could have regained control over a drama hastening towards its *dénouement*. Turgot, grave, philosophical and reckless, Calonne, intelligent and cynical, and even Necker, complacent in his rectitude, were ministers of the Enlightenment, men who could have brought their reforms to fruition in other lands, in the service of Frederick, Catherine or Joseph. But France, which had given to Europe its ideas of enlightened despotism, remained that very country where these ideas were not put into effect. If the Bourbons had thrown up a Bonaparte it is conceivable that they might have succeeded—scaled down Versailles to bureaucratic briskness, compelled nobles and clergy to pay fair taxation, bought out venal office-holders, crushed down the chaos of feudalism, provincialism, conflicting jurisdictions, ecclesiastical immunities, introduced equality and uniformity. And liberty? There is the question. An enlightened despot who steered France into this new era would have to be sufficiently enlightened to realize that his own absolutism must be sublimated. He must reform France, and then reform himself.

It is difficult to synthesize the subtle and paradoxical intellectual temper of these last years of the old régime. Rationalism still retained its sharp cutting-edge of criticism, but was being overlaid by *sensibilité*, which appealed to the natural against the sophisticated, venerated village patriarchs, lauded the *bon curé* and wept for star-crossed lovers, and which ran to seed in fashionable society with the marquise d'Urfé's sorcery, Cagliostro's dinners with the dead, Mesmerism, Swedenborgianism, illuminism, alchemy. But whatever we make of the intellectual atmosphere of the reign of Louis XVI, one thing is clear—a breath of liberty blows through it. This breeze came from the West, from newer lands across the Atlantic. Most Frenchmen had supported the rebels merely to score off England, and yet, once American independence was won, enthusiasm for the republic ousted Anglomania. The mingling of birth and wealth in high Parisian society and in capitalistic enterprises, and the victory of the *philosophes* in *salons* and the Academy were also bearing their fruits: 'people no longer ask a man's rank to admit him to their circle', wrote Sénac de Meilhan in 1787, 'but simply ask if he is agreeable'. New ideas of economic progress fostered a new respect for mechanical arts and technical education, and there was a fashionable, rather precious concern for the miseries of the poor which Fabre d'Eglantine was to satirize so bitterly. All this bright foam on the surface gives some indication of the direction in which the current of political insistence was setting. It is not easy to weigh the evidence; to concentrate on literature gets one into a world of ideas which cannot conclusively be shown to be moving events; the *cahiers*, making allowances for middle-class and clerical leadership, are honest documents, but were not suitable vehicles for expressions of political theory; the mass of petitions to the National Assembly is the sort of evidence we want, but it comes at a time when revolutionary events have already released inhibitions and falsified the original picture.

However, it is not difficult to sense feeling about monarchy. The king is taken for granted. The *cahiers* assume, not that a States-general is meeting to give France a constitution, but that there already is a constitution, and that the States-general is to clarify it. On the other hand, the *cahiers* are unambiguous in demanding an end of arbitrary rule and insisting upon individual liberty. There is a tension between these two ideas which gives us our clue for interpreting the Declaration of Rights, which was no flood of theory pouring down from a mountain range of philosophy, but a canal fed by springs arising from the work-a-day soil of France. When the Constituents proclaimed the separation of powers, which was fundamental, they were neither flourishing Montesquieu nor slavishly copying America; they were simply establishing a final guarantee of individual liberty in a state which they could only conceive of as monarchical.

Perhaps the key idea of '89, the formula which reconciled ideals of reforming government and individual liberty, was that of 'liberty under the law'. Law was to be sacred (that was why the Assembly set up a *Tribunal de Cassation* to watch over its execution), it was to be the expression of Rousseau's 'general will', of 'la volonté sociale'. Eighteenth-century France, with its myriad courts and complicated hierarchical society, was a fantastically litigious country; churchwardens could hardly allot a pew without being sued for it by someone. Hence, men looked forward with reverence to a day when law, co-ordinated and purified, would become an expression of the national will, and, then indeed, the king himself would be under it. The *parlements*, with naïve self-righteousness, were posing as representatives of the original fundamental law of the kingdom, the royal authority 'inaccessible aux surprises'. Archbishop Boisgelin, preaching before Louis XVI on the eve of his coronation, warned him (with an emphasis which the duc de Croy thought rather scandalous) that a king must be under the laws, and the civic oath of the Revolution was to the nation and the law as well as to the crown. A king of France, according to Quesnay, a Physiocratic supporter of enlightened despotism in theory, should 'do nothing'. 'And who would govern?' asked his royal pupil—'The laws'. Government by such a noble abstraction is an ambiguous formula awaiting interpretation, and it is probable that someone will end up by governing in the name of the laws as he sees them.

If it could have reformed France, and itself, that rôle might have fallen to the Bourbon monarchy.

To maintain its social leadership, to survive even, the crown had to strike at the heart of privilege, at exemptions from taxation. It did so, and evoked an aristocratic reaction with which the Revolution begins. Calonne and Brienne's demand for a universal land-tax with no privileged exemptions met with decisive opposition from the Notables, and from the *parlements* allied with great nobles of the sword and princes of the blood. The king, left with no alternative, summoned the States-general, and appealed to the Third Estate against this new Fronde. When *parlement* objected to the proposal to double the *Tiers*, it lost its popularity overnight. 'The privileged have dared to resist the king,' said Lamoignon, 'in two months' time there will be neither *parlements*, nobility nor clergy.' This is the language of a revolution directed by the throne. A Fronde, a regency, a defiance like that of the clerical order which defeated Machault in 1750, these were incidents of the old régime which the aristocracy was resurrecting. It was the crown which called in a new factor, and left the way open for the *bourgeoisie*. 'A change has come over the public dispute', wrote Mallet du Pan in January 1789, 'the king, despotism and the constitution are secondary questions: the main thing is a war between the Third Estate and the two other orders, against whom the court has called in the towns.'

The *révolte nobiliaire* was not a rising of a single coherent class. There were divisions between rich and poor, lay and clerical, robe and sword, court and country, between reactionary rebels and various brands of liberal ones. Intermarriage and a common life in polite society, the co-operation of sovereign courts with surviving provincial Estates, and, perhaps, the influence of Montesquieu in blending feudal and magisterial traditions had contributed to bring high robe and gilded sword into a political alliance, which only temporarily masked social distrust and rivalry. Great prelates playing at once for a constitution, the safety of the clerical order and the succession of Mazarin and Fleury, looked askance at sceptical *grands seigneurs* who were willing to give freedom of expression to Protestants and *philosophes*, and were more than half suspect of designs to use church property to finance national regeneration. Most magistrates of the *parlement* of Paris remained reactionaries, yet soon they were compelled to realize that their conservative discontents had given birth to a group of liberals, the so-called 'Americans'. One of these was Adrien Duport, whose home became a meeting place for the 'Committee of Thirty', an agency of propaganda directed by liberal aristocrats, rich bankers, and a few worldly ecclesiastics like Talleyrand and Sieyès. Clubs, masonic lodges, and the salons of titled ladies dabbling in politics drew together diverse groups of the 'patriotic party' and tangled the threads of liberal intrigue. There was a conspiracy against Marie Antoinette, there were pro-Necker and anti-Necker factions, and, above all, there was an Orleanist party, directed, suitably enough, by the author of *Les Liaisons dangereuses*. If an era of constitutionalism was approaching, magistrates of the red robe might reaffirm their position as guarantors of fundamental laws, or a second chamber representing high birth and high finance might be created: there would be ministerial posts for dukes or bishops or heroes of the American war; while a Bourbon prince who had dined with Fox, fought the English at sea, gone up in a *Montgolfière*, and issued model *cahiers* in favour of periodical States-general would surely reap his reward.

Poor, and indeed, rich provincial nobles had little to do with these cabals in Paris. If in May '88 they are found supporting the *parlements*, it is because Brienne's ill-calculated edicts were threatening their seigneurial jurisdictions, through which they enforced payment of disputed feudal dues. They wanted canonries in the church and commissions in the army for their sons, and places in better-class convents for their daughters, and were bitterly conscious that episcopal thrones, rich abbeys and colonelcies were reserved to the glittering nobles of Versailles. Read the marquis de Ferrières on 'pagodas' of the court battening on the pensions' list under the old dispensation, and conspiring with 'capitalists' under the new, or the comte d'Antraigues on the great 'who seem to form around the king a new nation, enemy of the people', and a fundamental cleavage of interest among the nobility becomes vividly apparent.

In provincial France, the revolt of the nobles was generally directed towards maintaining or reviving traditional assemblies under aristocratic domination, but this common theme only gave a modicum of unity to a diverse agitation. In Anjou, there was a directing intelligence, Walsh, comte de Serrant, who had a definite policy of enriching his class 'with the spoils of the *intendant*', and appealed to commoners to abandon 'vote-catching lawyers' and join him in plundering ecclesiastical property; Brittany was the scene of a blind defensive reaction on the part of a penurious squirearchy, the *épées de fer*; there was a reactionary party in Provence composed of two hundred or so fiefed nobles, a few higher clergy and the high robe, abetted by an *intendant* who was *premier président* of the *parlement* of Aix; in Franche-Comté there was a coalition of nobles and magistrates of the *parlement* of Besançon (many of the latter being commoners). It was a patchwork insurrection, and everywhere a few dissentient liberals appeared, drawing their inspiration from the shrewd and generous conduct of their class in Dauphiné, where nobles and middle classes worked in patriotic union for the fusion of orders and double representation for the *Tiers*. Other divisions in the aristocratic ranks were a result of foolish exclusiveness which alienated potential allies, and sometimes gave the commons powerful leaders—the newly ennobled of Nantes, officers of the local *Cour des Comptes* in other places, and in Provence five hundred unfiefed nobles led by no less a genius than Mirabeau.

Liberal nobles were a minority, and of this minority few wore their personal ambitions with dignity, like Lafayette or Stanislas de Clermont-Tonnerre, or brought to their achievement a lucid political intelligence like Mirabeau or Talleyrand. Yet the incoherent and anarchical flavour of aristocratic aspirations should not lead us to treat them as merely disreputable. Magistrates who burned Boncerf's brochure on feudal dues and set barriers to fair taxation, prelates who opposed toleration to Protestants or voting power to *curés*, had a genuine belief in their own indispensability. When they maintained that *parlement's* functions of registration and remonstrance, or the Assembly of Clergy's exclusive right to tax ecclesiastical incomes were 'remains of old national franchises' held in trust in the ark of privilege while despotism's waters covered the land, they were deluding themselves rather than other people. Social injustice warped and conditioned the minds of its beneficiaries as well as of those it disinherited. It was fatally easy, as de Ségur later explained, for young aristocrats to enjoy both the advantages which old institutions afforded them, and liberty which was the new intellectual fashion. Lafayette's naïve sincerity (Talleyrand put him just on the other side of the line where a man is deemed intelligent) makes his early career an illustration of the mental limitations which had to be overcome before a well-intentioned noble could achieve a genuinely liberal outlook. Like other lofty passions, liberty is rarely found unadulterated. It was possible, as Fénelon and Montesquieu had done, to identify it with an aristocratic revival as a barrier against despotism. Among the great there was a widespread recognition that exemptions must end and that control of taxation must be exercised through periodical States-general. They hoped, either by retaining the distinction of orders, or by forming a second chamber of birth and wealth, to retain political power in their own hands. Financial immunities had been a sort of bribe for the loss of political power: they meant to reverse this process, surrender immunities and regain domination.

What rôle could the king hope to play in the approaching battle between aristocracy and democracy which is the central theme of the Revolution? Louis XVI was not strong enough to dictate to either side. If the throne was regarded as a social necessity (and genuine republicanism did not arise until after the flight to Varennes), divine right was outmoded and sentimental loyalty to the wearer of the crown, while it survived, had passed out of politics. 'Today,' wrote the abbé de Véri, 'hardly anyone dare say in Parisian society, *I serve the king*. . . . You'd be taken for one of the chief valets at Versailles. *I serve the state*, is the expression most commonly used.' The army, subject to the abusive privileges which honeycombed civilian society, was unsure. In the spring of '88 there was a storm of discontent among officers when 'reforms' were announced which maintained court nobles in their right to facile promotion. During the aristocratic revolt precedents for disobedience were created, nobles who had fought in America threatening to draw their swords in defence of *parlement* and local officers refusing to be a party to repression in Brittany and Dauphiné. Appeals were being issued to soldiers not to fire on their brethren, which had their effect in June '89 when the *Gardes françaises* went over to the people. 'The defection of the army,' said Rivarol, 'is not a cause of the Revolution, it is the Revolution itself.' Thus only one effective line of action remained open to Louis. He was believed to be honest and his nation, atomized, reduced to confusion by interlocking abuses and rivalries, sought an impartial mediator.

But alas! when the States-general met, the government's plans were vague, although there was an all-too-definite request for money, and that at a time when the deficit was the nation's treasure, its only guarantee of radical reform. Moderates in the Third Estate and *curés* who wished to preserve the identity of the clerical order (as most of them did) were never offered a reasonable alternative to the extreme policy which ultimately prevailed in the vote of 17 June. The king had called in the people, then identified himself with reaction. There was only one mistake left for Louis to make, and that was to call on force. The movement of troops towards Paris and Necker's dismissal led to the fall of the Bastille. 14 July was a rising of Paris, not a rising of the *canaille* as Taine has it, or merely of the workers of the faubourg Saint-Antoine, but of the city as a whole. It was on 27 April, when a mob burned Réveillon's wallpaper factory, and on 1 August, when journeymen tailors met outside the Louvre to demand increased wages, that the starving working classes expressed their own particular and fundamental grievances. On 14 July they were rising with the aid of the mutinous *Gardes françaises*, with the *bourgeois* assembly of electors maintaining a cadre of revolutionary order, with financiers closing the Bourse in sympathy and providing arms for the people. Workers, middle classes and capitalists had been united by Louis XVI's blind plunge into reaction. Paris might have risen in any case, to walk the cobblestones free from the menace of privileged wheels, to sit in coffee-houses free from the ubiquitous *mouchard*, or, quite simply, for bread; but it was the royal folly which united the capital and created a new insurrectionary power, aimed directly against despotism in general, and against despotic control of the army in particular. With the fall of the Bastille, all possibility of a military coup vanished, the press censorship collapsed, an independent Parisian government and National Guard emerged, and a municipal revolution began all over France. It was an end of absolute rule. The Revolution passed to the control of the *bourgeoisie*.

After the October days had broken royal resistance to the decrees of 4 August, the Constituents exercised a legal dictatorship, and gave France new institutions. They swept away privilege and orders in the state, proclaimed the sovereignty of the nation, making their king a constitutional monarch, set up independent organs of local government, ended monastic vows and arbitrary imprisonment, and introduced religious toleration. We cannot here consider details: as our subject is government and society, the single question I would wish to ask is: Is this reformation of France fairly described as *'bourgeois'* in inspiration and intention? One may begin by admitting that use of this term is inevitable, and that it conveys a coherent impression of a complex pattern of events which would otherwise defy generalization. More than this, taking the programme as it stands, we find that liberalism everywhere has a flavour of *bourgeois* self-interest. A distinction between 'active' and 'passive' citizens embodies this in blatant political terms. Internal customs duties were ended and the internal corn trade freed, but tariffs and the colonial monopoly were maintained. An increase of taxation by 40 per cent could have cleared the debt in twenty years without selling Church property; instead, the Constituents chose the facile solution, one which would cost them least. Many of them were holders of venal offices, and it was no coincidence that they compelled themselves to accept reimbursement of their charges at the very moment ecclesiastical property was up for auction. Their basic land tax was designed to have none of the qualities of an income tax, and the long-term effects of this decision have been deplorable in French history. What was done for the urban poor? The *loi le Chapelier* forbade workmens' combinations, and public assistance to replace ecclesiastical charity was never satisfactorily organized. Even the later 'maximum' was a war-time measure forced upon rulers, who, like their predecessors in the first revolutionary assemblies, remained non-interventionist in economic principles. What was done for the peasants? As early as 3 November 1790 the original terms for the sale of Church property, which favoured small buyers, were revised, and had the papers of the *Caisse de l'Extraordinaire* and of the *Comité d'Aliénation* not been burnt in 1871, we should no doubt have heard more about peasant complaints. The Constituent Assembly did nothing for the landless, but presented tithes and islands and rivers of royal demesne to private proprietors. The Convention, which forbade associations of small buyers of *biens nationaux*, was as *bourgeois* as its predecessors. As early as 1790, a *curé* of Auvergne, with a terrible clairvoyance which Marat himself would have envied, ruthlessly defined the future social issue as a struggle against *bourgeois* domination. You have brought the aristocracy down to your level, he says, what if we, the people, ask you to bring us up to yours? 'In throwing stones, burning *châteaux* and murdering nobles it wasn't our intention merely to enably you to satisfy your vanity.'

But few contemporaries saw the situation in black and white like this, and those who did were seeing only half the truth. A comparison of the wide electorate set up by the *suffrage censitaire* of the Constituents with the electoral bases of the Restoration or July monarchy shows how genuinely liberal and egalitarian were the men of '89, in spite of all their prejudices in favour of property. And again, prejudices in favour of property can be of different kinds, and have widely divergent social implications. Economic *laissez-faire* was not meant to lead to oligarchical capitalism, but to a society inspired by the free competition of smaller men—that was why the *Cie des Indes* lost its monopoly, and why even Robespierre was silent in face of the *loi le Chapelier*. In agriculture, where *laissez-faire* would have helped big land-owners against smaller, customary grazing rights were maintained and the exportation of grain forbidden, in spite of a good harvest in 1790. Debates on the nationalization of mining rights in the first half of '91 reveal that it was small owners who wanted their property held sacred 'from the upper atmosphere to the centre of the earth', while it was big *concessionnaires* who wanted mineral rights declared national property. Only eighty members of the Constituent Assembly can be listed as agents of commercial or industrial interests, as against more than four hundred 'lawyers' of various kinds. All of which suggests that, when we describe the men of the Revolution as '*bourgeois*', we ought to rid our minds of Marxist technicalities. One should go back to Loyseau's picture (1613) of a man of reasonable means who does not work with his hands, except it be in some 'honourable' profession like jeweller, apothecary or draper; one should picture two contrasting ways of life, reflected in Chardin's solid interiors and in Watteau's ethereal landscapes. As Aynard says, it was not capitalism which constituted the *bourgeoisie*, but moral habits, intellectual prejudices and education.

We have seen that the nobility did not form a homogeneous class, and that the divisions of lay society ran clean through the ecclesiastical order: the diverse stratification of the Third Estate is more obvious still. One begins naturally by considering peasants, urban workers and *bourgeoisie*, only to find that these classifications are still not subtle or detailed enough to fit social facts. Consider rural France. In some areas there was a considerable *bourgeoisie* of the countryside, large-scale farmers of noble and ecclesiastical lands. Everywhere, especially in the South and Centre, there was a growing number of peasant proprietors, some very prosperous, like the honest farmers of Restif de la Bretonne's *Vie de mon Père*. These men, together with urban middle-classes seeking investment opportunities, were gainers by the sale of Church property. But there was also a vast mass of rural poor, *métayers*, peasant owners with plots too small to feed a family, landless labourers, and agricultural workers employed by urban merchants in part-time home industries. Very often, these folk only survived by leasing land from noble or ecclesiastical owners to supplement their own inadequate holdings, and most of them were as concerned as town artisans to have cheap food, as against more prosperous farmers who had a surplus of grain for sale. Thus, the richer half of peasant society wanted to buy more land, enclose commons, grow what crops it liked, and sell in the dearest market: the poorer half wanted land kept available, not for buying, but for cheap leases in small lots, it wanted to preserve commons and old grazing rights, and have government control of crop-planting and fixing of corn prices. Within these two interests, were many local and personal variations. Unable to read more than a few lines of the *Chemin du Ciel* or the *Petit Chrestien*, rarely moving more than a few miles from their own villages, and divided by sectional interests, the peasants did not constitute an effective social entity. The peasant risings which broke out in the spring of '89 were part of a separate autonomous non-political revolution caused by hunger, taxation, and hatred of privilege. They hastened the end of feudalism and contributed to a panic which led to the formation of militias and *bourgeois* domination, but they had no programme and could exercise no pressure for specific political action. Thus the Revolution had no agrarian policy. By removing feudal burdens and selling vast amounts of property, the revolutionary events widened the gulf between landowning peasants and the rural proletariat, who thus, by accident as it were, were left with the factory as their future destiny in national life.

Urban workers, like peasants, were not a class in the sense of a self-conscious entity. Big-scale industry had arrived in France, but it was the exception, and very small-scale industry was the rule. Struggles between journeymen and masters, masters and wholesalers, between urban and rural industry, between varying groups with differing privileges fragmented the cadres of artisan population. Strikes were growing more frequent in the eighteenth century, but they were strikes of individual trades in individual towns. There was hatred between rich and poor, but the whole mentality of the poor was pre-capitalist. A history of socialist theory finds an abundance of literary references in eighteenth-century France, from Montesquieu to Turgot and Necker to Marat, the *curés rouges* and Babeuf, but the theories remain in books or in journalism without infiltrating into working-class action or mentality. Urban *cahiers* were drawn up by the middle classes, the middle classes were sent as deputies to the States-general. The complaints of workers that are heard during the Revolution are, more often, complaints of consumers rather than producers. Even the *Enragés* have nothing better to demand than the maximum, a return to the regulatory policy of the old régime.

When we turn to the *bourgeoisie* then, the essential point to notice is that it constitutes a class, not as resisting pressure from below—for peasants and artisans were disunited and non-political in their demands—but as challenging privilege above. The issue is not possessions, but privilege. One might say, indeed, that the *bourgeoisie* in Marx's sense hardly existed under the old régime, or, if it did, it was not identical with the class which made the Revolution.

Bourgeois France begins somewhere among financiers ennobled by purchase, whose daughters have married great nobles, and among rich men newly dignified by holding high judicial office, like merchants of Montpellier who go on trading after they have become magistrates of the *Cour des Comptes* or a monied élite of Dijon which always ends up in the robe. Then comes a topmost circle of wealth, Parisian bankers and speculators, ship-owners and slave-traders of Western ports, San Domingo fortunes, great industrialists. Many of these, by strict definition, could hardly be called *bourgeois*, for they moved luxuriously on the fringe of the aristocracy. Wherever money was found, a patent of nobility was never very far away. Success was not quite complete without it—even Merlin of Douai, who drew up the law of suspects, had once bought an office of *secrétaire du roi* to achieve personal ennoblement. Then come wide layers of society which are strictly *bourgeois*, but even so, sharply subdivided into proud cliques and corporations, and consumed by envious desires for precedence. Status was based, apparently, on the aristocratic idea that to work with one's hands was derogatory; thus pride of place went to *rentiers* and those living 'noblement et de leurs biens'; then came office-holders and those exercising liberal professions; next merchants, provided they were wholesalers; then shopkeepers and the common run of professions and trades. Yet all the while this scale of status was bending and yielding under pressure from another type of judgement, for sheer naked wealth was demanding recognition, resentful of the traditional necessity to buy idleness or office before being deemed respectable. In these middle ranks of society, where the process of osmosis towards the aristocracy functioned but rarely and tardily, the more explosive hatred of privilege was found. There were doctors, surgeons, apothecaries, merchants and, above all, there were *avocats* and notaries, who at Brest, Saint-Malo, Angers, Guingamp and many another town were found organizing middle-class opposition to the aristocracy, whether it be the feudal nobility of the countryside, or ennobled aldermen of municipal oligarchies. In capitation registers and provincial almanachs we catch glimpses of a middle-class divided into a whole hierarchy of wealth and status. Writing of the little town of Gray in Franche-Comté, where his own family of rich peasant stock had purchased office, Cournot says: 'In customs and social habits, the nobility and *bourgeoisie* consisted of a multitude of layers, of social strata each separate and distinct, running from a prince of the blood to the humblest artisan.' But there were certain clear lines of separation, drawn by privilege. While society at the end of the old régime was infinitely complex, there were points on the social scale where these lines of separation became a fundamental cleavage, and privilege at these points of cleavage was the key issue of the Revolution.

It is on the eve of the flight to Varennes that *bourgeois* revisionism arises, an instinctive drawing together of property owners for fear of that class which André Chénier described as one that 'knows nothing, has nothing, takes interest in nothing, and knows only how to sell itself to those willing to buy it'. But until then, the attack is against privilege and its driving force is a class compounded of many diverse social layers, fused together for political action by hatreds, ideals and ambitions. The *bourgeoisie* which made the Revolution was not, essentially, a capitalist class. It was a coalition of the educated and ambitious. 'The old régime made a crucial error,' said Danton; 'I was educated by it as an exhibitioner at the collège du Plessis. I studied there with great nobles who . . . lived with me on equal terms. My studies once finished, I had nothing . . . my former comrades turned their backs on me. The Revolution came: I and all those like me—we threw ourselves into it. The old régime drove us to it by giving us a good education without opening any opportunity for our talents.' In 1783, Barnave wrote in his *Journal* of the disillusionment which tortured 'a man born with a great soul' who found 'the roads barred everywhere . . . only limited and trivial careers are open to him'. It was the royal appeal to the nation which called to life the *bourgeoisie* of '89, a temporarily united, yet irresistible force, determined to end privilege, open careers to talent, obtain a say in government, strike off medieval fetters on enterprise. De Tocqueville regrets that their ruthless passion for equality burned so much more fiercely within them than the nobler desire for liberty; but to their minds, these two were inseparable, and it is not very surprising that men who wanted free government—truly free government, not Malouet's 'deceptive appearance of unanimity for innovations tending towards something which resembled a free government'—should have pictured themselves as its administrators, orators and officials. United by hatred of privilege and despotism, they swept away the restrictions of the old régime, and, by so doing, they left a way open for the emergence of the *bourgeoisie* in the Marxist sense of that word, a development which many of them, could they have forseen it, would have regretted.

For the old régime, whose abuses they were condemning, was nevertheless their world, and they could not guess, in 1789, at the nature of a new age which would be created by the failure of royal leadership, the breach with Catholicism, by war and inflation, and by the relentless combinations arising from their own ambitions. 'Années fécondes en emotions vives et douces,' wrote one of them, looking back on those days, when he had been an Oratorian schoolmaster, teaching physics at the college of Arras, knowing Masillon's sermons by heart and half in love with Charlotte Robespierre—'O years rich in lively sweet emotions!' This was in 1816, and by then he was duke of Otranto, ex-Chief of police of Napoleon, ex-terrorist, ex-Dechristianizer, ex-Oratorian—Fouché.

BIBLIOGRAPHICAL NOTE

Since this chapter was first published, the whole subject has been renewed by innumerable publications. The bibliography which follows no longer reflects the sources from which the text was derived. For the sake of brevity, the list has been confined, where possible, to works in English, and the reader is assumed to be using the book list accompanying Professor Bromley's chapter for works concerning social structure at the end of the old régime.

I. FRANCE AT THE END OF THE OLD RÉGIME, AND THE COMING OF THE REVOLUTION

DAKIN, D. *Turgot and the Ancien Régime in France* (1939).

EGRET, J. *La Pré-Révolution française, 1787-8* (1962).

GOTTSCHALK, L. *Lafayette between the American and French Revolutions, 1783-89* (Chicago, 1950).

GRUDER, V. R. *The Royal Provincial Intendants* (1968).

LEFEBVRE, G. *The Coming of the French Revolution* (trans. R. R. Palmer, Princeton, 1949).

For the economic background, the monographs of C.-E. Labrousse are essential. M. Labrousse has summarized his views in R. Mousnier and Labrousse, *Le XVIIIe siècle, révolution intellectuelle, technique et politique* (Hist. Gén. des civilisations V, 1953); see also Lefebvre, 'Le Mouvement des prix et les origines de la Révolution', *Annales historiques de la Révolution française* XIV 1937).

For a controversial view of the events of 1789, see F. Braesch, *1789: l'année cruciale* (1941).

II. GENERAL STUDIES OF THE REVOLUTION

Professor Goodwin's brief introduction (1953) and the Rev. J. M. Thompson's narrative history (1951) retain their value. The best up-to-date volume in English is Norman Hampson's *A Social History of the French Revolution* (1963). G. Lefebvre's *La Révolution Française* (1951), a synthesis by the greatest of the historians of the Revolution, is available in English translation (2 vols., 1962-4).

For a controversial interpretation of the events in France in a world setting, see R. R. Palmer, *The Age of the Democratic Revolution* (2 vols. 1959-64).

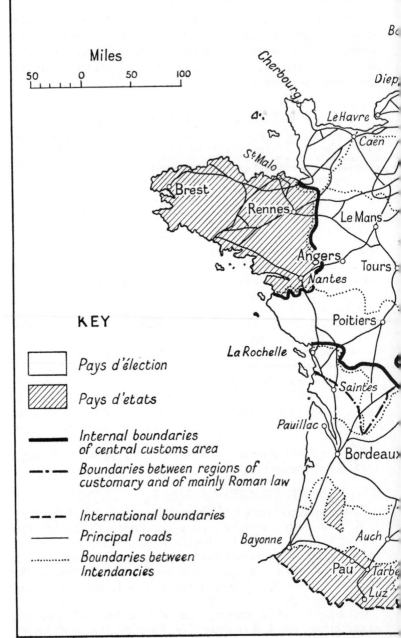

Miles

50   0   50   100

KEY

Pays d'élection

Pays d'etats

Internal boundaries
of central customs area

Boundaries between regions of
customary and of mainly Roman law

International boundaries

Principal roads

Boundaries between
Intendancies

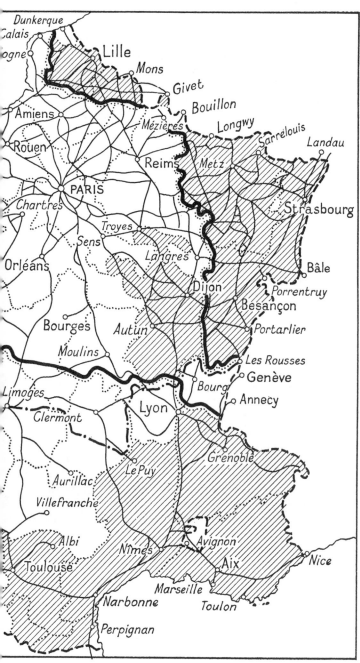

Dunkerque
Calais
ogne
Lille
Mons
Givet
Bouillon
Amiens
Méziéres
Longwy
Sarrélouis
Landau
Rouen
Reims
Metz
Strasbourg
PARIS
Chartres
Troyes
Langres
Bâle
Sens
Dijon
Porrentruy
Orléans
Besançon
Bourges
Autun
Portarlier
Moulins
Les Rousses
Limoges
Bourg
Genéve
Clermont
Lyon
Annecy
Grenoble
Le Puy
Aurillac
Villefranche
Albi
Avignon
Nîmes
Aix
Nice
Toulouse
Marseille
Narbonne
Toulon
Perpignan

HE ANCIEN RÉGIME   [By Mary Potter

Demographers are now making important contributions to revolutionary history; see M. Bouloiseau (ed.), *Contributions à l'histoire démographique de la Révolution* (1962). For institutional history, J. Godechot, *Histoire des Institutions de la France sous la Révolution et l'Empire* (1951). For the changing attitudes of historians to the Revolution, see G. Rudé, *Interpretations of the French Revolution* (Historical Association pamphlet, 1961), and J. McManners, 'The Historiography of the Revolution', *New Cambridge Modern History*, vol. viii, ed. A. Goodwin (1965).

A brilliant and monumental work which is changing our whole approach to the Revolution and which cuts across all the 'orthodoxies' is Richard Cobb's *Les armées révolutionnaires* (2 vols., 1961-3).

III. SOME PARTICULAR TOPICS

1. THE ARMY

LÉONARD, E. G. *L'Armée et ses problèmes au 18e siècle* (1958).

HARTMANN, L. 'Les Officiers de l'armée royale à la veille de la Révolution', *Revue Historique* C & CI (1909).

2. THE CHURCH

There are useful general histories in French by

A. Latreille (1946), A. Dansette (1948, English trans. 1961) and D. Rops (1960). See also, J. McManners, *The French Revolution and the Church* (1969), and B. Plongeron, *Conscience religieuse en Révolution: regards sur l'historiographie religieuse de la Révolution Française* (1969).

3. THE MOVEMENT OF IDEAS

BELIN, J. *La Logique d'une idée-force. L'idée d'utilité sociale pendant la Révolution, 1789-92* (1939).

DUCLOS, P. *La Notion de constitution dans l'œuvre de l'Assemblée constituante de 1789* (Poitiers, 1932).

LEROY, M. *Histoire des idées socialistes en France de Montesquieu à Robespierre* (1946).

MAUZI, R. *L'Idée de Bonheur dans la littérature et la pensée françaises au 18e siècle* (1960).

TRAHARD, P. *La Sensibilité révolutionnaire 1789-94* (1936).

4. INDIVIDUAL TOWNS

HUFTON, O. *Bayeux in the late 18th century* (1967).

KAPLOW, J. *Elbeuf during the Revolutionary Period* (1964).

MCMANNERS, J. *French Ecclesiastical Society under the Ancien Régime: A Study of Angers in the Eighteenth Century* (1960).

5. ARTISANS AND WORKPEOPLE IN THE REVOLUTION

COBB, R. 'The Revolutionary Mentality in France, 1793-94', *History*, XLII (1957).

ROSE, R. B. *The Enragés: Socialists of the French Revolution?* (1965).

RUDÉ, G. *The Crowd in the French Revolution* (1959).

SOBOUL, A. *Les sans-culottes Parisiens en l'an II* (English trs. abridged, 1964).

WILLIAMS, GWYN A. *Artisans and Sans-Culottes: Popular Movements in France and Britain during the French Revolution* (1968).

6. THE BOURGEOISIE

AYNARD, J. *La Bourgeoisie française, essai de psychologie* (1934).

LEUILLOT, P. 'Réflexions sur l'histoire économique et sociale à propos de la Bourgeoisie de 1789', *Rev. d'histoire moderne et contemporaine* (1954).

SAGNAC, P. 'La Révolution et sa concept de la propriété, 1789–1904', *Cahiers d'histoire de la Révolution française* (1946).

THORE, P. H. 'Essai de classification des categories sociales a l'intérieur du Tiers État de Toulouse', *78ᵉ Congrès des Sociétés savantes à Toulouse* (1954).

For controversy about Lefebvre's interpretation of the role of the bourgeoisie, see A. Cobban, *The Social Interpretation of the French Revolution* (1964), and B. Behrens, 'Straight History and History in Depth', *Historical Journal* VIII (I) 1960). See also G. V. Taylor, 'Types of Capitalism in 18th-century France', *English Historical Review,* LXXIX (1964).

For plans for a comparative study of the bourgeoisie of Western Europe, see E. Labrousse, P. Léon *et al.* in *Relazioni, 10 congresso internazionale di scienze storiche* (Florence, 1955).

7. THE PEASANTS AND RURAL FRANCE

BOIS, P. *Les Paysans de l'Ouest* (1960).

DAVIES, ALUN 'The Origins of the French Peasant Revolution', *History,* XLIX (1964).

DE SAINT-JACOB, P. *Les Paysans de la Bourgogne du Nord au dernier siècle de l'Ancien Régime* (1960).

LEFEBVRE, G. 'La Révolution française et les paysans', *Annales historiques de la Révolution française,* X (1933).

LEFEBVRE, G. *Les Paysans du Nord pendant la Révolution Française* (1924).

LEFEBVRE, G. *Questions agraires au temps de la Terreur* (1932).

MASSÉ, P. *Varennes et ses maîtres 1779–1848* (1956).

MERLE, L. *La métairie et l'évolution agraire de la Gatine poitevine* (1958).

TILLY, C. *The Vendée* (1964).

F. M. H. MARKHAM

Napoleonic France

—◆◎◎◆—

Any analysis of the institutions of Napoleonic France
presents the historian at once with a striking and significant contrast. Whereas the political institutions of the
First Empire proved ephemeral, its legal and administrative
institutions proved to be permanent. The Council of State, the
Prefects, the Codes, the Legion of Honour, the Bank of France,
all remind us that the Consulate is one of the most important
and formative periods in the development of France. It was then
that the framework of the modern French state was stamped for
good or ill on a society still fluid and malleable from the melting-
pot of the Revolution. De Maistre recognized this fact when he
said of the restored Bourbon monarchy: 'Louis XVIII has not
been restored to the throne of his ancestors: he has simply
ascended the throne of Bonaparte.' Guizot complained under the
July Monarchy that 'a natural and important incompatibility
exists between the representative government instituted by the
Charter, and the administrative monarchy founded by Louis XIV
and Napoleon'. Louis Napoleon argued plausibly in 1851 that
'as France has lived on the administrative and judicial institutions
of the First Empire for 100 years, why should not the political
institutions of the Empire be equally beneficial?'

The Napoleonic reforms proved to be lasting precisely because
they were not original. Napoleon despised ideology, based on
abstract principles, and did not claim to be an innovator. He
aimed to satisfy the need of the dominant classes in French
society and to follow the trends of historical development of the
French state. 'From Clovis to the Committee of Public Safety,
I embrace it all,' he said in 1809. Napoleon claimed to represent
the Revolution, and also to have ended it. This claim can only
be understood if the complexity of the Revolution is borne in
mind. De Tocqueville has shown in his *Ancien Régime et la*

Révolution that the aim of the Revolution was to modernize French government and society in one convulsive leap. It was at the same time a political, a social, and an administrative revolution. When the political revolution foundered in the Terror, there still remained the social and administrative revolutions, the achievement of equality and efficient government, which seemed to the mass of Frenchmen the more important aims of the Revolution. Many of the philosophers of the eighteenth century had looked to an enlightened despotism to carry out these reforms, and Napoleon appeared to be the ideal of the enlightened despot in action.

The success of the *coup d'état* of Brumaire is explained by this change of attitude of public opinion. Since the *coup* of Fructidor 1797 the Constitution of the Year III had ceased to function normally: the government of the Directory could only keep going by a *politique de bascule*—alternating purges of royalists and Jacobins. The Directory had inherited a fearful legacy of debt and inflation, and it had made repeated and genuine efforts to restore the currency by repudiating the paper money of the *assignats*, to balance the budget, and ensure a regular revenue by taxation. But all these efforts broke down through the weakness of the central government and the division of power between the Directory and the legislative Councils. Chronic weakness of finance threatened the payment and supply of the armies, and deserters swelled the bands of brigands which infested whole areas of France. The defeats in the war of the Second Coalition had caused a revival of Jacobinism and a marked swing to the left in the elections of May 1799. The Council of Five Hundred had voted a Law of Hostages, authorizing the imprisonment of relatives of *émigrés*, which recalled the worst days of the Terror; and a progressive income tax, which frightened the financiers and the *bourgeoisie*.

The idea of a revision of the Constitution to strengthen the executive power was already in the air from the beginning of the year 1799. A group of politicians such as Daunou, Roederer and Talleyrand, who were to form the party of the Brumairians, was forming round Sieyès, who entered the Directory in May 1799. Sieyès thought of using General Joubert to carry out his *coup d'état*, but Joubert was killed at the battle of Novi in August 1799. Moreau was approached, but when he heard of Napoleon's return from Egypt he told Sieyès: 'There's your man: he will carry out your *coup d'état* much better than I.' Napoleon's journey to Paris from the south developed into a triumphal procession of popular enthusiasm and acclaim. The failure in Egypt and Syria had been eclipsed by the news of the victory of Aboukir over the Turks and Napoleon was remembered as the conqueror of Campo Formio and the founder of the Cisalpine Republic, the one man who could bring order and a victorious peace to France. His return thus precipitated a crisis which had been slowly developing, and in Paris he found himself at once wooed by every political faction—by the Director Barras, his old patron, by Sieyès, and by the Jacobins. He determined to ally himself with Sieyès, reckoning that in the outcome it would not be he who would be Sieyès' tool, but the reverse. Thus it was Sieyès who was allowed to plan the *journée* at St Cloud which nearly miscarried and was only saved by Lucien Bonaparte's quick wit, and the expulsion of the Jacobin deputies by the conciliar guard. But once the new government of the three Consuls had been approved, it was Napoleon who turned the tables on Sieyès and the Brumairians, whose aim in supporting the *coup d'état* was not a dictatorship but a Constitution with a strengthened executive under parliamentary control. Napoleon's *coup d'état* against Sieyès took place in the secret meeting which hammered out the draft constitution. He accepted Sieyès' proposals for strengthening the control of the central government, and for a system of representation based on the principle of 'Authority from above, confidence from below'. The communal and departmental electors were to draw up lists of local and national 'notables', from which the government would nominate officials and members of the legislature. But Sieyès' plan for an executive composed of a powerless Grand Elector, with two co-equal Consuls, was rejected. Instead there was to be a First Consul with all executive power, and the Second and Third Consuls were to be merely advisory. In compensation for this defeat, Sieyès was given the Presidency of the new Senate, with power to nominate the members, who in turn would nominate to the Legislature and Tribunate. Thus firmly entrenched in the legislative assemblies the Brumairians still hoped to be able to control the First Consul.

A plebiscite approved the new Constitution of the Year VIII by three million votes, with fifteen hundred dissenting, but the new régime was by no means secure until after the victory of Marengo. During Napoleon's absence in Italy, the opposition in the Tribunate grumbled and intrigued and canvassed possible successors to Napoleon, such as Carnot, Moreau or the duc d'Orlèans. After Marengo, and still more after the Concordat and the Peace of Amiens, Napoleon was able step by step to eliminate all opposition, and extend his autocracy. In 1802, one-fifth of the membership of the Tribunate was due for renewal, and the Senate was persuaded to nominate the members who were to retire. In this way twenty of the prominent members of the opposition were removed. The Tribunate was then induced to reorganize itself into three sections, for legislation, finance, and domestic affairs, meeting separately—and henceforward its debates were deprived of all life. Its final suppression in 1807 caused no stir.

Popular enthusiasm for the Concordat and the signature of the Peace of Amiens (March–April 1802), gave Napoleon the opportunity to extend the Consulate from a ten-year tenure to a life-tenure. The Senate proposed that the Consulate should be extended for a further ten years, but Napoleon took the matter out of their hands by insisting on a plebiscite. This was prepared by the Council of State and asked the electorate to vote on the Consulate to Napoleon for life.

After the plebiscite Napoleon induced the Senate to make important modifications to the Constitution by the procedure of *senatus-consultum*. The First Consul could now nominate his own successor for confirmation by the Senate, and could negotiate treaties without submitting them for approval. A new Privy Council was created, encroaching on the functions of the Council of State, which had proved too independent for Napoleon's liking. The powers of the Senate were increased. It could now revise the Constitution, dissolve the Legislature and Tribunate, nominate the Consuls. But at the same time the Senate was made more servile. The First Consul was to preside over the Senate, and he could nominate an unlimited number of Senators. The independence of individual Senators was undermined. The First Consul could award '*Senatoreries*'—national estates—up to one-third of the number of Senators, and Senators were no longer excluded from administrative posts. The electoral system was also changed. Instead of the system of the 'national list' (which had never, in fact, been put into operation since the national list was not drawn up till 1801), there were to be assemblies of *cantons* and *arrondissements*, elected by universal suffrage. These assemblies chose the members of electoral colleges of *départements*, but only among the six hundred most highly taxed citizens of the *département*, who were elected for life, and nominated candidates to the Senate and Legislature. The President and up to twenty members of the electoral colleges were to be nominated directly by the First Consul. This electoral system survived the Empire and was used, with modifications, under the Restoration.

The Constitution of the Life-Consulate gave Napoleon practically the power of an absolute monarch: it only remained to add the façade of the imperial title. Both Napoleon's ambition, and the logic of the situation, led irresistibly to the solution of the hereditary Empire. As a youth Napoleon had been an ardent admirer of Rousseau, but his visit to Paris in 1792 and the spectacle of mob-violence had soon disillusioned him. By 1800 he was saying that 'Rousseau was a madman who has brought us to the state we are in now'. He came to share the view held by Mirabeau in 1790 who had urged the king, in his secret correspondence with the court, to continue the work of Richelieu and lead the Revolution, by completing the destruction of feudal privilege and modernizing the administration. The Revolution was not to be regarded as essentially incompatible with monarchy. In Napoleon's view the fall of the throne had been due to the 'vanity' of the *bourgeoisie* and the feebleness of Louis XVI. The Bourbon dynasty had failed to rise to the occasion: it was therefore open to Napoleon to 'pick a crown out of the gutter'. He saw no reason why a 'fourth dynasty' of France should not establish itself in France, based on the changes brought about by the Revolution. The coronation in Notre Dame, the elaborate ceremonial of the imperial court, and the Austrian marriage, reflected Napoleon's obsession with the idea of making his dynasty permanent and legitimate. After the marriage with Marie Louise, niece of Marie Antoinette, he even adopted the rather ridiculous habit of referring to Louis XVI as 'mon oncle'.

The proclamation of the hereditary empire also satisfied the claims and allayed the fears of the classes which had been the main beneficiaries of the Revolution. The regicides, the *bourgeoisie*, and the peasantry, who had acquiesced with relief in the *coup* of Brumaire, could never feel safe so long as the survival of the régime depended solely on Napoleon's life. If he were assassinated or killed in battle, they were threatened with a return to Jacobin anarchy or a Bourbon restoration. Louis XVIII had given no assurance in his Declaration of Verona in 1797 that he would not restore the lands of the Church and the *émigrés* to their former owners. It is highly significant that Napoleon's coronation oath contained a specific pledge to maintain the settlement of the *biens nationaux*.

The prolonged alarm and uncertainty caused by the royalist plot of Georges Cadoudal in 1804, culminating in the execution of the duc d'Enghien, prepared public opinion for the proclamation of the Empire. The execution of Enghien put an end to the assassination plots, and, by making Napoleon the accomplice of the regicides, ruled out the possibility of a Bourbon restoration.

Given Napoleon's attitude of mind and assessment of the situation, we should expect to find in his reorganization of France a mingling of revolutionary and reactionary elements. The reforms of the Consulate and Empire look both ways. From one aspect they are a realization of reforms projected in the Revolution, from another, a surreptitious return to the institutions of the Bourbon monarchy. Even in the early days of the Consulate, Napoleon was heard to say that 'the old administration was the most perfect that ever existed. While conserving every useful innovation produced by the Revolution, I would not reject the good institutions which it wrongly destroyed.' Napoleon's personal influence in the reforms must not, however, be exaggerated, and it would be misleading to describe the government of the Consulate as a military dictatorship. Napoleon insisted that 'it is not as a general that I am governing France; it is because the nation believes that I possess the civil qualities of a ruler'. The success of the Consulate was in direct proportion to Napoleon's success in attracting to his government the ablest men, regardless of their past. Former servants of the monarchy like Gaudin and Portalis rubbed shoulders with ex-revolutionaries like Merlin de Douai, Treilhard, and Thibaudeau. Napoleon's contribution was to get things done: for the first time since Louis XIV (with the exception of the great Committee of Public Safety of 1793–4) France felt the impulse of a powerful, unified will. Esmein, the legal historian, comments on the making of the Civil Code that 'interesting as Napoleon's observations occasionally are, he cannot be considered as a serious collaborator in the great work'. But he was the driving force that pushed it through, and he presided at thirty-six out of the eighty-four sessions of the Council of State devoted to the Code.

The first and one of the most important reforms of the Consulate was in finance, by the creation of a centralized administration for the assessment and collection of taxes. Since 1790 the yield from direct taxation, being in the hands of local authorities, had been slow and uncertain. The Directory had made an effort to deal with this problem in 1797 but was not strong enough to carry it through. Gaudin, a financial official of the *ancien régime*, who was called in by Napoleon, brought the tax-returns up to date by the end of 1800. The Bank of France was founded in 1800 as an independent corporation, in alliance with the government, and in 1803 it was given the monopoly of the issue of bank-notes. In 1804 the *droits réunis* revived the indirect taxes of the *ancien régime*—a rationalized *gabelle* and excise on liquor and tobacco. In 1811, tobacco became a government monopoly. These taxes yielded a large and expanding revenue up to the end of the Empire.

Despite the wars and the economic dislocation of the Continental System and the British blockade, the finances of the régime remained fairly strong up to 1813. Till the Russian campaign, war paid for itself through indemnities and contributions from vassal-states which went into a separate *domaine extraordinaire* under the personal control of the Emperor. Even at his fall in 1814 the public debt amounted to no more than 60 million francs, and the rapid recovery of the public finances under the Restoration is an indication of their strength under the Empire.

The reform of local government was frankly a return to the centralization of the Bourbon monarchy, untrammelled by the checks which had existed in the *ancien régime*. By the law of February 1800, Prefects, appointed by the First Consul, were to be in sole charge of the *départements*. The elected councils of *départements*, *cantons* and *communes* were reduced to advisory functions, and mayors were to be nominated by the central government. As de Tocqueville first pointed out in his *Ancien*

Régime et la Révolution, the Prefects were a reprint, writ large, of the *intendants.*

The Civil Code, issued in 1804, and renamed *Code Napoléon* in 1807, was the realization of a project conceived at the outset of the Revolution. In 1792 the Convention had appointed a drafting Committee which produced a plan for a Code. In all, five plans had been discussed by 1800. Such a Code defining the rights and relations of persons and property was urgently needed. In 1789 legal unity of the French nation did not exist. There were over three hundred local Codes in force, and a fundamental division between the law of the north and the south. In the south, property rights were based on written Roman law, the Code of Justinian; in the north, on customary Teutonic law. On top of this were the accretions of later feudal custom, canon law and royal ordinance. The Revolution had caused a drastic upheaval in the property system. It had swept away feudal rights and had redistributed a large amount of land by the nationalization and sale of the lands of the Church and the *noblesse.* This new situation needed to be defined and stabilized.

Controversy during the revolutionary period turned on the choice of principle on which to base the new legal system. Was it to be an abstract *loi naturel,* ignoring the traditions and pre-judices of the past, or one of the existing systems—Roman, customary, or feudal law? The Code of 1804 was in the end a compromise between these different principles, reflecting in its emphasis the changing trend of opinion since 1789. The plan of the Convention represented the high water-mark of the philo-sophic, rationalist influence. It recognized the equality of persons, civil marriage, divorce on grounds of incompatibility, adoption, inheritance by illegitimate children if recognized by the parents, and equal division of property among the heirs. It was hostile to Roman law which enforced the despotic authority of the father and gave absolute freedom to dispose of property by bequest: and inclined more to customary law, because it limited paternal authority and safeguarded the division of inheritance in the family. From 1795 onwards a reaction in favour of Roman law and traditional juristic concepts is perceptible. Sagnac (in his *Législation Civile de la Révolution*) sums up the spirit of the Code as 'la réaction de l'esprit juridique contre l'esprit philosophique'.

In the drafting sessions of the Council of State Berlier and

Thibaudeau, who were former revolutionaries, defended the principles of customary law: Napoleon, Cambacérès and Portalis favoured reaction to Roman law. Hence the compromise which preserved the main revolutionary principles of equality, but modified them in accordance with the reactionary trend of the Consulate. Paternal authority was restored, and the subjection of married women. Grounds for divorce were severely restricted; adulterous wives could even be imprisoned by their husbands. Property up to one-quarter of the whole could be bequeathed away from the family. The recognition of illegitimate children was discouraged. These provisions were deliberately intended as an antidote to the moral laxity of the period of the Directory, resulting from the breakdown of the social order in war and inflation. The general character of the Code reflects the ideas of the middle class, which had benefited from the Revolution. It emphasized the rights of individual property, and, above all, it reassured the holders of national lands, by confirming the revolutionary land-settlement. Fisher points out (in *Cambridge Modern History*, vol. IX, Ch. 6) that 'A few years earlier the Code would have been steeped in revolutionary extravagance; a few years later it would have borne the hard imprint of despotism'.

The four later Codes—those of Civil Procedure, Criminal Procedure, the Penal Code and the Commercial Code—follow more closely the rules of the *ancien régime*. The jury-system, introduced in the revolutionary period, was severely curtailed, especially in criminal cases, and special courts without juries, reminiscent of the *cours prévotales* of the *ancien régime* were authorized for cases of rebellion, coining, smuggling, assassination by armed bands. In addition to the hierarchy of civil and criminal courts, the *conseils de préfecture* and the *Conseil d'État* dealt with administrative justice, litigation between private citizens and the state. *Lettres de cachet* were openly revived by a decree of 1810, which gave the *Conseil Privé* powers of arbitrary arrest.

The institution of the Legion of Honour and the negotiation of the Concordat were, much more clearly than the Civil Code, the personal policy of Napoleon. They were a more conspicuous breach with revolutionary principles, and they aroused considerable opposition in the *Conseil d'État*, and the assemblies. The Orders and decorations of the monarchy, such as the Saint-Esprit, St Michel, St Louis, had been abolished by the Convention as contrary to equality. The Revolution was not opposed to some form of recognition for outstanding services to the nation, and occasionally 'civic crowns' were awarded to individuals by decree. As First Consul, Napoleon awarded 'swords of honour' to soldiers. In 1802 he brought forward a project for a Legion of Honour which would be open both to soldiers and civilians with a hierarchy of grades and pensions. The members were to be appointed by a Grand Council, presided over by the First Consul. This provision was the one to which Napoleon attached most importance. He was determined that patronage and honours should be in his own hands, and Sieyès' national list of notabilities, which had been completed by the end of 1801, was a privileged body beyond his control. In defending his project in the *Conseil d'État* he revealed the counter-revolutionary trend of his ideas. 'I do not believe the French love liberty and equality. They are not changed by ten years of revolution. They are like the Gauls, proud and fickle, they have only one sentiment, honour.' When Thibaudeau objected that decorations were 'baubles', Napoleon retorted: 'You are pleased to call them baubles; well, it is with baubles that mankind is governed.'

When the Empire was proclaimed Napoleon attached great importance to the creation of an imperial nobility. As more and more of the *émigré* aristocrats rallied to the new court and dynasty, he wished to efface the prestige of the *ancien régime* titles, to fuse the new and the old, and to bind everyone of importance to his person and his fortunes.

But he had to proceed cautiously, to lessen the shock to the principle of equality. In 1804, six Grand Imperial Dignitaries were created, and the new Marshals of the Empire. In 1806, the first hereditary fiefs were granted to certain soldiers and civilians from Italian territories, for example, the principality of Pontecorvo to Bernadotte, that of Benevento to Talleyrand. In 1807, Marshal Lefèbvre was made Duke of Danzig, with a grant of lands within the Empire. The choice of Lefèbvre for the first hereditary dukedom was deliberate: for he was an old veteran of the Republic, and his wife was reputed to be a former washerwoman. In 1808, a hierarchy of hereditary titles was established. The *ralliement* of the old *noblesse* was to a large extent accomplished, but Napoleon was less successful in his policy of lavishing grants and titles to his followers. The more they received, the less they had to look for in advancement, and the less inclined they were to risk their gains in endless adventures. It is curious that in the *débâcle* of the Empire many of the former royalists proved more loyal to Napoleon than the Marshals and the ennobled revolutionaries.

There can be little doubt that Napoleon's attitude to religion was that of an agnostic, educated as he was in the Voltairian scepticism and anti-clericalism of the Enlightenment. But he was too intelligent to be a dogmatic atheist, and he was profoundly convinced of the social and political importance of religion. He remarked to Gourgaud, his aide-de-camp at St Helena: 'A religion is necessary to cement the union of men in society.' His early experience of government in Italy and Egypt had impressed on him the power of religion. In his dealings with the Papacy in 1797 he had refused to follow the Jacobin anti-clerical policy of the Directory: in Egypt he had studiously respected the religion of Islam. In defending the Concordat he maintained that 'Society is impossible without inequality, inequality intolerable without a code of morality, and a code of morality unacceptable without religion. The people need a religion; this religion must be in the hands of the Government.'

Apart from these general tenets of his statecraft, Napoleon saw the immediate advantage of a religious settlement. When he came to power, the religious question opened by the Revolution was still unsolved and was a cause of grave internal weakness.

The Civil Constitution of the Clergy, passed by the Constituent Assembly in 1791, had been condemned by the Pope as uncanonical, because it subjected the bishops and clergy to popular election. A schism ensued between the Constitutional Church which accepted the Civil Constitution, and the non-juring bishops and priests. The Convention had been forced into the position of persecuting not only the non-juring priests but catholicism as such, and had provoked civil war in La Vendée. Robespierre had realized the danger of a religious war, and had tried in his Cult of the Supreme Being to find a formula to appease the religious strife. After his fall the official policy of the Directory was one of toleration and neutrality towards religious sects, varied by outbursts of repression of non-juring priests suspected of royalism, and attempts to foster new cults of rationalistic religion, such as La Revellière's cult of Theophilanthropy.

As First Consul Napoleon saw the immediate advantages to be gained by a religious settlement. The reports of his Prefects confirmed his impression that, whatever the attitude of the politicians, the peasants were still obstinately attached to their churches and their priests. Even in intellectual circles religious scepticism was no longer the undisputed, fashionable doctrine. A religious revival, allied with the romantic movement in literature and a counter-revolutionary trend in political thought, was already challenging the scepticism of the Enlightenment. Bonald, Maistre, Chateaubriand and Fontanes were the leaders of an intellectual movement, which ascribed the anarchy of the Revolution to the decay of religious faith and authority. Reaching its zenith under the Restoration, this movement was growing in influence under the Consulate and Empire and gave support for Napoleon's authoritarian policy. The *émigré noblesse*, headed by the Comte d'Artois, were the first to be influenced, and had already returned to religious orthodoxy.

Napoleon saw that a Concordat with the Pope would drive a wedge between catholicism and royalism, complete the pacification of La Vendée, and reassure the buyers of Church lands. A settlement based on the schismatic Constitutional Church, or on protestantism, would bring none of these advantages. Only a comprehensive agreement with the Pope would suffice. Napoleon argued that 'Fifty *émigré* bishops in English pay are the present leaders of the French clergy. Their influence must be destroyed and for this I must have the authority of the Pope.'

Before he left Italy in June 1800 after the Marengo campaign, Napoleon had got into touch with the newly elected Pope Pius VII, proposing a Concordat. It was not till a year later, after protracted bargaining, that agreement was reached. Napoleon instructed his agents to 'treat the Pope as if he had 200,000 men'. The Concordat recognized the Roman Catholic religion as 'the religion of the majority of Frenchmen' (not, as the Pope had demanded, as the 'established' or 'dominant' religion) and guaranteed liberty of worship subject to the maintenance of public order. The schism between the constitutional and the non-juring clergy was to be ended by the resignation of all existing bishops and the appointment of a new episcopate. The right of the First Consul to nominate, and of the Pope to institute bishops was recognized. The French government undertook to pay the salaries of the clergy, thus securing the recognition that the sale of Church lands in the Revolution was irrevocable. In the event the schism was not completely healed. Half of the non-juring bishops refused to resign or acknowledge the Concordat, and some of them maintained dwindling congregations in France, known as the *Petite Église*. The Pope refused to institute twelve of the former Constitutional bishops nominated by Napoleon.

The way in which the Concordat was finally passed into law in April 1802 further diminished the advantages which the Pope had hoped for. It was presented as a general 'Law of Public Worship', which regulated other sects as well as Roman Catholicism, and Organic Articles were added, without consulting the Pope, which reasserted Gallican principles and subjected religious worship to minute governmental regulation. Even so the anti-clerical majority in the Legislature and Tribunate reacted strongly against the Concordat. The law had to be withdrawn after the first discussion, and it was only after the Tribunate had been purged, and after the Peace of Amiens had given Napoleon overwhelming popularity, that it finally passed. The generals signified their displeasure at the official Te Deum to celebrate the Concordat by forcibly turning the priests out of their seats in Notre Dame. General Delmas boldly commented to Napoleon after the service: 'A fine monkish show. The only thing missing was the 100,000 men who gave their lives to suppress all that.'

Despite all disappointments and persecutions Pius VII never forgot that Napoleon was the 'restorer of the altars', and he showed his gratitude by coming to Paris for Napoleon's corona-tion. But friendly relations did not last long, as the Concordat was based on a fundamental clash of views. Napoleon looked on the Pope and the bishops as his 'moral Prefects', and, with his growing appetite for domination, revived the pretensions of Charlemagne and even the Caesaro-papism of Constantine. At St Helena he said: 'I should have controlled the religious as well as the political world, and summoned Church Councils like Constantine.' Pius was no political prelate but a devout priest who was determined to preserve the spiritual independence of the Church and the temporal independence of the Papacy, even at the cost of martyrdom.

In 1806, when the Bourbons had been expelled from Naples and Eugène had been installed as Viceroy of the Kingdom of

Italy, Napoleon wrote to the Pope that 'Your Holiness is sovereign of Rome, but I am its Emperor. My enemies must also be yours.' After Tilsit he summoned the Pope to join the Continental System and close his ports to the English. When the Pope refused, he occupied the Papal States. Finally in 1809, during the Wagram campaign, he proclaimed the annexation of Rome to the French Empire. He wrote to Murat that 'the Pope is a madman who should be shut up'. The Pope was arrested in the Vatican and removed to imprisonment at Savona.

Despite this outrage there was little open unrest in the French Church and a majority of the French bishops supported Napoleon in his attempts to reach agreement with the Pope in his isolation at Savona and later at Fontainebleau. Pius held firm, and countered by refusing to confirm the appointment of bishops. After the Moscow campaign Napoleon relaxed his terms and offered Pius the Treaty of Fontainebleau. In June 1814 the Pope was allowed to return to Rome without conditions.

Although most Catholics recognized that the quarrel between Emperor and Pope was on temporal and not spiritual questions, it undermined the moral strength of Napoleon's position. In 1808 Napoleon had been received with enthusiasm on a visit to La Vendée; by 1813 this region was again a centre of royalism.

Education was regarded by Napoleon, like religion, as a 'source de pouvoir' through the control of opinion. 'My principal aim in the establishment of an official body of teachers is to have the means of directing political and moral opinion. Such an institution will be a safeguard against the re-establishment of the monks.' The constitution of the University of France was produced in 1808 after long deliberation in the Council of State. It was not a university in the normal sense of the term, but rather a Ministry of Education, which, under a Grand Master, was to license and control all teachers. Napoleon conceived it as a sort of lay Jesuit order, to combat clerical education, which had since 1800 recaptured the field of primary education and more than half the sphere of secondary education. The Revolution had produced grandiose schemes on paper for free state education, but in fact by 1800 primary education had sunk to a level lower than in 1789. Secondary education had made some progress with the founding of the *École Polytechnique* in 1794, and of some hundred *Écoles Centrales*. These were, however, boycotted by middle-class families as being irreligious. In 1802 they were suppressed and replaced by *lycées* of an increasingly militarized character. They were no more popular with the middle classes than the *Écoles Centrales*, and the powers given to the *Université* were partly intended to force pupils into the *lycées*.

It transpired that Napoleon's aim was largely frustrated by the growing pressure of the counter-revolutionary and clerical movement. He contributed to his own defeat by appointing as Grand Master of the University Fontanes, a poet and classicist and a crypto-royalist instead of the scientist Fourcroy, who had been Director of Public Instruction since 1802. Fontanes used his authority to favour clerical education and purely classical and literary studies. Napoleon himself emphasized the importance of scientific and historical training, and wrote a remarkably far-sighted memorandum in 1807 from the depths of Poland, envisaging an institute of advanced historical study. Under Fontanes' régime primary education remained in the hands of the Church, and classics, rhetoric and law remained predominant in the university faculties. Nevertheless, university education in France became the most advanced in Europe, with over 6,000 students in 1813. Yet nothing shows more clearly than the development of educational policy under the Empire the strength of the counter-revolution which was to culminate in the Restoration.

Napoleon was firmly convinced that he could not dispense with a secret police and a censorship of the Press. He said in 1800: 'If the press is not bridled I shall not remain three days in power.' Napoleon had not only his daily police bulletin from Fouché's Ministry of Police, but his *cabinet noir* for censoring correspondence, and his own secret agents who kept him informed on the state of public opinion. Censorship of the Press was established by a decree of June 1800. By 1811 there were only four daily papers in Paris, and one for each *département*. In 1810 he detached the censorship of books from the Ministry of Police, and put it under Portalis as *Directeur-Général de l'Imprimerie*. A year later he was complaining that it was too arbitrary and pettifogging in its methods. Napoleon clung to censorship but he wished to disguise it as much as possible. The arts and the theatre were also elaborately state-subsidized and state-controlled. It is not surprising that the art and literature of the Empire were generally lifeless and heavy. The leaders of the new romantic movement, Chateaubriand and Madame de Staël, were both opponents of the Empire.

After the heroic and constructive period of the Consulate the Empire has an increasingly sombre and sterile character. Napoleon's appetite for domination grew on him with power. One by one his more independent advisers were got rid of—such as Roederer, Chaptal, Talleyrand, Fouché—and replaced by second-rate men such as Maret, Champagny, Savary, who knew only how to carry out orders. Chaptal said of Napoleon that 'he wanted valets not counsellors'. Although those who knew him intimately agree in testifying that he was in temperament kind-hearted, fascinating, and indulgent (and Josephine once remarked to her daughter Hortense that 'people would have a better idea of him if he did not resist sentiment which he regards as weakness'), Napoleon set himself to act on the principle that power could only be exercised through fear and constant supervision. 'Abroad and at home I reign only through the fear I inspire.' He aimed at keeping his ministers and generals in awe, playing them off against each other, and maintaining a constant tension of jealous rivalry for his favours. He would allow nothing like a system of collective ministerial responsibility to develop, but co-ordinated the ministries through Maret, his Minister of State. Mollien said that 'in the midst of his camp and during military operations he wished not only to govern but to administer France by himself, and he succeeded'. It is estimated that he dictated about 80,000 letters and orders during the fifteen years of his rule—an average of fifteen a day. One of his civil servants remarked in his memoirs that 'the Emperor exercised the miracle of his actual presence upon his servants, however far they might be away from him. Napoleon himself once remarked: "What will they say of me when I am gone? They will say 'Ouf!'"'

Napoleon was not deceived by the trappings of power and a servile court. His inmost thoughts were revealed when he said: 'Conquest has made me what I am and conquest can alone maintain me.' He was extremely perturbed by the Malet conspiracy which was partly responsible for his hurried return from Vilna in December 1812. Malet, a mad Republican general, announced that Napoleon had died during the retreat from Moscow and proclaimed the Republic. His *coup d'état* made some headway before he was arrested: but the significance of the episode was that none of the officials who had been deceived by Malet thought of proclaiming the accession of Napoleon II. When the Legislature met at the beginning of 1813, it began to demand reforms. Napoleon's intransigence in the peace negotiations of 1813 and 1814 was largely due to his realization that the loss of the Grand Empire would mean the collapse of the autocracy in France. On his return from Elba in 1815 he was disgusted by the strength of liberal opinion to which he was forced to make concessions in the *Acte Additionel*, which guaranteed a constitutional monarchy on the lines of the Charter granted by Louis XVIII in the First Restoration. 'If I had known what it would be like,' he said, 'I would never have come back.'

The Napoleonic autocracy had indeed an inherent self-contradiction of which Napoleon was aware when he said: 'All this may last my lifetime but my son will have to govern very differently.' The constitutional balance of the Restoration and the July Monarchy is already foreshadowed in the late Empire and the Hundred Days. It was the Napoleonic Senate which deposed Napoleon and recalled Louis XVIII with guarantees in 1814. The autocracy had been built up on the support of the propertied classes, particularly the middle class which had been the chief beneficiary of the Revolution and the Empire. As they gained in wealth and confidence they were bound to demand a larger share in government.

Napoleon had done much to foster the development of industry and his protectionist policy accorded with the ideas of French manufacturers. He had effectively exorcized the menace of popular insurrection provoked by hunger, by elaborate measures for ensuring the food-supply of Paris and providing relief in times of unemployment. But the hardships and dislocations caused by the Continental System lost him the confidence of the industrial and commercial classes. The commercial sea-ports were ruined by the British blockade, and the prolonged industrial depression which set in in 1810–11 was ascribed to the policy of the Continental System. The tightening of conscription and taxation in 1813 and 1814 completed the alienation of public opinion. The crisis of the allied invasion in 1814 was met with apathy and weariness. When Napoleon arrived in Paris from Elba in 1815 he said in a moment of disillusion: 'They have let me come as they have let the others go.' This apathy was as much spiritual as material in origin. Napoleon had overstrained the nerves of the nation with too much *gloire*, and he had sapped its vitality by substituting his own will for popular initiative and demanding nothing but passive obedience. When his ministers in 1814 talked of the need to revive the spirit of 1793, Napoleon said: 'Rouse the nation? When the Revolution has destroyed the nobles and priests, and I myself have destroyed the Revolution.'

BIBLIOGRAPHICAL NOTE

General

The numerous biographies of Napoleon are too well known to need mention. For English readers the most recent treatment is by J. M. Thompson, *Napoleon Bonaparte*, Oxford, 1952 and by Felix Markham, *Napoleon*, 1963.

Full bibliographies may be found in:

BRUUN, G. *Europe and the French Imperium*, New York, 1938.

GODECHOT, J. *Les Institutions de la France sous la Révolution et l'Empire*, 1951.

LEFEBVRE, G. *Napoléon*, 4th edn., 1953.

VILLAT, L. *La Révolution et l'Empire*, vol. 2, 1936.

GEYL, P. *Napoleon—For and Against*, 1949, gives a critical analysis of French historical writing on Napoleon.

Memoirs and Letters

J. M. Thompson, *Napoleon's Letters*, Oxford, 1934, provides a representative selection and translation from the *Correspondance de Napoléon* (1858–69).

The following memoirs are useful for the Napoleonic system of government:

BEUGNOT, *Life* (1871).

CHAPTAL, *Souvenirs* (1893).

FAIN, *Mémoires* (1908).

ROEDERER, *Journal* (1909).

THIBAUDEAU, *Mémoires sur le Consulat* (1827).

Law and Government

AULARD, A. *La Centralisation napoléonienne. Etudes et leçons*, vol. VII, 1913.

BOURDON, J. *La Réforme judiciaire de l'an VIII* (Rodez, 1941).

DURAND, C. *Le Conseil d'État napoléonien*, 1949.

DURAND, C. *Les Auditeurs au Conseil d'Etat,* 1958.

FISHER, H. A. L. 'The Codes', *Cambridge Modern History*, vol. IX, ch. 6.

HANOTAUX, G. 'Du Consulat à l'Empire', *Revue des Deux Mondes*, 7th Series, vol. 26, 1925.

LEROY, M. *L'Esprit de la législation napoléonienne* (1898).

SAGNAC, P. *La Législation civile de la Révolution* (1898).

PONTEIL, C. *Napoléon I et l'organisation autoritaire de la France,* 1956.

VANDAL, A. *L'Avènement de Bonaparte*, vol. 2, 1905.

WELSCHINGER, A. *La Censure sous le premier Empire*, 1882.

Social, Religious and Economic Aspects

AULARD, A. *Napoleon Ier et le monopole universitaire* (1911).

BALDENSPERGER, F. *Le Mouvement des idées dans l'émigration française*, 1925.

BALLOT, C. *L'Introduction du machinisme dans l'industrie française*, 1923.

CROUZET, F. *L'Economie Britannique et les Blocus continental,* 1958.

HANOTAUX, G. 'La Transformation sociale à l'époque napoléonienne', *Revue des Deux Mondes*, 7th series, vols. 33, 34, 1926.

DE LABORIE, LANZAC. *Paris sous Napoléon*, 1910.

LATREILLE, A. *L'Église catholique et la Révolution française*, 1950.

DE LOMÉNIE, E. BEAU, *Les Responsabilités des dynasties bourgeoises*, vol. I, 1943.

MARION, M. *Histoire financière de la France*, vol. IV, 1914.

POUTHAS, C. H. *La Jeunesse de Guizot*, 1936.

TARLÉ, E. 'Napoléon Ier et les intérêts économiques de la France', *Revue des études napoléoniennes*, vol. 1, 1926.

VIENNET, O. *Napoléon et l'industrie française*, 1947.

A. F. THOMPSON

From Restoration to Republic

After Waterloo, Louis XVIII, like other kings, crept out into the sun again. There was little hope of reviving the old order, for the France he had known lay buried beneath the upheavals of a generation. For too long too many had done too well out of its demise. Louis was ready to accept most changes of the recent past, and sought security in compromise with those who had much to lose at his return. Bourbon divinity was dead, and one dealt in constitutions nowadays; though understandable, the vindictive greed of the *émigrés* was unrealistic folly. The *ancien régime*, duly restored, must be reconciled with *bourgeoisie* and peasantry, the heirs of 1789 and the great Napoleon. When conflicts of interest could not be resolved, they should be ignored, and all might perhaps be well. Eighty years later, Méline, favourite son of peasant and *bourgeois*, alarmed by the venerable passions aroused by the Dreyfus affair, declared that the policy of sensible men was always 'neither revolution nor reaction'. Unless one compromised, appreciating that problems were usually insoluble and that optimism was out of place, then government, like life, became impossible. Prudent and defeatist as the most moderate of monarchs, Méline saw dogs stirring which Louis had tried to put to sleep, and was afraid.

In 1898 as in 1815, fear, deep-rooted and many-sided, remained a prime condition of French politics. The difficulties, it seemed, were eternal: except by appeasement and evasion, nothing could be done. Governments still feared to act; and the actions of governments were still feared. Yet, though he fell, Méline need not have worried as Louis had, with good reason. The process of elimination begun in the latter's day, and sheer exhaustion with experiment, had at last produced the system which divided Frenchmen least. For success, a way had to be found of doing nothing tolerably: nothing especially to injure or disturb the vested interests created by the Revolution and consolidated under both Empires, to whom government was at best a protective necessity. The Third Republic might be a last resort, incapable of inspiring enthusiasm even among its beneficiaries before Dreyfus. But there was now no alternative, and one problem at least had been solved. However roughly, the essential shape of French society in the nineteenth century was determined by 1815. What had followed was primarily a search for the constitutional framework which might adequately contain those who were contented and those who were not. In Louis' time, men could still hope for the perfect answer. By Méline's, that hope had been abandoned, and, unlike the Bourbons, the Third Republic had come to stay.

Between the Restoration and the Affair the history of France is a history of negatives. Failure to restore or modify monarchy and to maintain the revived Empire culminated in the reluctant, imprecise establishment of a republic, at the second attempt, as *pis aller*. The Napoleonic revolution in law and administration, with its vices as well as its virtues, was imposed upon, not adapted to, an individualistic society. Within an economic and social structure dominated by the peasant and petty *bourgeois*, despite much advance, there did not emerge the industrial basis vital to the modern state, nor its counterpart, the social policy demanded by an urban proletariat, here so deeply imbued with a violent, extremist tradition. Superficially, this was a period of upheaval and oscillation, of a cyclical rhythm in constitutional development which enthralled contemporaries and has bewitched the historian, a joy to theorists since Marx and Tocqueville. Yet between 1815 and the turn of the century no European community, certainly no great power, changed less in essentials. The end-product was the Third Republic, with its basic conservatism on both right and left, the obsolescent issues of its politics, its backward economy and ossified social structure.

The past lay heavy on Frenchmen, not least because they wished it so: the search had been for preservation and protection, rather than novelty or change. 1789 and its aftermath, especially the consolidation under the first Napoleon of the supersession of the old order, had created a great vested interest. How could this best be preserved? Or, rather, what could be restored, by way of monarchy, empire or republic, which did not threaten or constrict the gains of forces which remained dominant, at least in the last resort? Within sixty years five forms of government were tried; and, at the end of the century, when four had failed, the prospects of the fifth could still be doubted.

Previous lectures have defined this vested interest, and described its emergence. The nervous but determined legatees of 1789 and the original Empire were the *bourgeoisie*, great and small, and the property-owning peasantry. Through decades of experiment, over and over again, the initiative, whether destructive or constructive, came from the former. From the latter, particularly after 1848, any régime had to secure for success and survival at least acceptance. The association of these groups was often unconscious but always present. Adumbrated in 1830, clear in the June Days of 1848 and in 1852, their alliance was sealed, signed and delivered in 1875. Their suspicions once aroused, the partners invariably resisted the more extreme pretensions of the monarchists, especially when legitimist and ultramontane; and, with greater alacrity, the threat to property and order from a Left which became stronger and more socialist than Babeuf had ever been. For long they had a soft spot for the Bonapartes, as well they might; until the Napoleonic legend was shattered at Sedan, and the Commune pointed the moral that imperialist war could prove a more serious menace to the stability they craved than the distrusted republic.

Constitutionally the answer was found in a system of free but limited government, weighted against both Right and Left, under the management of those who bridged the gap between the two groups: the professionals of the provincial *bourgeoisie*. These were the men whom Daniel Halévy saw as the typical servants of the Third Republic in its early years. 'Provincials provided with decent patrimonies; politically republican, but in everything connected with money and the vested interests determined conservatives.' They came to their inheritance after the elimination of alternatives, *faute de mieux*; and laid feeble if grasping hands upon it. Boulanger, that chocolate soldier, could reduce them to paralysis, and it needed all the stimulus of the Dreyfus affair to make them masters of a régime of which they had hitherto been little more than caretakers. By 1905, however, there could be no doubt that *la France bourgeoise* had found its institutional framework.

The process had taken time. Back in 1815, Louis XVIII, shrewd, old and weak, had returned to a defeated, suspicious France in the baggage train of the Allies. The new vested interests were already twenty-five years old, and had become strong enough to doubt and even oppose Napoleon in the last phase of his power. Unlike the rest of his family, Louis had learnt lessons which he hoped to apply in restoring the dynasty. But round his neck, as opposing but unequal weights, hung both the Charters and the *émigrés*, led by his brother, Artois. Louis did his best; yet from the days of the *Chambre introuvable* his failure to find a balance was certain. Even before the ominous symbolism of Charles X's coronation, with its sham medievalism, the prospects of the Bourbons were gloomy; for the moment to attempt reconciliation soon passed and discontent mounted, still finding parliamentary expression despite distortion of the constitution. Their political shortcomings are notorious; but the trouble went deeper. Suspicion of the *ancien régime* had been strong from the start: Charles X came to appear as the incarnation of vengeful, absolute reaction. His attitude to the Church and the grievances of his friends in exile suggested that he might be ready to disturb the settlement which had given the peasant his land; and to mulct the middle class, especially the big *bourgeoisie*, of something of its gains, while denying it a share in power. Moreover, this might only be the beginning, and where would it end? Exaggerated or not, such fears sprang from profound, acquisitive sources; and, as Chambord was to discover, were far from laid half a century later. In 1830 the barricades were redundant, except as a gesture of dismissal. Charles and Polignac could find no one to defend them, and quietly faded away, leaving a monarchist solution still possible. If only the Charters had been respected, men felt, then one's suspicion need not have become certainty. All that was required was a return to the broken promises of 1815, and an end to the aspirations of the *émigrés*.

For a moment, the July revolution peopled the stage with the stock figures of nineteenth-century France. Even the peasantry, inarticulate but not unnoticed, stood in the wings, restraining throughout the provinces the enthusiasm of the *hobereaux* for their over-zealous king, and silencing the priests. In Paris, backed by the great cities, the middle class, particularly the big *bourgeoisie*, asserted its dominance behind a front of liberal intellectuals, disgruntled ex-Bonapartists, and elderly professional revolutionaries. For the last time, his figure not what it had been, Lafayette played the *jeune premier*, with the gold-digging Louis Philippe as his leading lady, and more than a hint of pantomime. The theme of the set was the tricolour, and the crowd scenes, if not altogether necessary, were magnificent. Once again, and not for the last time, the Parisian masses were called on to the streets by hopes that were to be bitterly disappointed, both by their leaders and by the régime which they helped to create. From the revolution and its sequel, in Lyon as well as Paris, men like Thiers and Louis Blanc drew very different conclusions. Here, too, the Orleanists appeared as the first of 'enemies on the left'; and, benefiting from this point of vantage upon success, moved sedately to the right.

With Louis Philippe, epitome of all the *bourgeois* virtues, quasi-constitutional monarchy replaced neo-legitimist, and proved to be no more satisfactory. Promises, real or implied, were again broken. The king was shifty and calculating, determined to rule as well as reign: though more subtly than before, the revised Charters were nullified a second time. Guizot, his chosen instrument, lecturing a pliant *parlement* packed with functionaries, moved complacently towards disaster, shedding support as he went. Certainly the narrow limits of the *pays légal*, and the betrayals of the early years, made enemies almost from the start. Certainly there was also a failure to reward or silence the lower orders, to evolve a social policy to cater for the growing problem of the urban working class. But, above all, the system alienated its makers, the men of 1830, by excluding them from an effective share in power, which they came to believe they could have wielded so much better, at home and abroad. When troubles multiplied and government lost its grip, placemen were no substitute for solid citizens like Thiers or Tocqueville. With more auspicious origins than its predecessor, the July Monarchy by 1848 had lost its adherents even more completely than had Charles X eighteen years before; and fell to revolution by banquet, leaving a vacuum to be filled. Indeed, unlike 1830, a revolution hardly had to be made: discontent, variously and disjointedly demonstrated, merely called attention to the absence of control. 'The time for kings is past,' said Thiers; monarchy in both its variants had failed.

Paris had again played the dominant rôle, which alone made some sort of republic inevitable. Moderates and radicals were agreed upon this, if upon little else: only a few old men, and the optimistic Louis Napoleon, thought of the Bonapartes. The disillusioned creators of the deposed monarchy had reached Thiers' conclusion with reluctance. They did not make the second revolution, and they had no plans ready. Moreover, after 1830, they were distrusted in Paris and the great cities as self-seeking and treacherous. Economic as well as political conditions had favoured the growth of a radical republican movement, drawing its support from the petty *bourgeois* as well as the working man, in which a vague and variegated socialism played a part. The impetus, such as it was, to the overthrow of the July Monarchy came from these men, fortifying their convictions at reform banquets, and thinking of social as well as political change. The Second Republic, in its first phase, emerged in an atmosphere of leftist extremism, soon to be symbolized by the National Workshops, which profoundly alarmed the men of property. Here was a menace far more serious than the mere failure to satisfy of Louis Philippe; and, in its novelty, perhaps more frightening than the threat they thought they had found in the aspirations of Charles X. The masses had not been used to make a revolution, clearly and visibly, as in 1830. Since it had occurred, they must not be allowed to control it, now that they were infected with such dangerous notions.

In the June Days of 1848 the new Babeuf Plot was brought to a violent end as Cavaignac cleared the streets of Paris. The servant of a *bourgeoisie* temporarily sure of its real enemy, his efficiency as a counter-revolutionary was applauded not only by the middle classes; but also by articulate peasant opinion. The rural volunteers who came to reinforce the General's troops voted with their feet, expressing an identity of interest which had been implied in 1830. Here in token was evidence of the importance of the peasantry, in the year in which they acquired the suffrage. In the last resort, the figures of the Daumier·cartoon and the Courbet landscape would move and work together in defence of their place in the sun. After June, in the second phase of the Second Republic, there was little doubt who had to be satisfied. Monarchy was dead, and the masses cowed; terms could now be made to provide for those who really mattered.

If a republic was unavoidable, it must be conservative in form; as far as was feasible, restricted in electoral basis; and with a strong executive, to make the world safe for the common man of property. A substitute was required which might fulfil the expectations of constitutional monarchy in 1830, without recourse to kings. But, despite the elimination of alternatives, the idea of a republic remained repugnant to many Frenchmen; and traditional doubts and half-formulated fears had been given force by events in Paris before the views of right-thinking men were asserted by Cavaignac. The origins of the Second Republic, tainted by 'socialism' and the prominence of the poor, would have made its reformation difficult enough for the new masters had they made no mistakes. To promote the election of Louis Napoleon as first President was to be too clever by half. They knew they faced a heavy task, and hoped to bring a great name to their assistance in the choice of a man of straw. But, in uneasy circumstances where confidence is lacking, it is dangerous to tamper with explosive myths. An elected President, given real power and a wide popular appeal, might outmanœuvre and destroy those who had intended to employ him for their own secure establishment. For all their careful calculations, the liberal intellectuals, still talking and scheming, were soon driven from the scene by what Marx aptly called 'the eighteenth Brumaire of Louis Napoleon', less by force than by a legend.

Over the past generation a Bonapartist myth had been gradually built up. There were always mourners anxious to commemorate, embellish and inflate the achievements of the great Emperor. In and after 1848, the legend, based upon a solid foundation of fact, was found to possess an irresistible attraction, and the snags of empire were forgotten. Among the difficulties of making the republic viable and respectable, there appeared another solution, urged upon a hesitant but receptive France by the mystical self-confidence of Louis Napoleon. Greatness and stability might be restored with the Empire; and, after all, who had done most to create what *bourgeois* and peasant wanted to preserve and cherish? Louis Philippe had failed in his task, and one's support was withheld; then his immediate heirs came to seem as bad as Charles X, if not worse in their very different way. Even after June, could the republic ever be trusted? Hard as the Thiers and Tocquevilles struggled they were trapped by the past; by their own constitution-making and over-smart politics; and by the adroit exploitation of a perfect opportunity by his uncle's nephew.

Louis Napoleon as President displayed an ostentatious concern for the defence of interests he rightly identified as vital, accumulating much credit. What was wanted, he believed, was firm administration, resting upon a semblance of representative government, and conducted with a suitable *panache* and in the hope of glory. The latter was especially important if the loyalty of the Army was to be secured for the *coup d'état*. In fact, those who might have erected the barricades were exiled, cowed, or saw nothing to defend; while comfortable scholars do not fight in the streets. Personified and in action, the legend found no opposition worth the name from men who retired with what grace they could muster, confidently and indeed accurately predicting disaster.

Resounding approval of this easy victory came through one legacy of 1848, universal suffrage, which had brought the peasant fully into politics, visibly at the side of the *bourgeois*. 'Le suffrage universal finit toujours par discerner et récompenser ses véritables amis,' said the optimistic Gambetta. Whatever might happen in the long run, Louis Napoleon's experience taught conservatives a lesson concerning the initial results of such a change which was not lost upon either Bismarck or Disraeli. In Namier's phrase, demagogic despotism is 'the desperate shift of communities broken from their moorings'; and in the drifting, dissatisfied France of 1852 the promise of bread and circuses was well timed. For a while at least, Church, peasant, business man and soldier could all be bribed to support a retrial of the one previous system not recently discredited. Indeed, little bribery was needed: most Frenchmen surrendered happily to the tyranny of the plausible myth, abandoning liberty and the freedom to choose their masters.

The Second Empire often appears as a feeble echo of its great predecessor. That truly weak man, Napoleon III, was a derivative, conjuring up strength from the legend which carried him to power. In his policies, at home and abroad, aping of the original is obvious time and time again. Yet he was something more than a mere plagiarist, and even careful copying might ensure a modicum of success. From the start the régime had its enemies; later, notably through the twists and turns of a doctrinaire foreign policy incompetently executed, it acquired more. But there were many who did well, and dramatically well, out of this latest experiment. Rigged as they were, the plebiscites of 1870 show a broad measure of continuing support; while the void after Sedan, and the difficulty of finding a replacement, are notorious. The available evidence suggests that the revived Empire provided real benefits on a considerable scale; and, above all, that it proved the system which least displeased most Frenchmen. Napoleon III destroyed his own creation: he was not overthrown, any more than the Third Republic in 1940, by critics turned revolutionaries, as were the régimes of 1815, 1830 and 1848. This Chekovian romantic could produce results, and as master of the most politically 'mature' nation in Europe. There had been much to enjoy; when he fell to the Germans, there was much to regret.

Especially in the economic sphere, success was due to good luck as well as good management. In the nineteenth century France never experienced an industrial revolution comparable to those in England or Germany. At the end of the century it remained largely what it had been in 1815: the country of localized, small-scale industrial development, tending to be antiquated if highly skilled in its methods, and more concerned with secondary than primary production. Still preponderantly an agrarian economy, its characteristic figures were those of the property-owning peasant, his cultivation as conservative as his outlook, and the *bourgeois* merchant, shopkeeper, small master and professional man, only in Paris and a few of the greatest towns far from the land and the psychology of the petty rural proprietor. Under the July Monarchy, with its high tariffs and concern for the business men and farmers of Balzac and Flaubert, the difficulties of the post-war period diminished, and the trend was generally if patchily upward. Increased prosperity at some levels and in certain groups did not necessarily imply a reflection elsewhere, as the condition of the urban working class before 1848 demonstrated. Nevertheless, the peasant and the *bourgeois* were better off by the time of the *coup d'état* than they had been a generation earlier, with more to protect or lose. Improvements in technique in well-established trades, enhanced efficiency in financial organization and the extension of communications, combined with a slow growth of population and a favourable fiscal policy, promised further gains. This promise was not disappointed; and it seems certain that the Second Empire was a period of increased general prosperity, as it was undoubtedly one of considerable economic innovation.

How far the régime itself contributed to this development is not yet clear. Napoleon III set the fashion for dictators in promoting public works, and the largesse was widely distributed. His motives might be mixed: the streets of Paris had to be rendered unsafe for barricades, and avenues cleared for the whiff of grapeshot.

However, Haussmann's truly imperial planning meant money in the contractor's pocket and wages for the working man. Here was a more effective substitute for the National Workshops, producing visible and magnificent results. Of more general importance was the encouragement of easier credit, and more adventurous banking, calculated to assist and please the commercial and industrial *entrepreneur*; and, while reactions here might be more variable, notably to the Cobden treaty, fiscal policy was designed to cater for the friends of the system. Most of all, perhaps, the state played a significant part in the greatest and most beneficial change of these years, the improvement of communications by road, rail and water, which tapped the potentialities of a well-established economy without revolutionizing it. Here indeed were echoes of the First Empire.

Whatever the true explanation, Napoleon III got the praise for changes when they were good, as he got the blame when they were not. There is little doubt where the balance lay. Even among the urban workers, with whom earlier régimes had so notably failed, life improved. The agitations of the 'sixties for improved status, especially for the unions, were those of men more concerned with conditions of work than with politics—which, in the French context, is to say a great deal. However, the greatest gains went elsewhere, to the *bourgeoisie* and, above all, to the peasantry. For the latter a vastly better standard of living began to emerge, which was to deepen further an innate conservatism and to prove so important under the Third Republic. Materially, the Second Empire served well those whose dominant position in French society the First had done much to determine; and from his investments, so fortunate as well as so well-placed, Napoleon III drew a handsome political dividend. Moreover, the task of his enemies was increased, as their numbers and vehemence were reduced, by a prosperity for which government could fairly claim some credit.

Nevertheless, the weaknesses of the revived Empire are obvious. Like the great Napoleon, a lesser man, under less propitious circumstances for his country and himself, had to face and overcome all the dangers which beset the usurping despot, especially when he appeals to 'the people' for survival without an efficient army and an effective secret police. The possibility of serious external failure, invariably disastrous, was always present after 1859; while at home the autocrat, particularly when he is successful enough to have the problem of securing a succession, makes a multiplicity of enemies, not least through rigidity and exclusion, the stigmata of an aging dictatorship. To Napoleon III the first of these dangers, catastrophe in foreign policy, came with a vengeance; but in dealing with the second, it is less clear that he failed.

The 'Liberal Empire' presents a fascinating problem: how far can autocracy modify itself and placate its critics without losing control? To assert that the last of the Bonapartes was defeated by this difficulty would be rash. Modification under pressure, before it became too strong for comfort, was his strategy from 1860; as indeed he had promised earlier, remembering the underlying weakness of his uncle even at the height of his vast powers. Those who felt they had extorted concessions thought often enough of alternatives, but the system managed to contain them; and after 1869 it is doubtful whether the most dangerous opponents had not been bought off. Moreover, beyond the reconciliation, precarious perhaps, of men like Thiers and Ollivier, the plebiscites suggested a firm basis of support. What were such squibs as the Belleville programme compared with this? In 1870 few substantial citizens were seeking more than amendment of the régime. Sedan forced them to do so, and they found the search exceedingly difficult. In the eyes of many Frenchmen, Napoleon III had lived up to his own precept: 'un gouvernement n'est donc pas un ulcère nécessaire, mais c'est plutôt le moteur bienfaisant de tout organisme social'. What could take his place?

The interregnum of the years between 1870 and 1875 presents the last, most intense phase of half a century of experiment; and stands as a tribute to the Second Empire, though far from mute. In confusion and despair, was France once again to run the whole gamut of institutional forms? The republic had its adherents, conservative and radical, squabbling over the true title to the heritage of the Jacobins. But 1848 remained a depressing memory, with old doubts reinforced by experience; while the defiant misery of the Commune sharply revived familiar fears. For others, at least until Chambord proved himself impossible, the long-awaited opportunity for a return to monarchy seemed to have arrived. In the chaos of defeat bewildered little men had turned to their social superiors as representatives, and filled the National Assembly with *notables* surprised at their own resurrection and determined to seize this unexpected chance. The most realistic of royalists could be forgiven if they felt an upsurge of optimism under such remarkable circumstances. Even the unrepentant Bonapartists, after a brief but hardly decent interval, came to have hopes of imperial rehabilitation. For the collapse of the Empire made everything, including its return, seem feasible in this time of delusion.

The fundamental problem was still the same. What form of government could best placate and satisfy the dominant elements in French society, the great vested interests who had provoked or conditioned all experiment since 1815? Probably they preferred the liberalized Empire to any alternative: in the aftermath of Sedan, they knew its revival to be out of the question. If positive benefits could not be secured, then they wanted the régime least likely to injure them. Primarily through the efforts of an improbable combination, Gambetta and Thiers, they were now to get this, though time was needed for their full conviction. Between them, these two men forced a predominantly monarchist Assembly, under the leadership of dukes with Orleanist leanings, to create a republic, reluctantly, vaguely, and not without hope of reversion to something more congenial. No system of government was ever more shuffled into, nor approached in so crabwise a fashion as the Third Republic. Indeed, the decisive vote of 1875, on the Wallon amendment, is symbolic of the mode and atmosphere of its appearance. The amendment was carried by a single vote. Yet a member of the Assembly, arriving panting a few minutes late for the division, protested that he would have voted against had he come in time. However, the thing was done; and, in view of the history of the past five years and the lessons they had taught about attitudes moulded over a century, it is hard to believe that anything else could have been done. The two great protagonists of the republic saw what was possible and made it happen.

In 1871, very late in the day, Thiers came into his own at last. Convinced that 'the republic is one of the things left us by the empire', he was clear about the course to be taken. Law, order and prosperity must first be restored; but as chief of the executive power he would discreetly prepare the way, among conflicting claims, for the conservative republic he had failed to establish after 1848. 'He sought', said Daniel Halévy, 'the republican future through the vision of a Consulate of which he himself was the hero.' Bullying and bamboozling, dominating the Germans, the Assembly and indeed all France, Thiers promoted and guided an astonishingly rapid recovery with ruthless, dictatorial efficiency. Because of his concrete achievements and his skill in managing both friends and enemies, the solution he desired was made infinitely more likely than it had appeared in the false dawn of monarchism in the summer of 1871. Even without the ludicrous intransigence of Chambord, it is difficult to believe that the latter's prospects were ever good, particularly in view of the newly strident ultramontanism of his supporters. The self-styled Henri V seemed the reincarnation of Charles X, a distant yet all too audible echo of the *ancien régime*. But the reign of Thiers was needed to provide time for the idea of a republic to become tolerable; while his successes did much to make it respectable. By 1873 intelligent royalists, like De Broglie, could see that the republic must come if only as an interlude, and concentrated upon the attempt to find a safe and malleable version.

The work of Thiers was complemented by Gambetta's campaign to make provincial France accept what it had so long rejected. Few political agitations have been more remarkable. In the eyes of many, Gambetta was the firebrand of Belleville, and the man who had wanted to continue an impossible war, imagining himself a second Danton. Nevertheless, by patient persuasion and carefully selected argument and exhortation, he managed to convince the average Frenchman, in town and country, that a republic was the answer. Conjuring up plausibility and avoiding precision, he advocated peace and prosperity, allaying fears by asserting that 'there is no social problem'. With perceptive genius, the attack was concentrated upon clericalism; for there was the immediate enemy. To most of his hearers this was not a religious or rationalist question: their concern was wider and more material. Like the Bourbons, clericalism meant the *ancien régime*, whose ghost stalked the 'seventies under the unattractive patronage of Pio Nono and Chambord. Gambetta set out to discredit monarchy beyond redemption by playing upon the hereditary distrust which had destroyed Charles X; and, with the assistance of the monarchists, he succeeded. Thiers had already suggested that the republic might work as well as the Empire; and that it would be safe from and against left-wing deviations after the effective suppression of the Commune. Very early, by-elections for the Assembly showed which way the wind was blowing; by 1879 the new republic was in the hands of the republicans, all the more completely because of the illustration provided for Gambetta's case by the ill-considered *putsch* of the *Seize Mai*. Obviously the time for dukes as well as kings was past. The process of settlement by elimination was over, and an adequate half-way house between right and left had been found.

Despite the rout of its opponents, however, the Third Republic for long carried an air of the conditional and uncertain. Those who believed it to be the best or only solution remained preoccupied with making 'the provisional permanent'; but such a party of compromise could not call upon the myths, the deep emotions and firm attachments, which stirred the defeated of both extremes. In the aftermath of victory, the aptly named 'opportunists' did little to consolidate their conversion of France. The 'eighties were marked by timid conservatism, a drab complacency of unimaginative, narrow-minded men, whose policy at home and abroad was based upon the simple principle of appeasement, though they could have claimed the credit for restoring the classic liberties of the subject. The attitude of these new Girondins was personified in Ferry, a greater man than his contemporaries, but still the archetype of their evasive mediocrity. Given the complexity of the French problem, this approach had some merit. How could everyone be satisfied, and how far did it matter so long as the dominant groups felt there was no real alternative? Like Louis XVIII and the latter-day Thiers, Ferry and his friends considered that one should do enough to keep the peace and no more. Every dog that would sleep must be allowed to lie undisturbed.

But, as always, here was the snag. Before long the protagonists of 'movement', of whatever persuasion, become impatient of 'order'; and, above all when government appears too humiliating and corrupt, are encouraged to attack, eternally optimistic. Moderates in power find disillusioned supporters drifting to the left, while their opponents on the right tend to acquire a new unity and zest. This was the fate of the 'opportunists'. Domestic policy provoked their enemies without satisfying their more ardent friends; both were infuriated by a grasping colonialism which seemed a craven abdication of France's greatness as a European power, designed to fill capacious pockets. In the end, in the Wilson scandals, corruption was revealed at the Élysée itself. This combination of circumstances made possible the strange career of Boulanger, based upon 'the syndicate of the discontented', which was perhaps the last genuine threat to the survival of the Third Republic as the best that could be done. Until he realized that he had created a Frankenstein and tried to rally republicans in defence of their system, Clemenceau saw this vain and timorous soldier, so susceptible to social and sexual seduction, as a Cromwell for the Left. Soon he was St. Arnaud to the Bonapartists and Monk to the monarchists, a means to their various ends. All things to all men, Boulanger failed each of his promoters in turn, through sheer inability to take command and act.

Nevertheless, the rise and fall of the General, 'dying as he had lived, a subaltern', demonstrated the fundamental strength of a régime still unsure of itself. With a profound tenacity stemming from the sources of their power, the men of the establishment displayed just enough courage, just enough capacity for decision, in action or inaction, to hang on until Boulangism evaporated; and the remnants of this half-baked Caesarism could be swept away by a whiff of verbal grapeshot, since no more was needed. Clearly, by very force of caricature, the General had shown the absence of an attainable alternative. Moreover, those who claimed that this existed were hopelessly involved in the ultimate absurdities of Boulangism. For the first time, and despite Panama, the Third Republic in the nineties began to win 'national acceptance'. This was indicated dramatically by the *ralliement*; and in the break-up of monarchism and what remained of Bonapartism, both under-mined and divided by the association with Boulanger. In addition, those upon whom the republic primarily depended were courted more actively than at any time since Gambetta's heyday, notably through the Méline tariff, which cushioned the *bourgeoisie* and peasantry against the harsh facts of a changing economic context. Colonialism might continue, for too many in politics were concerned for it to be otherwise; but the Franco-Russian alliance suggested that this was not incompatible with a positive and successful European policy. Whatever might be said, in practice the old order, every old order, accepted a defeat which there seemed no prospect of reversing. The despised, makeshift republic had come to stay.

For these reasons, it is easy to understand the irritated alarm of Méline when he tried to stifle the Dreyfusards. A system had been devised which worked, because it had acquired the solid support of those whom its predecessors had flouted, aroused or failed; and because its enemies were weak or already half-reconciled. What more could one hope for? To disturb this happy situation would be madness; and there might be ways of dealing with the lunatics. Méline agreed with M. Queuille: 'dans la politique il ne s'agit pas de résoudre les problèmes, mais de faire taire ceux qui les posent'. But on this occasion the prudent were wrong; for the Dreyfus affair provided a splendid opportunity for consolidating a régime still partly on sufferance upon a thoroughly secure basis. The political or electoral victory of the 'seventies and 'eighties found its counterpart in the closer, fuller control of a republic run by republicans over the lives of Frenchmen which followed from the reduction in the authority of the Church, and the displacement from positions of power in the civil and military administration of men who were 'internal *émigrés*'. Moreover, especially among the intellectuals, the Affair created a republican myth, a legend which was to strengthen and sustain something which had hitherto seemed only 'beautiful under the Empire'. Upon its own, sometimes dubious merits, the Third Republic had at last established a claim to positive, enthusiastic loyalty. Politics might remain 'a matter of taste', in Robert de Jouvenel's phrase; but the taste could be admitted by an honest man. Indeed, Jaurès particularly came to adorn the system which he tried to defend and make defensible, and he was not alone. In these years of high excitement the ivory tower lost many distinguished tenants, to the great gain of public life.

Balance, however, is never easy to maintain. The politics of the Third Republic have often been described as the politics of fear: fear that government might neglect or invade one's private preserves; fear of the extremist that the ideal might be submerged in the possible; or fear of the moderate and satisfied that either Left or Right might upset a plodding apple-cart. Even after Dreyfus, the old Right, in essence monarchist, could still be used as a bogey by adroit politicians; but what·came to matter more was the growing power of the socialist Left, inside and outside the Chambers. For most of the past century the urban working class had played a rôle intermittently important, but usually peripheral and subsidiary. When they acted more independently, as in the early months of 1848 or during the Commune, the spectacle had been horrifying. By the 'nineties, under a liberal régime, the revival of left-wing traditions was being hastened by economic and social change, in this second major phase of French industrial development in the nineteenth century, as well as by novel influences like Marxism. Initially the full significance of what was occurring was masked by its limited reflection in *parlement*, largely due to the attractions of syndicalism. Nevertheless, Waldeck-Rousseau's 'government of national defence' at the height of the Dreyfus affair found it desirable to include a socialist in Millerand, who was permitted to make a first, tentative approach to the mounting problem of the condition of the proletariat. Shifts in society, relatively stable for so long, began to threaten a hard-won stability in government.

Under universal suffrage in the second generation, following the familiar pattern, the masses were moving towards the centre of the stage. Few supporters of the Third Republic, protector of peasant and *bourgeois,* wished to see them there, a force more disturbing than the old Right had been. Their coming made the ostensible issues in politics seem obsolescent and often irrelevant: with all the more fervour, those issues had to be kept alive. To neutralize the 'enemy on the left' became more than ever important, and yet increasingly difficult without paying excessive blackmail or associating too closely with ancient opponents whose enmity was still required for electoral purposes. For a very long time, however, the men of the Third Republic proved able to do very little. The Radicals, successors to the 'opportunists' as the party of the establishment and the core of all governments until 1940, usually managed to retain the friends of the régime while at least containing its critics and its enemies. Elimination had done its work better than most Frenchmen had expected or dared to hope for: the *pis aller* of 1875, it was demonstrated, could be a solution after all.

Or rather, perhaps, a solution of sorts, too rarely seen as anything more. For the Third Republic, at least until the aftermath of the Affair, represented the grave of high and varied hopes, sustained for almost a century. Once enshrined, its *mystique* was a poor and feeble thing, of which apologists, even Alain, could make little. However, especially if paradoxically to Frenchmen, forms of government are not everything, particularly when quarrels about them reflect the stability of a society and not the reverse, as was true of much of the nineteenth century. Between the Restoration and the Affair, France was a great power, once the greatest of powers, in decline. Certainly the iridescence of decay may be seen in a period of remarkable brilliance in the history of its culture. The richest of feasts was prepared for body, mind and spirit: from the arts to food and wine the individual was never better served. Talleyrand boasted of the *douceur de vivre* under the *ancien régime*; but whether even the life of a nobleman before 1789 compared with the existence of an alert contemporary of Flaubert or of Renoir is a nice point for controversy. So long, that is to say, as one was not an impoverished aristocrat, deprived of the past, or a working man, looking to the future; for *la France bourgeoise* was limited in the bestowal of its benefits. Nevertheless, under the Third Republic the good life was possible as never before, with every embellishment of civilization. Both Louis XVIII and Méline were right: in 1815 there was much to gain, in 1898 much to lose.

BIBLIOGRAPHICAL NOTE

The following suggestions are intended solely as a practical guide to further reading. Especially useful works are marked with an asterisk.

1. *General Histories*
BURY, J. P. T. *France, 1814–1940*, 1969.
COBBAN, A. *A History of Modern France,* vols. ii and iii, 1965.
*WRIGHT, G. *France in Modern Times,* 1962.

2. *Particular Periods*
(a)
*PONTEIL, F. *La Monarchie parlementaire, 1815–48,* 1949.
ARTZ, F. B. *France under the Bourbon Restoration.* Cambridge, Mass, 1931.
BERTIER DE SAUVIGNY, G. DE, *La Restauration,* 1963.
DE LA GORCE, P. *Louis Philippe,* 1931.
POMARET, CH. *M. Thiers et son siècle,* 1948.
JOHNSON, D. *Guizot,* 1963.
(b)
*DANSETTE, A. *Deuxième République et Second Empire,* 1942.
PONTEIL, F. *1848,* 1937.
MACKAY, D. C. *The National Workshops,* Cambridge, Mass., 1933.
*DE TOCQUEVILLE, A. *Souvenirs,* 1942.

SIMPSON, F. A. *The Rise of Louis Napoleon,* 1950.
(c)
THOMPSON, J. M. *Louis Napoleon and the Second Empire,* Oxford, 1954.
DE LA GORCE, P. *Napoléon III et sa politique,* 1933.
ZELDIN, T. *The Political System of Napoleon III,* 1958.
DUVEAU, G. *La Vie ouvrière en France sous le Second Empire,* 1946.
(d)
*BROGAN, D. W. *The Development of Modern France, 1870–1939,* 1967.
BOURGIN, G. *La Troisième République,* 1939.
*GOGUEL, FR. *La Politique des partis sous la Troisième République,* vol. i, 1946.
HALÉVY, D. *La Fin des Notables,* 1930.
HALÉVY, D. *La République des ducs,* 1937.
DANSETTE, A. *Le Boulangisme,* 1938.
CHAPMAN, G. *The Dreyfus Case,* 1955.
JOHNSON, D. *France and the Dreyfus Affair,* 1966.

3. *Economic and Social Problems*

*CLAPHAM, J. H. *Economic Development of France and Germany, 1815–1914,* Cambridge, 1936.
SÉE, H. *Histoire économique de la France,* vol. ii, 1951.
MORAZÉ, CH. *La France bourgeoise,* 1952.
DOLLÉANS, E. *Histoire du mouvement ouvrier,* 2 vols., 1936 and 1939.
LORWIN, V. R. *The French Labor Movement,* Cambridge, Mass., 1954.
PHILLIPS, C. S. *The Church in France, 1789–1907,* 2 vols., 1929 and 1936.

4. *Critical Essays on various aspects of the period*

BEAU DE LOMÉNIE, E. *Les Responsabilités des dynasties bourgeoises,* 2 vols., 1947–8
PLAMENATZ, J. *The Revolutionary Movement in France, 1815–71,* 1952.
RÉMOND, R. *La Droite en France de 1815 à nos jours,* 1954.
*THOMSON, D. *Democracy in France,* 1964.
BODLEY, J. E. C. *France,* 1902.
*SIEGFRIED, A. *Tableau des partis en France,* 1930.
JOUVENEL, R. DE. *La République des camarades,* 1934.
THIBAUDET, A. *Les Idées politiques de la France,* 1932.

From Dreyfus to Vichy

━━━━◥◖◗◤━━━━

The Third Republic was established, as previous lecturers have shown, by a process of elimination. It came into being because, to the great *bourgeois* and peasant vested interest created by the Revolution, it seemed more satisfactory than any of the previous régimes; and these dominant sections preferred it, not because they thought it likely to bring them benefits, but because it appeared unlikely to injure them.

The politics of these established groups were the politics of fear: but they had two causes for alarm and not one. The Right remained for them permanently tarred with the landlord and clerical brush. Their grandfathers had believed that their property might be threatened by a counter-attack of the *ancien régime*; and the descendants preserved a hereditary mistrust of the forces of reaction, which attached them to 'Left' principles and habits of mind. Yet, in the present, the Right was no longer an economic, even if it might still be regarded as a political and ideological, menace. Now the threat to property came from the Socialists, a growing power on the Left. The men of the middle course feared both sources of disturbance; and the domestic history of the Third Republic depended on which danger was uppermost in their minds.

The answer to that question varied both in time and place. In the old-fashioned, economically individualist regions, where small independent businesses predominated, working for local markets and unconcerned with the activities of the state, the little men who ultimately ruled the country could safely indulge their ideological preference for the Left; in the modernized areas of big business, growing trade unions, national markets, a developing economy needing state aid and transport facilities, more immediate interests prevailed. At the beginning of the twentieth century France was a prosperous, self-sufficient land, a great exporter of capital, where politics were, in Robert de Jouvenel's phrase, a matter of taste, not a factor governing men's daily lives. Questions of principle, the naming of streets or the celebration of Good Friday in the navy, could arouse passionate feeling (of which the dispute over education in Britain during the same years gives a faint indication). But as national politics came to be dominated by economic questions, and to make a real difference to the life of the average man, then the conflicts of interest proved the more powerful influence. Between the Dreyfus affair and Hitler's war, the middle of the road groups hesitated between their twin aversions. The Radicals who represented them in the new century, like the Opportunists who had done so in the old, preferred to fight elections in alliance with the Left, but to govern with conservative support. Their dearest wish was to do nothing, their favourite slogan 'neither reaction nor revolution'. They were appropriately compared to the radish, 'red outside, white inside, and sitting in the middle of the butter-dish'.

The decisive factor, then, was fear of the dynamic groups in society, which could not be allowed power lest they should set Frenchmen once again at one another's throats. So the Third Republic, which had come into existence because it divided the country least, set out in 1875 on the line of least resistance, guided by the shortest-sighted, most unconstructive elements in France. These groups, the middle *bourgeoisie* and the propertied peasantry, were numerically important, but they took care to buttress their voting power by institutional devices. Of the sixteen Chambers of the Third Republic, thirteen were elected under a system which helped the parties of the centre against the extremists. In the Senate, the countryside and small towns were so over-weighted against the developing and modernized regions, that enemies of the régime on both sides were almost unrepresented. Constitutional conventions served similar ends: the office of President of the Republic had been shorn of effective power, but to make quite sure that no ambitious President would emulate Napoleon III, the parliamentarians were careful to elect only the most colourless candidates to the post. They preferred a weak executive with weak men managing it: and over the years a sort of political natural selection developed, so that leaders were no longer bred. When France needed a strong man in 1917, she turned to one who had been kept out of office for all but three years of his career (and later repaid his services by refusing him the Presidency of the Republic). When the need recurred in 1940, there was no one in politics to answer the call.

The moderate groups could thus manipulate the political system in their favour. In addition they formed the largest single block of opinion in the country. But they could never confidently rely on the support of a clear majority of the voters, and at election times they needed an understanding with one or other of their rivals. To seek support from the Right, except in an emergency and for a short period, would shock their own clients, still ferociously hostile to the reactionaries. At the polls, therefore, the Radical strategy was 'no enemies on the Left'. This course too was dangerous, for these allies had unwelcome social and economic aspirations; but their attention could usually be diverted into the harmless channels of anti-clericalism.

The Third Republic, then, was based on the predominance of a great vested interest and the discredit or exhaustion of the rival social forces. Such a régime could never hope to attract enthusiasm or escape mediocrity. President Grévy, attending an exhibition in the 'eighties, was told that there were few outstanding items but that the average standard was high. 'A good average,' he replied 'but that's just as it should be in a democracy.' With this state of affairs many groups, and those the most influential, were reasonably content; but others, and these among the most vigorous and active, always felt themselves excluded from effective citizenship.

These 'internal *émigrés*', spiritually disinherited in the Republic, came of very diverse origins. Some were attached to an older social order, devout Catholics and members of fashionable society. But others belonged to the modern economic world, the industrial workers and, especially after 1930, the managers and technicians. Moreover, at all times the discontented were numerous in the new generation; the ardent idealism of youth could feel little loyalty and no enthusiasm for the prudent, uninspiring, even corrupt régime. Indeed just before the Dreyfus case J. E. C. Bodley went so far as to suggest that most of the best Frenchmen were among the three million who never voted. It did not greatly concern him that the governing class of the country had no contact with fashionable society, for he regarded both as utterly worthless. But it was equally out of touch with the practical men who managed the affairs of France. The British Parliament was dominated by commerce, agriculture and industry, the French

Chambers by the professions. Yet, Bodley pointed out, the élite even of the intellectuals held aloof from the sordid trade of politics; the parliamentarians were professional men indeed, but third-rate ones.

It was in just these characteristics of the Third Republic that 'Alain', its chief philosophical defender, found matter for rejoicing. In his view the function of the deputy was precisely to represent the ordinary undistinguished citizen against the eternal conspiracy of the strong, the rich, and the successful—those who have 'arrived' and have consequently been corrupted by the embrace of society. Alain's argument is not to be lightly dismissed; it helps to explain why the roots of the régime in popular affection went so much deeper than might have been expected, and why Bodley's plausible belief that the slightest strain would upset a system wholly unsuited to the French was soon resoundingly disproved in the Dreyfus affair, the syndicalist troubles, and the First World War. But the fear and suspicion of leadership, which characterized Alain's point of view, were weaknesses for which a price had to be paid. Because of the detachment from the Republic of the most powerful groups in society, France drew many of her political representatives from sections standing outside the 'natural' governing class and even, it was claimed, outside the main stream of national tradition. Charles Maurras, the great reactionary pamphleteer, was exaggerating but not romancing when he maintained that under the Republic politics were dominated by the 'four confederated states', the Jews, Protestants, Freemasons, and *métèques*. This situation, felt by many good Frenchmen to be unnatural, imposed a further strain on national unity. To those who could not look upon the Republic as *their* régime, Maurras' distinction between the *pays légal* and the *pays réel* seemed to expose a fundamental fault (in both senses) in French society.

Despite these difficulties the system justified itself triumphantly in 1914. For all the attacks on Republican inefficiency, its military performance contrasted favourably with that of the Second Empire; for all the divisions among Frenchmen, the despised democracy proved capable even in adversity of maintaining national unity for longer than any of the autocratic belligerents. But if in the short run the crisis of the war was surmounted, over the years it undermined the foundations of the régime, accelerating all the forces making for disintegration. For the do-nothing, *immobiliste* outlook of the dominant groups, the aversion from power of the men who held power, was only one of many paradoxes. The population was failing to reproduce itself—except in the benighted regions where the party of enlightenment and progress had proved unable to destroy the influence of clerical reaction. In politics it was impossible to strengthen the executive because this was demanded by the Right, who sought to modernize government only in order to halt the evolution of society. Consequently, in social policy effective progress was blocked by the intransigence of the Left, who rejected on political grounds the institutional changes indispensable to a reforming policy. And in the economic race France was falling behind during, and indeed because of, the democratic régime. Napoleon III had made himself unpopular by imposing free trade to foster industrial development. But leaders of the Third Republic had more respect for the electorate. In 1892 Jules Méline discovered the political advantages of high protection. A French Baldwin, a bogus-bucolic spokesman of industrial interests, Méline (unlike Baldwin) did win votes, especially peasant votes, by his tariffs. Existing farms and firms secured a comfortable life and easy profits. Industry progressed, though less rapidly than in other countries. But in time foreign markets contracted, enterprise came to seem unnecessary and unmannerly, new businesses found it hard to enter the charmed circle. Fiscal and social as well as commercial policy helped to protect small, weak, inefficient units against the threat of competition, to 'close the windows' of the French economy against the menace of fresh air. This commitment to backwardness was accepted not only by a short-sighted peasantry and petty *bourgeoisie*, but equally by the most respectable sections of informed opinion. Georges Duhamel had tried in vain to win election to the *Académie française*: he owed his eventual success in 1930 to his satire on the machine civilization of the United States.

The war inflicted terrible material losses on France, and exacerbated all the conflicts and strains in society. Economically, paying the price for her easy-going policies, she fell farther behind other powers. Internationally, both through the greed and ambition of her dominant groups and through unforgivable abdication of responsibility by America and Britain, France overstrained herself by trying to play a rôle which had been far beyond her strength for more than a century. And under the pressure of social backwardness, economic depression and international insecurity, the political foundations cracked. When politics came to centre on the real conflicts of the twentieth century instead of the abstract preferences of the eighteenth, the differences among Frenchmen proved too sharp to be resolved by the normal processes of democracy. By 1938 the parliamentary system was half suspended; in the well-known phrase, the crisis of 1940 did not kill the Third Republic, it merely drew attention to the fact that it was dead.

The reactionaries welcomed that crisis as a 'divine surprise'. By this remark Maurras was of course greeting not the victory of the hated Germans, but the unexpected chance to sweep away the no less detested Republic. The counter-revolutionaries were to have yet another opportunity to display that bankruptcy of statesmanship which had for a hundred and fifty years been their political hall-mark. Pétain's alleged dictum, 'France will never be great again until the wolves are howling round the doors of her villages', is at least *ben trovato*. For four years the motley parade of enemies of the Republic, some respectable but inept, others disreputable but clever, yet others traitorous and barbaric, displayed in succession their shoddy wares to an increasingly resentful public. The Vichy experiment showed once for all that that favourite scapegoat for France's ills, her governmental system, was a mere symptom of weaknesses deep-rooted in French society.

It was a reopening of old wounds that drained French strength in the 'thirties and 'forties. Past conflicts were renewed, often by the former protagonists or their heirs. Admiral Darlan's father, Minister of Justice in Méline's cabinet, had wished to prosecute the first Dreyfusard pamphleteer. Captain Maxime Weygand subscribed to the memorial for Colonel Henry the forger. A du Paty de Clam became commissioner for Jewish affairs under Vichy.[1] Maurras, sentenced for collaboration, exclaimed: 'The revenge of Dreyfus!'

The main French parties, Communists excepted, were born in the aftermath of the Affair: Radical party, *Alliance démocratique*, *Fédération républicaine*, Socialist party all appear in the first five

[1] But du Paty was a very lukewarm anti-semite; and Darlan *père* came to doubt Dreyfus' guilt and was dropped from office. (Méline, true to the Baldwinesque principle of letting sleeping dogs lie, had refused to prosecute the pamphleteer, Bernard Lazare.)

years of the century. Outside parliament the monarchist *Ligue de l'Action française* and the united *Confédération générale du travail* date from the same period; the Christian Democratic *Sillon* movement from which M.R.P. was to spring, and the 'Mascuraud committee' which raised Radical funds, are a little older. Many leaders of the 'twenties and 'thirties were ministers, supporters or collaborators of Waldeck-Rousseau: Barthou, Caillaux, Doumer, Doumergue, Herriot, Paul-Boncour, Poincaré, Reynaud, Sarraut, Tardieu. Briand entered the Chamber in 1902; Léon Blum, Charles Maurras, Marc Sangnier awoke to interest in politics through the Affair; Chautemps, Darlan and Flandin were the sons of politicians who began ministerial careers in the 'nineties.

There is thus a real unity about the period from Dreyfus to Vichy. It was in the 'nineties that the Republic first won national acceptance with the *Ralliement* of the Church, the Méline tariff, and the Russian treaty.[1] In the 1893 election, despite the resounding scandal of Panama, only 16 per cent of the votes went to reactionaries (compared with 45 per cent eight years before) and only three *départements* (against thirty in 1885) showed a majority against the Republic. In parliament Léon Bourgeois, in 1895, was the first prime minister to depend on the support of the Socialists (and also the first to be ejected by the Senate); and his successor Méline was the first republican to rely on the Right for his majority.

In the country the great political tendencies were themselves changing. The Left came increasingly under Socialist influence and turned away from its historic nationalism towards a passionate anti-militarism. The Right accommodated itself to a new world of manhood suffrage, general education, mass organization and propaganda, where mere social prestige no longer sufficed. A new, noisy, urban, popular movement developed, very different from the old conservatism of the respectable classes. Led by the journalistic firebrands of the *Action française* and the demagogic priests of the Assumptionist order, these forces were violently nationalist, bitterly anti-parliamentary, and closely linked with the new plebeian forms of revivalist Catholicism. It was a sign of the times that in 1900 the turbulent city of Paris elected its first right-wing municipal council.

The Radicals too were changing; abandoning the Left position

[1] I owe this point to Mr R. S. C. Donald. Each of the three sections of the Right—clerical, *bourgeois*, and nationalist—was affected by these events.

they occupied in the early years of the Republic for the cautious respectability of the centre, they were ceasing to be a movement of intransigent opposition and becoming a party of government and compromise, which soon established almost a permanent claim to the Ministry of the Interior. In this process they lost their traditional hold on the great cities, especially the capital, but acquired in compensation a new provincial clientèle among the prosperous peasantry and the small-town *bourgeoisie*, the lawyers, doctors and shopkeepers who dominated the politics of the Third Republic. The Freemasons transferred their support—and the only effective political machine in France—from the Opportunists to the Radicals, and the lodges soon became the driving force of thriving Radical local committees. With this more powerful and yet more moderate Radicalism many Opportunist Republicans, conservatives with important business and press interests, found it easy to co-operate. This combination was influential but uninspiring; and in the first decade of the new century intellectual leaders of all shades of opinion—Barrès and Bergson, Maurras and Péguy and Sorel—threw down their various challenges to the dreary régime and the quiet life it had been created to preserve. So clearly did they recognize their common enemy that Maurras himself, the prophet of order, strong government, and nationalism, the bitter opponent of popular movements, the believer in 'politics above all', for some years gave open sympathy and encouragement to the revolutionary, semi-anarchist, anti-militarist, anti-political syndicalists of the C.G.T.

The peculiar importance of the Dreyfus case was that it brought into bitter conflict the three institutions which, according to Bodley, were the foundation-stones of French social stability. He had denounced the worthless parliamentary and fashionable classes, but he had given high praise to the useful work and honourable devotion of the army, the clergy, and the *Université*, the teaching profession. Hardly had his book appeared when the Dreyfus affair arrayed the first two in a savage struggle against the third. Already, in the 'eighties, Jules Ferry's educational laws had provoked conflict between Church and *Université*. Yet these professions had something in common, for both were recruited from the people, drawing on *boursiers* either of the State or of the Church; and their mutual hostility had apparently been abated by the *Ralliement*. The army on the contrary was the last stronghold of the gentleman in the governmental system, the one form of public service which the scions of the old aristocracy felt able to undertake. But until the Dreyfus case it was popular among republicans. This general esteem was abruptly forfeited by the arrogant claim of its leaders to preserve it as a state within the state, independent of the hated republican politicians, and by the contention of its champions, led by Maurras, that social order and social hierarchy should take precedence over justice to the individual. It is now becoming fashionable to maintain that the ruin by forgery and perjury of an innocent man is comparatively venial, provided the motive were an impersonal devotion to a social class or an official department. To France's credit this repulsive view, though widely held and vigorously propagated, did not prevail.

Yet the anti-Dreyfusards were right in maintaining that more than the fate of an obscure though wealthy Jewish captain was at stake. The partisan legends of both sides might be equally false: there was neither a plot against the Republic as the Left alleged, nor a conspiracy to subvert the social order as the Right pretended. But once the battle was joined, great political consequences were bound to follow, since the winning side was almost certain to abuse its victory. It did. Under the Combes ministry which held office from 1902 to 1905, the doctrines of the Left went far to wreck the machinery of government. Camille Pelletan, the Minister of Marine (Alain's ideal minister), reduced the navy to a state of sorry inefficiency. General André, appointed to the War Ministry as one of the few reliable republican generals, overplayed his hand by using the masonic lodges as sources of information about Catholic officers. This scandal of the *fiches* made it impossible to carry through the purge of the army, which though no longer a law unto itself remained a stronghold of the men of the old order, a 'permanent *ralliement*' as it has been called. Through it such men could, like Lyautey, work honourably for France outside her own borders, building a great empire for which voters and politicians showed only indifference or distaste. They could, like Foch, serve her in war; and like Pétain, Weygand, and Franchet d'Esperey, they could unhappily justify the Left's suspicion that few senior officers were trustworthy guardians of democratic government.

The second loser from the Dreyfus struggle was the Church. Though many of its responsible leaders would have preferred an attitude of prudence, the noisy popular priests and press, under

Assumptionist leadership, threw themselves into the engagement and contributed to the anti-semitic venom of the reactionary side. Inevitably the whole Church suffered from their defeat. But though the anti-clerical campaigns were a direct consequence of the Affair, another motive played its part. Waldeck-Rousseau's coalition, assembled in June 1899 to defend the Republic, embraced many shades of opinion, from the wealthy *bourgeoisie* who later formed the *Alliance démocratique* to the Jaurès wing of the Socialists. The cabinet itself for the first time included a Socialist, Alexandre Millerand, later a reactionary President of the Republic, the pioneer on the well-travelled road to fame and power which winds its tortuous way from Left to Right. Dangerous firebrands like this, toying with notions of introducing income-tax or facilitating strikes, alarmed the Opportunist wing of the majority; the attack on the religious congregations proved an admirable way of diverting their attention.[1] 'Old General Hokum leads an unbeatable army'; and the anti-clerical campaign thus inaugurated was to dominate politics for the next five years. No more was heard of the strike bill; the proposed income-tax was quietly abandoned; and the *Alliance démocratique* group rallied to the republican cause and the separation of Church and State. In the intransigently Left Combes government, to which Alain pointed with pride, the Minister of Finance was Maurice Rouvier, the archetype of the shady business man in politics, who had been kept from office since the Panama scandal.

With the separation of Church and State in 1905, the clerical dispute lost much of its bitterness. The class struggle became the focus of politics; the ideological quarrels of the old society were overlaid by the conflicts of interest of the modern world. In all western Europe, Sir John Clapham has remarked, France had least 'practical socialism' (public ownership, welfare legislation, co-operation, redistributive taxation, etc.). Ill-paid, ill-housed workers followed the revolutionary syndicalists, who repudiated capitalism,

[1] The dates are significant. Millerand announced his strike bill at a Socialist meeting on 15 October 1899. As soon as the Chamber met the business republicans attacked Waldeck-Rousseau, who in his reply promised to act against the congregations. For a year nothing happened. Then on 7 October 1900 Millerand, under Socialist pressure, reaffirmed his intention to introduce the strike bill; on the 22nd Barthou, leader of the business group, warned the prime minister that his majority was in danger; and on the 28th Waldeck-Rousseau promised to deal with the congregations at once.

democracy, army and nation. When the terrible Radical guerrilla Clemenceau came to power he relied on the Right for support against strikes in the country and Socialists in the Chamber. Aristide Briand, in turn revolutionary agitator, parliamentary broker in Church affairs, and prime minister, broke a railway strike by calling up the workers he had once championed to the army he had traduced. Socialists joined reactionaries in demanding electoral reform, loathed by Radicals. The *bloc des gauches* was splintered.

Germany exploited these rifts in French unity. In 1905 she took advantage of the separation crisis, the Pelletan-André régime and the Russo-Japanese war to force out the Foreign Minister Delcassé, maker of the *entente cordiale*, whose premier Rouvier was bent on appeasing Berlin. Six years later, in a second Moroccan crisis, another business prime minister, Joseph Caillaux, took the same line. But the panic mood of 1905 had gone; and Caillaux's successor was the unyielding Raymond Poincaré, who in 1913 became President of the Republic. Against Briand's conservatism and Poincaré's nationalism Radicals and Socialists drew together again. The 1914 election was won by a Left reunited under Caillaux in support of an income-tax and opposition to longer military service.

The flood of war swept differences away, and for three years Frenchmen stood together in *union sacrée*. When this foundered, Poincaré in 1917 called to power the last of the Jacobins, Clemenceau, who promptly arrested Caillaux and his disreputable ally Jean-Louis Malvy, Minister of the Interior since 1914, accused of tenderness to defeatists. Clemenceau brought the country through to a victory which solved none of the major problems that had confronted France on the eve of war. In the next decade Poincaré, Briand and Caillaux still faced Germany abroad and financial troubles at home; and if the war had temporarily eased the former difficulty, it had aggravated the latter.

By 1914 France's easy-going economic policy was beginning to show its weaknesses. Competitive effort was discouraged by high protection, thwarted by Malthusian habits of mind, starved by the policy of the banks. These had chosen (for huge commissions) to place French savings abroad rather than at home; 36 per cent of all French investments were outside the country, especially in Russia and Turkey, and much of this vast stake was lost through the war. Moreover the burdens of government were inequitably distributed. The war increased these burdens enormously, but diminished no whit the stubborn selfishness of the wealthy. War-time finance was profligate; the whole cost was borne by loans, raised on ever stiffer terms as the conflict dragged on. Not until 1916 was the income-tax at last imposed. And after the victory the business men and rich peasants continued to fight bitterly for as long as they could against new taxes, and then to evade them. Their policy was to make Germany pay, and the vain effort to do so weakened France's international position by offending her allies. In the end the Germans and the French rich both resisted successfully, and it was the *rentier* who bore the cost of the war when, in 1926, Poincaré devalued the franc.

The immediate political effects were surprising. The small saver in France had seen what had happened to the currencies of central Europe, and so far from blaming Poincaré for the loss of four-fifths of his capital, he was grateful for retaining what was left to him. The country moved towards the Right. Already, in the 1919 elections, fear of Bolshevism had given the conservatives their first victory at the polls. They overreached themselves in the occupation of the Ruhr. But the *cartel des gauches*, victorious in 1924, fell to pieces when it tackled the financial problem; Clemenceau dismissed it with contemptuous comment, 'O + O + O = O'. In 1928 Poincaré's prestige produced a repetition of the 1919 miracle and another right-wing Chamber. When the world slump came belatedly to France, successive Ministers of Finance (always safe and orthodox men) pursued a policy of deflation and economy which exasperated salaried classes and wage-earners alike. Disgruntled *rentiers*, resentful workers and petty *bourgeoisie* were all affected by the smouldering discontent; and in 1934 the spark of the Stavisky scandal caused a furious blaze where previous affairs of the kind had died away (or been smothered) without attracting much attention.

The Concorde riots of 6 February 1934 were the first since 1848 to destroy a government. So began the critical phase of the Third Republic. Devaluation, even though it might have been worse, had yet struck a heavy blow at confidence in the domestic future. The rise of the Nazis destroyed the hope of security abroad. The effects were none the less powerful for taking time to show themselves. Fear of ruin and fear of war became the dominant motives in men's minds; and the régime was too fragile a construction to stand the strain. The change was sudden; in the summer of 1933 a shrewd English observer had described France as the most stable country in Europe; barely six months later the convulsions had begun.

The immediate mood in the 6 February riots was not of fear but of rage. Abuses, tolerated in prosperity, aroused fury in a time of economic distress, among the small men who had lost their savings, the ex-servicemen, the lower middle class who pride themselves on not being proletarians, who stand aloof from normal political activity, and who participate only in an occasional violent eruptive movement under a Boulanger, a Déroulède, or even a de Gaulle. Their wrath was directed against the Radicals, back in office since the 1932 elections, corrupt and easy-going as they had been for so long. The party had indeed its 'Young Turks' such as Pierre Cot, Léon Martinaud-Déplat and Pierre Mendès-France, a strangely assorted trio as they seem today. But though their hopes and ambitions were high, their influence as yet was small; and their seniors were incapable of dealing with any form of political demonstration more violent than a parliamentary interpellation. Under the pressure of the rioters the government resigned. But power, so far from being seized by a young and dangerous Fascist movement, was peacefully transferred to a self-satisfied octogenarian ex-President of the Republic, Gaston Doumergue. This, however, did little to diminish the resentment and alarm of the Left at the triumph of the riotous leagues, at the deflationary economic policy of successive cabinets, at the menace of Nazi Germany. For motives which differed widely, Radicals, Socialists and Communists buried their feuds, and combined to win the 1936 election. The Popular Front government introduced a series of overdue reforms. But with its victory came a wave of spontaneous strikes, bloodless, but terrifying to an intensely class-conscious *bourgeoisie*; and the reforms, though in the long run fully justified, were unfortunately timed when Germany was organizing for war.

For French foreign policy had broken down. Conscious of France's inferiority against her dangerous neighbour, Marshal Foch had in 1919 wanted to perpetuate her temporary ascendancy by dismembering the enemy, detaching the Rhineland from the Reich. This safeguard, unpopular with the United States and

Britain, had been renounced by Clemenceau in return for a guarantee of support from these two powers, which the prospective allies had almost immediately repudiated. Alone, or even with her Eastern European clients, France was too weak to pursue successfully either a 'hard' or a 'soft' course towards Germany. Poincaré's policy of the strong hand failed in 1924, for neither French nor international opinion would accept it for any length of time. But Briand's attempt to trust the Germans paid no better dividends; reparations were scaled down, allied troops evacuated the Rhineland five years before the treaty required—and the Nazi vote promptly rose to six million. In 1926 Poincaré had dealt with the financial crisis while there was still something to be saved; eight years later his old friend Barthou was assassinated before his attempt to check Germany's diplomatic progress could bring results. From that day forward, except for an intermittent and futile pursuit of the will o' the wisp of Mussolini's goodwill, the Quai d'Orsay abandoned any serious effort to halt the Nazi advance, and sank into increasingly abject dependence on Whitehall.

Domestic disputes and foreign alarms combined to make 1936 the year of schism, when French national unity broke under the strain. The Germans, unopposed, reoccupied the Rhineland in March, and thenceforth the self-styled realists worked more and more openly for an understanding with Hitler. Pierre Laval in the foreground, Caillaux and Malvy in the shadows provided continuity between the new defeatists and their predecessors in the previous war.[1] At the same time internal tensions were brought to a head by the election of seventy Communist deputies and by the great stay-in strikes which greeted the advent of the Popular Front government. Conservative leaders were growing more and more hostile to the parliamentary system. Capitalist magnates like Ernest Mercier, influential right-wing politicians like André Tardieu, prominent figures in the army and police, flirted openly

[1] Laval had first entered office as an associate of Caillaux, whose followers now included Emile Roche, who first proposed ceding the Sudetenland to Hitler: Montigny, Laval's chief ally in July 1940: and Baudouin, once a protégé of Rouvier and later Vichy Foreign Minister. Peyrouton, Malvy's son-in-law, became Pétain's Minister of the Interior—and Eisenhower's Governor-General of Algiers.

with authoritarian ideas. French politics became a cold civil war. Just before becoming prime minister, Léon Blum was savagely beaten in the street by *Action française* thugs: his Minister of the Interior was driven to suicide by the slanders of the right-wing press[1]; and the *cagoulards*, a group of Fascist dissidents from *Action française*, begun their campaign of terrorism and murder. With the Spanish war and the Munich crisis, the internal and external conflicts became inseparably bound together. Most domestic conservatives drifted into a defeatist acceptance of a Europe dominated by Germany; many actively preferred Hitler to Blum. But some attitudes to Nazism were not decided by class-war motives. A minority on the Right remained anti-German (though often pro-Italian). Pacifism was strong among Radicals, Socialists and trade unionists. And the most vociferous pro-Nazi agitators were an ex-Socialist, Marcel Déat, and an ex-Communist, Jacques Doriot.

These furious disputes proved too much for a political régime designed expressly to provide a weak government. It was a fair-weather system, constructed by groups which wanted a quiet life, and worked by men whose talents flourished in peaceful circumstances. Specialists in lobby politics like Camille Chautemps, or eloquent orators like Édouard Herriot, rose to the top; men of action like Clemenceau or his former secretary Georges Mandel were frustrated at every turn. The nominal leaders, as Daniel Halévy remarked, thought with Alain that their duty was to defend the interests of the little man against attack—not to govern the country. When the years of crisis came there was no one to rise to the occasion. At home the deputies abdicated, abandoning their powers and authorizing the government to legislate by decree. Abroad, under the sly Georges Bonnet 'whose long nose', as Mandel bitterly said, 'sniffs danger and responsibility from afar [and who] will hide under any flat stone to avoid it', French foreign policy fell into complete subservience towards Britain. In 1939 France declared war only with extreme reluctance and hesitation; characteristically the Chambers, despite the requirements of the constitution, were never called on to vote the decision[2].

During the months of 'phony war' defeatism was rampant. The

[1] Fascist papers like *Gringoire* led this abominable campaign; but the dishonour of starting the slanders belongs to the Communists.

[2] Credits were voted; their purpose was of course known, but was prudishly not specified.

Communists, outlawed after the Nazi-Soviet pact, began an underground anti-war campaign among the workers which strengthened the hand of the pro-Germans and pacifists (who were not identical, for many of those least eager to fight Hitler were ardent to attack Stalin). When the invasion came, panic spread rapidly. Most of the politicians behaved badly enough; but the moral collapse of the old governing class was still more complete, and the leaders of the army, the first to despair of the Republic, themselves became the militant chieftains of the defeatist camp. One man alone among those in a position of power might have provided a rallying-point. But Mandel, handicapped by being a Jew, was also the most unpopular and isolated man in political life.

Thus the Third Republic, which had confronted the ordeal of the First World War with such unexpected success, failed ignominiously in the second. The reasons were material as well as moral. Behind her economic Maginot line France was falling farther and farther behind her rivals. It is true that after 1918 (as after 1945) the pace of her impressive post-war recovery matched that of her neighbours. But in 1928 she had less than half as much industrial machinery per head as the other industrial nations of Europe. And in the decade before Hitler's war her economy, unlike that of others, declined. Between 1929 and 1938 French industrial production fell by a quarter, while Germany's rose by the same proportion and Britain's increased by a sixth. In agriculture it was much the same story. Corn prices in France exceeded the world price by 30 per cent in 1913, by 200 per cent in 1939.

In manpower, again, France suffered terribly in the First World War: of eight million men mobilized no less than three-quarters were killed or wounded. The economic handicap was severe; allowing for the indirect losses such as the shortfall in the birth-rate, it has been calculated that by the end of the century war and war preparation will have cost France a third of her potential male labour force. The direct military consequences were serious too. The population was not reproducing itself. In 1870 France could call on as many men of military age as Germany; in 1940, less than half as many. Moreover the leadership of her army had stagnated under the soporific effect of victory, while the Germans had learned from the stimulus of defeat. The Riom trial, intended to save the reputations of the soldiers at the expense of the hated politicians, was to show instead how completely the military chieftains had failed either to foresee the development of modern warfare, or even to use the men and materials available to them in the battle.

Yet whatever weight is given to these factors, the moral collapse remains undeniable. The partisan prophets of the Third Republic, Maurras and Alain, had each played their part in the demoralization of their countrymen. The one found his audience among the wealthy, the well-born, the powerful and *bien-pensant* classes which dominated industry and administration and the armed forces. For forty years he had preached unrelenting hatred, exposed or invented scandal, and persuaded the 'élite' of France that the people were cowardly and degenerate, the political leadership rotten with corruption, the country ripe for a terrible and deserved catastrophe. The other's disciples filled the teaching profession, the enormously influential 'republican clergy'; and with equal persistence he had taught them to mistrust all leaders, to discount talk of foreign danger as a mere device to cover sinister designs at home, to mock at appeals for sacrifice or discipline, and to identify civic virtue with comfortable and anarchic individualism. So the masses distrusted those who might have led, and the classes hated and despised those who might have followed. Maurras with his exclusive nationalist passion, Alain with his fanatical democratic zeal, each striving to undermine the foundations on which the rival idol rested, helped to bring the whole temple crashing to the ground.

Yet the downfall of the Third Republic cannot be blamed only on the weakness of the régime, the violence of ideological conflict, or the fear and hatred of the workers which gripped a middle class deprived of its sense of security. In addition, Frenchmen of all opinions knew well enough that their country could no longer hope to police Europe alone, and the years between the wars showed them that they could expect no Anglo-Saxon help until too late. When Germany revived, stronger and more aggressive than ever, the struggle to resist came to seem increasingly hopeless. It is significant that the German propaganda campaign of 1940 was directed at French patriotism rather than at French individual selfishness. Its theme was not 'Why throw your life away for a hopeless cause?', but 'Why sacrifice the future of the nation by another blood-letting in the interests of the foreigner?' Such ideas influenced many of the defeatists and pacifist leaders, who resigned themselves with regret to France's decline, and sought only the comfortable dependent status of a satellite power which no longer attempts to determine her own fate or influence that of others. The Republic had chosen to travel on the line of least resistance; Vichy was the terminus.

So the Third Republic committed suicide in due constitutional form, and by a seven-to-one majority the National Assembly voted to confer on Marshal Pétain powers not only to govern without parliamentary control, but to legislate and draw up the new constitutional settlement as well. During the four years of authoritarian rule which followed, France once again proved herself, as Bodley had called her, 'the land of political surprises where lost causes come to life again'. One after another the alternatives to the Republic were tried and discarded.

In the early months the old-fashioned reactionaries held power, dominant in the Marshal's entourage and numerous in the cabinet. Most of them had belonged to or sympathized with *Action française*, many had been active in the 6 February riots or victims of the Popular Front, and their aim was to replace the detested democratic system with a traditionalist, authoritarian, Catholic régime. Marshal Pétain's *Ordre nouveau* was nothing but Marshal MacMahon's *Ordre moral*, taken out of storage rather than brought up to date. These men had no love for either Britain or Germany; their external policy was *attentiste*, and after their Pyrrhic victory in overthrowing Laval in December 1940, most of them were soon driven from power by Nazi pressure.

Next came the leaders of the financial, industrial and academic worlds. Men of this type had once formed the core of the Orleanist party, had rallied to the conservative republic when it seemed better able to protect their privileges, and were as prompt to desert it in adversity. The Darlan cabinet was full of distinguished professors and energetic business men. Thirdly (though all these groups overlapped) there were the technicians, resentful of politicians who interfered with the smooth running of their services, or convinced that a democratic state was too unstable a base for positive or constructive activity. During the 'thirties the admirals, the *conseillers d'état*, the *inspecteurs des finances*, had grown more and more exasperated with the Republic. So general was the disaffection that the Vichy régime has been called 'the French state stripped of its democratic façade'. Concerned for efficient administration, usually contemptuous of archaic reaction, but indifferent or hostile towards political liberty, such men (including some of those from private business) were heirs of the Bonapartist tradition.

All these groups collaborated with the Germans, while often trying to moderate their demands by the passive obstruction at which Frenchmen excel. By 1944 all had failed, and the newest enemies of democracy came into their own: Darnand with his ruthless militia, Déat and Doriot and the Paris Fascists who, under German protection, had bitterly denounced the traditionalists of Vichy, and loudly demanded a popular, national-socialist system. Manœuvring with his customary skill among the factions, Laval employed his disreputable talents to bargain—though on ever less favourable terms—on his country's and his own behalf.

The men of Vichy fulfilled none of their promises. Government, dependent on the whims of an easily influenced octogenarian, grew less firm than ever. Ministers changed as rapidly. Policies became even less coherent. The factional struggle for power went on with unabated fury. Class antagonisms were not resolved but aggravated by Vichy's blatant favouritism for the rich. Centralization and bureaucracy were not relaxed but carried further. The new masters had charged that justice was tainted under the rule of their adversaries; under their own it was poisoned. The new moral order had corruption, delation and cruelty for its fruits. And the very factions which had once proclaimed themselves the only true Frenchmen, which had implied that their opponents were outside the pale of the nation, now committed themselves to collaboration with the enemy. Seventy years had been needed to discredit the Third Republic. Its authoritarian critics condemned themselves in four.

In resistance to the Germans and to the Frenchmen who increasingly became their tools, many of the 'internal *émigrés*' found a full part to play. In some right-wing and even royalist circles, especially in the army, the resistance early gained a foothold. The Catholic democrats, growing in numbers and activity under the inspiration of the *Sillon* for half a century, now 'found themselves' as an organized movement. When in June 1941 French national interests came to coincide with those of the Soviet Union, the heroic conduct of the Communist rank and file wiped out among the less politically minded resisters the memory of past and the suspicion of future betrayals by the party bosses. And, like any revolutionary movement, the resistance was largely an affair of youth. So men hoped that from the trials of war, occupation and liberation a genuinely new democracy would arise. In 1945 only one voter in twenty-five favoured the restoration of the Third Republic. Only one in eight voted for the old Right, even under its resistance leadership. The former republican figure-heads had forfeited their claims to power by their defeatism before the war, and the anti-republican 'élite' by collaboration during it. It was time for new men. For a brief moment it seemed that the Republic had at last won over the best of those who had stood aloof: that devout Catholics, militant workers, and youthful idealists could take their place as full citizens, helping to build the Fourth Republic, *la République dure et pure*.

BIBLIOGRAPHICAL NOTE

General Histories

BROGAN, D. W. *The Development of Modern France, 1870–1939*, 1967 (an excellent detailed narrative history).
COBBAN, A. *A History of Modern France, vol. 3: 1871–1962*, 1965.
WRIGHT, G. *France in Modern Times*, 1962.

Critical essays on the history of the period

BEAU DE LOMÉNIE, E. *Les Responsabilités des dynasties bourgeoises:* t. 2, *de MacMahon à Poincaré*, 1947; t. 3, *la guerre et l'immédiat aprés-guerre*, 1954.
THOMSON, D. *Democracy in France*, Oxford, 1964.

Essays on the state of France

BODLEY, J. E. C. *France* (2 vols.), 1898 (an invaluable description of politics and society at the opening of the period).
EARLE, E. M., ed. *Modern France: Problems of the Third and Fourth Republics*, Princeton, 1951 (twenty-eight American studies).
HALÉVY, D. *La République des comites*, 1934.
JOUVENEL, R. DE. *La République des camarades*, 1934 (two critics, one bitter and one sardonic, of French political practice under the rule of the Radicals).
MAILLAUD, P. *France*, Oxford, 1942 (a penetrating sketch).

Particular periods and men

ARON, R. *Histoire de Vichy 1940–44*, 1954 (abridged as *The Vichy Regime*, 1958).

BINION, R. *Defeated Leaders,* New York, 1960 (Caillaux, Jouvenel, Tardieu).

CHAPMAN, G. *The Dreyfus Case, a Reassessment*, 1955.

CHASTENET, J. *La République triomphante (1893–1906)*, 1955.

CHASTENET, J. *La France de Monsieur Fallières (1905–14), 1949.*

COLTON, J. *Léon Blum,* New York, 1966.

FARMER, P. *Vichy, Political Dilemma,* New York, 1955.

GOGUEL, F. *La Politique des partis sous la Troisième République*, 1946 (a most useful general history, mainly on the inter-war years).

GOLDBERG, H. *The Life of Jean Jaurès,* Madison, Wis., 1962.

JACKSON, J. H. *Clemenceau and the Third Republic*, 1946.

LACOUTURE, J. *De Gaulle,* Paris, 1965; New York, 1968.

THOMSON, D. *Two Frenchmen: Pierre Laval and Charles de Gaulle,* 1951.

Particular topics and points of view

ALAIN (pseud. of E. CHARTIER) *Eléments d'une doctrine radicale*, 1925.

BLOCH, M. *Strange Defeat,* 1949.

DANSETTE, A. *Religious History of Contemporary France*, 1961.

GIRARDET, R. *La Société militaire dans la France contemporaine, 1815–1939,* 1953.

JOLL, J., ed. *Decline of the Third Republic,* 1959.

KINDLEBERGER, C. P. *Economic Growth in France and Britain 1851–1950,* Cambridge, Mass., 1964.

LORWIN, V. R. *The French Labor Movement,* Cambridge, Mass., 1954.

MAURRAS, C. *Devant l'Allemagne éternelle*, 1937.

RÉMOND, R. *The Right Wing in France from 1815 to de Gaulle,* Philadelphia, Oxford, 1966.

SHARP, W. R. *The Government of the French Republic,* New York, 1939.

SIEGFRIED, A. *Tableau des partis en France,* 1930 (tr.: *France, a Study in Nationality,* Yale, 1930; an excellent discussion of French political psychology).

TARDIEU, A. *La Révolution à refaire:* t.I, *Le Souverain captif,* 1936; t.2, *La Profession parlementaire,* 1937 (a denunciation of democracy by the leading conservative of his day).

THIBAUDET, A. *Les Idées politiques de la France,* 1932.

MAX BELOFF

The Fourth Republic (1945-55)

➤➤➤⟩⟨⊙⟩⟨⊙⟩⟨⟨⟨

The first volume of the war memoirs of General de Gaulle
begins with a passage whose sombre eloquence defies
translation—a passage in which the leader of the Fighting
France of war-time describes that conception of his native country
which has always inspired his thought and conduct. For him,
France cannot by her very nature support mediocrity. Her history
must inevitably be composed of glorious achievements and
exemplary catastrophes. Her people carry within themselves
centrifugal tendencies only held in check when their energies are
devoted to some vast collective enterprise. Greatness is inseparable
from de Gaulle's idea of France.[1]

Yet when this book was published in 1954, at a time when the
political influence of de Gaulle had seemingly sunk into insignificance and when his erstwhile parliamentary following had
disintegrated into a leaderless and divided flock of mere politicians,
a passage of this kind came as something of a shock to the
ordinary reader, so far did it seem to be in fact, and in spirit, from
the France of everyday experience under the Fourth Republic.
The contrast between the ideal and the reality is to our minds one
major distinction between the contemporary France which is our
present subject, and the France of any period since the late fifteenth century. France is no longer a Great Power by the standards
of the global political constellation within which she has her being.
Just as the France of the late fifteenth century irrupted on to the
Italian scene and by so doing dwarfed the petty states of the
Peninsula, so France since the liberation has been overshadowed
by the world powers, the Soviet Union and the United States.
The transformation has by no means been a sudden one; at the
very time that de Gaulle was growing up in the atmosphere of
intensified patriotism that he describes, the inexorable curves of

[1] See Charles de Gaulle, *Mémoires de Guerre*, Vol. I, p. 1 (1954).

247

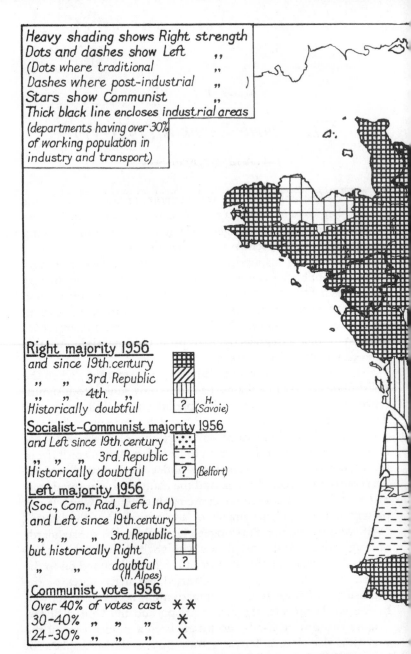

Heavy shading shows Right strength
Dots and dashes show Left ,,
(Dots where traditional ,,
Dashes where post-industrial ,,)
Stars show Communist ,,
Thick black line encloses industrial areas
(departments having over 30%
of working population in
industry and transport)

<u>Right majority 1956</u>
and since 19th.century
  ,,   ,,   3rd. Republic
  ,,   ,,   4th.   ,,
Historically doubtful   ? H. (Savoie)

<u>Socialist–Communist majority 1956</u>
and Left since 19th. century
  ,,   ,,   ,, 3rd. Republic
Historically doubtful   ? (Belfort)

<u>Left majority 1956</u>
(Soc., Com., Rad., Left Ind)
and Left since 19th.century
  ,,   ,,   ,, 3rd. Republic
but historically Right
  ,,   ,,   doubtful
           (H. Alpes)

<u>Communist vote 1956</u>
Over 40% of votes cast ✶✶
30-40% ,, ,, ,, ✶
24-30% ,, ,, ,, X

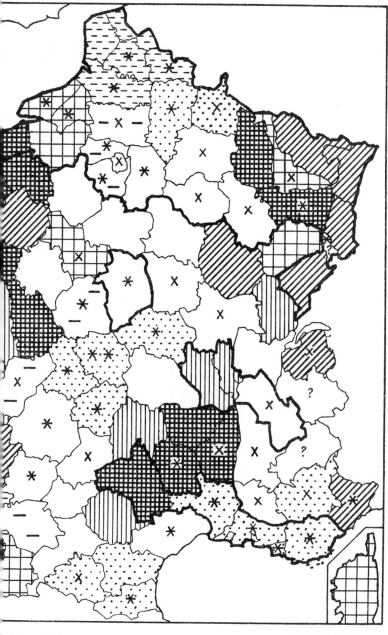

population, of the production of coal and steel, and of all that goes
to make up industrial and military strength were tending against
her. Germany was striding ahead; just as beyond Germany, the
Slavs in their turn were setting out on the upward path of national
growth. But the essentials of France's relative decline were
partially concealed by the outcome of the First World War; France,
saved in the short run by Russian strength, in the long run by
American strength, yet saw herself as a Great Power—and the
ultimate reckoning was delayed.

After the events of 1940, only a superb anachronism like de
Gaulle could altogether ignore the realities of the situation; and
the relations between French government and French society in
the decade since the liberation and the armistice cannot be understood unless one appreciates as a necessary background to the
constitutional and party struggle and to the structural reforms,
actual or attempted, the psychological problem of learning to live
as a Power of the second or even the third rank. It has been a
particularly difficult task because, although the United States and
Russia were both prepared in their different ways to accept the
1940 *débâcle* as conclusive proof of France's decline, it was an
axiom of British policy—though one little understood or appreciated in France—that France should be given the formal status of
a Great Power both in the post-war arrangements for Europe and
in the arrangements for a world security system. Let me quote
Mr Bohlen's minutes of the Yalta Conference:

'The Prime Minister felt that the question of the zones of
occupation in Germany "brought up the whole question of the
future role of France in Europe and that he personally felt that
France should play a very important role. He pointed out that
France had had a long experience in dealing with the Germans,
that they were the largest naval power, and could be of great help
in the administration of Germany. He went on to say that Great
Britain did not want to bear the whole weight of an attack by
Germany in the future, and for this reason they would like to see
France strong and in possession of a large army. He said it was
problematical how long the United States forces would be able
to stay in Europe and therefore it was essential that France be
relied upon to assist in the long term control of Germany." In
countering the Russian arguments against French participation,

Mr. Churchill said: "British public opinion would not understand why France was being excluded from a problem which was of such direct concern to her." "France had gone down before the attack of the new German tank and air units" . . . but . . . "He observed that the destiny of great nations was not decided by the temporary state of their technical apparatus".[1]

This optimistic view was even more natural to Frenchmen who, impressed by the achievements of the Resistance and of the forces of Fighting France, tended to overlook the fact that France's salvation had come from outside, even more conclusively this time than in 1914–18.

Nevertheless the defeat itself could not be overlooked, and a number of alternative solutions to the problem of relations between France and the rest of the world presented themselves, and have ever since continued to furnish much of the stuff of French politics. Indeed, one could go further and say that the cleavages in French society which France had inherited from her past and which coloured the history of the Third Republic lived on into the Fourth, which added new ones. Into the conflicts between clerical and anti-clerical, between collectivist and capitalist, between democrat and anti-democrat, were injected the new conflicts between partisans of different approaches to this overriding problem of external affairs.

There were five main types of solution; though some of them naturally overlapped in their application and as to their supporters. There were, first, those who like General de Gaulle himself fundamentally denied that the problem existed at all. What had let France down, had been the weakness of her institutions, and the greed of sections of the community who had placed their interests before that of the nation. Let France equip herself with a stable governmental system, let her reform her armed forces, allowing the inventiveness of her people to serve as remedy for their paucity in numbers—numbers again reduced though not, as it proved, devitalized by war-time losses—let her cultivate the military virtues of self-sacrifice and obedience, and all would yet be well.

A lead along these lines had been given by de Gaulle himself

[1] See the proceedings of the Yalta Conference of February 1945 published in the *New York Times*, 17 March 1955.

and had inspired much of the Resistance. One French régime paralysed by its own anarchic weakness had abdicated in defeat; another which was the product of a criminal surrender to the enemy had tried to meet France's problems by an unwarrantable recourse to personal authority. The French nation repudiated the Third Republic as it repudiated Vichy. The struggle for liberation from the German yoke was also the struggle for a new Revolution.[1]

Some historians of the early years of the Fourth Republic have seen its story as essentially that of a Revolution that failed. They have argued that, quite apart from the Communist leadership which had its own plans for the kind of Revolution it wanted, there was in France at the time of the liberation a general determination to transform the social order by the united action of the entire nation. To discover the reason why this desire was frustrated seems to them to be the main problem which faces the historian of this period.

Various explanations in these terms have been given. It could be argued that essentially the desire for a Revolution was an illusion. What had bound the nation together, what had held together the centrifugal forces of which de Gaulle writes, was the desire to get rid of foreign rule. Once the invader had gone, the old divisions reasserted themselves; and Gaullism turned out to be not something transcending classes and parties but as just one more political attitude among many. De Gaulle on French soil could not be the universally accepted national leader that the necessities of the struggle had imposed upon all the resistance groups—including even and especially the Communists—but only the leader of a national movement. Thence the descent was easy to being the leader of a party, and thence in turn to a new solitude, awaiting more or less alone some new crisis which might cause the country to turn once more to him and to his ideas. Nor was this in itself surprising. If the sufferings of war, the horrors of captivity and deportation and the risks of the Resistance had built new bridges between members of different groups it had not obliterated their identities. And for the non-heroic masses, the divisions of the country enforced by the Occupying Power and the different effects of war-time economic developments upon different classes in the community had not made for unity; rather the reverse. Finally, it was to be expected that for the heroic and non-heroic

[1] See e.g. de Gaulle, op. cit., p. 678.

alike, the war would come to be seen mainly as an unwelcome interruption in their personal lives, and that their energies would as soon as possible be diverted to private rather than public purposes. In post-war France—and not in France alone—the private sphere bulked large.

There is also one more specific explanation. The time when large-scale structural alterations would have been easiest would have been the period immediately after the liberation. The new French political system which then emerged was essentially composed of a double strand: Fighting France, that is to say de Gaulle, and the Resistance, meaning in fact mainly the Communists, whose 176 martyrs were inflated into 75,000 for the sake of electoral propaganda.[1] The Communists were not interested in reforms which would merely strengthen and purify the existing social order. Ultimately, they desired a Soviet-type revolution at the moment when this should fit into the plan of their Russian mentors. For the time being, however, they were prepared to help France to recover, and the discipline in production which their presence in the Government made possible laid the foundations of this recovery on the technical side, even though France failed on the vital financial front owing to the successful opposition of new or revived interest groups. In these circumstances, what the Communists did was to seize what levers of command they could and use the Vichy interlude as an excuse for a 'purge' on as large a scale as possible. They came to infiltrate and divide, not to reform and unite. Without the Communists, given their control over the trade unions, there was no real majority for reform.

Externally too, the peculiar position of the Communists at this stage is vital for an understanding of the weakness of de Gaulle's position. The original Gaullist attitude to the problem of France's place in the world had taken the traditional nationalist line of dealing with the German threat by means of territorial annexations on the Rhine, and the fragmentation of what was left of Germany. By a curious paradox this produced in the immediately post-liberation period, a belief that France could rely on the Soviet Union as being the only one of the Great Powers likely to sympathize with such aims. Stalin's contempt for France had been missed by the French, who had been more upset by the open tactlessness of Roosevelt, especially where de Gaulle himself was

[1] H. Lüthy, *A l'heure de son clocher* (1955), p. 83.

concerned. Almost the first sequel to de Gaulle's triumphal return to Paris was his visit to Moscow and his conclusion there of the treaty with the Soviet Union. This also was based, of course, upon an intolerable misunderstanding of Soviet aims and of the whole international constellation. In the end the position was untenable; there could not be a European settlement on these lines any more than there could, in the long run, be a French Government based on an internal alliance of so paradoxical a kind as that between de Gaulle and Thorez. Within a short time, de Gaulle himself was to use for his recent allies the term 'separatists'—true enough in the sense in which he used it, but doubled-edged nevertheless.

A second approach to the problem of France's relation to the rest of the world could be described as a modified Gaullism, in that it accepted the view that France could only become great once more by an enormous effort of self-disciplined reform; but different from de Gaulle's own creed in two ways. In the first place, it did not accept the view of which de Gaulle made himself the principal exponent from the time of the debates about the constitutional form which the Fourth Republic should take, namely, that France could only get a stronger executive by abandoning the parliamentary in favour of the presidential type of government. Whether de Gaulle ever correctly understood that the United States constitution presents very serious inconveniences to an Executive as soon as his policies require either legislation or appropriations, is not clear. At any rate he himself was clearly convinced, largely as a result of his unavailing efforts to get his own defence policies adopted in the pre-war period, that France would get nowhere with governments dependent for their existence upon shifting parliamentary majorities. Constitutional reform of some kind was bound to be on the agenda as soon as it was seen that de Gaulle's gloomy predictions about the probable result of the constitution actually adopted were justified by the event; but for this group, constitutional reform was not as for de Gaulle, the *sine qua non* of all action. In the second place, it tended to take the view that what France needed was not only more resources but more discrimination in their application—a readier acceptance of the need for bringing ends into harmony with means. This was the essence of the Mendès-France programme of 1954-5. And it is significant that it was on the imperial front, by the truce in Indo-China and by attempted concessions in North Africa that

Mendès-France made his attempt to reduce the scale of France's commitments.

This eventually brought Mendès-France and those who thought with him into a rather sharp conflict with another group—those who had hoped to remedy France's weakness in Europe by calling in new worlds in Asia and above all in Africa to redress the balance of the old. Just as Britain was preserved as a Great Power not by virtue of her island resources but because of the existence of the Empire and Commonwealth—and French opinion was manifestly cloudy about both—so, it was now argued, the French Union could be made to serve the destiny and interests of France. That in a world of awakening nationalisms, the Union might demand as much or more from France as it contributed to her, was masked partially by the tendency to ascribe any difficulties that arose to the intrigues and jealousies of rival powers, first Britain, and then America—and neither can be accounted wholly blameless in this regard—and partially by the fact that imperial interests, and particularly North African interests, were themselves among the most powerful of the sectional interests which dominated French politics at home.

In the event, the French in Indo-China fought a war against Communism which many Frenchmen felt not to be their war, and in defence of positions which many Frenchmen felt should not be held, and would not have been but for private interests involved. In North Africa, the situation was grimmer, since the position of the French settlers could not be disregarded, and since the settlers themselves were more than prepared to use force to maintain themselves in lands which owed what prosperity they enjoyed largely to their own enterprise. In no case was it possible to work out a consistent policy or to keep to it; nor was it certain that any clearer line would emerge when the problem of policy towards tropical Africa came up for solution in its turn.

Indeed there ran through the whole imperial idea as now advocated, a veritable series of contradictions including an attempt to combine a policy of a limited assimilationism for an indigenous élite as the sole answer to political demands, with an unwillingness to do anything that might make the relationship between the metropolis and the Empire a two-way one, especially in the economic sense. The idea of developing the real resources of the Empire, other than those in military manpower, had never made any real headway except for different reasons in Indo-China and Morocco, and was now largely beyond France's powers. For the French, for all the sentiment attached to the projects for a French Union as a result of the share of the African territories in resistance and liberation, had no political doctrine suitable for the task they were now setting themselves. The imperial idea had never had any but a most exiguous appeal and on the Left anti-colonialism was rampant. And not only the Left lacked the foundations for a new policy.

It has indeed been argued that France presents the paradox of having an overseas empire without possessing a theory with which to justify its existence; that no French intellectual even of the Right had advanced a theory of the mission of the white races or of France's civilizing role; though these have been among the commonplaces of politicians. And it is possible that in France more than elsewhere the lack of doctrine is a serious political handicap.[1]

These three schools of thought were essentially in agreement in acting according to the presuppositions of sovereign states of the traditional kind. In contrast to them there emerged a relatively new element: the 'Europeans'. It would take us too far outside the proper limits of our subject to analyse the progress and decline of the European idea; though it is possible to give an account of the French problem almost wholly in these terms.[2] To analyse the rôles of the various institutions, both consultative and executive, both international and supra-national, that were set up in the period would take one beyond the horizon of French thought and politics. Nor were the French responsible for what did most harm to the European idea, its premature linking with the alleged need for German rearmament, so suddenly perceived by Washington in the summer of 1950, and the consequent endeavour through the European Defence Community (EDC) to make the European framework bear more than could reasonably be expected of it. Now that the line of German integration with the West has been found to lie through a North Atlantic rather than a European link—as could indeed have been foreseen—and now that this too is beginning to be seen as a beginning rather than an end, it is also too early to say whether we have seen the last of the European

[1] See R. Aron, 'Les Intellectuels français et l'Utopie', *Preuves*, April 1955.
[2] See e.g. H. Lüthy, op. cit.

idea as an important factor in French politics. Clearly, there were still, in 1955, important men in France who thought otherwise.

What one can say is that the idea had during the first post-war decade a multiple and often contradictory appeal. It certainly had appealed as one way to end the Franco-German conflict—that conflict which is to Frenchmen still the real core of all international problems: more real certainly, than the remoter threat of Communist Russia. It also seemed a possible way of escape from the economic difficulties which beset France long before the political *débâcle* of 1940.

It is almost universally admitted—and one does not need to linger upon it—that France's problems arise in considerable measure from the fact that her price-structure is out of line with that of the rest of the world, and that this springs in part at least from the excesses of protectionism in which the country has increasingly indulged. Protected from external competition, and unaffected by the teachings of Keynesian economics, French business in many fields lacks incentive to increase production and lower costs because it prefers to work on high profit margins from a smaller output. Protectionism of another kind in the form of concealed or overt subsidies multiplies not only small producers, but small distributors, making a relatively weak productive sector support an unbearably high overhead; a celebrated instance is the fantastic distortion of French food distribution through the virtual monopoly of the Paris *Halles*.

The idea of creating a European market appeals to two different schools of thought about the remedy. The liberal economists believe in the virtues of open competition. Destroy the edifice of protection, and French industry will be forced to compete or go under! Nothing less brutal will provide the necessary incentive; and those sectors that make their way will have a wider market in which they can profit by the economy of scale that Frenchmen believe to be the main if not the sole source of American prosperity.

The other group—the planners—believe that the same results can be achieved if international planning of the 'Schuman' Coal and Steel Community type is extended to other fields, and that such planning would help to eliminate some of the unpleasant by-products which would otherwise follow from a direct exposure of France to naked competition.

But although the economic argument attracts the technocrat, the ideological drive is political; and it is here that it runs into difficulties. Federalism, it has been pointed out, is a difficult conception for a country that knows nothing of intermediate authorities in its own internal life, where indeed the destruction of such authorities was one of the unreversed consequences of Bourbon absolutism, the doctrinaire centralism of the triumphant Revolution, and the Napoleonic genius for administration. French writings on federalism never make sufficiently plain the fact that federal Europe and French sovereignty are incompatible. But French politicians of all parties are aware of the implied threat to their own authority.

There is however a special as well as a general problem. As has been shown repeatedly, the price of going any distance with supra-national institutions, either economic or political, is to create a division between Continental Europe and Great Britain. But to proceed without Great Britain means, for France, finding herself face to face with a disquietingly recovering Germany, and taking part in a Europe moved by an ideology strongly Catholic in inspiration. Both of these perspectives have alarmed elements on the French Left, particularly among the Socialists. Thus the European idea has been an important factor of division in French politics quite apart from whatever reality it may have or may not have had in itself. It would not be altogether true to say that 'Little Europe'—a federation of Western Europe without Britain and Scandinavia—has been the party preserve, almost the *raison d'être*, of the MRP—preventing this party of Catholic democrats from relapsing into the insignificance which most people expected would be their fate when once the extreme Right had recovered from its post-Vichy ostracism—but it would not be so far from the truth as all that. The venom with which partisans of 'Little Europe' —and not only in France—swung into action against Mendès-France for his failure to press the ratification of EDC in 1954 is significant enough.

The only other element in France which has a policy of its own is of course the Communist Party. The exploitation of their rôle in the Resistance, and of their position in the early governments of the post-liberation period, has given the Communists a position from which they have shown no serious signs of being dislodged. Indeed it is perhaps one of the minor miracles of our time that they did not succeed so in infiltrating the machinery of the state as to create a situation not unlike that of Czechoslovakia in 1948; it is something that France has not had to be preserved from a Communist coup by foreign arms. The position they have retained is however a vital one. They control from the point of view of vote-getting a large proportion of the French proletariat, and have an important access to other elements of the population whose particular grievances, as a party perpetually in opposition, it costs them nothing to exploit. Even the weighting of the electoral law against them before the 1951 elections could not do more than affect the representation of the party in the National Assembly: the 5,431,000 Communist voters in 1946 getting 183 seats; the 4,934,000 in 1951 getting 101. In 1956 the party could claim to represent almost 26 per cent of the voters as against 15½ per cent in 1936. Furthermore the lack of a sense of the political situation as a whole on the part of certain groups and their proneness to act on a narrow view of their particular interests, the accessibility of so large a proportion of the electorate to the slogan of no enemies on the 'Left', the ability of the Communists to play upon the fear of Germany and the dislike of the American 'occupation', and finally the political imbecility of some important French intellectuals—Sartre for instance—all combine to give the Communists a sphere of activity beyond that provided by their nominal adherents.

There is perhaps no need to go deeply into the suggestion that the French are peculiarly vulnerable to Communism because they do not, for historical reasons, find the Soviet example as repellent as do some other western peoples—and this, because in many respects, such as its concern for doctrinal purity and its use of terror, it resembles their own Revolution which they are brought up to admire. It might equally well be urged that a country which has exalted individualism, and in which the idea of individual self-fulfilment is still regarded as something to which social goals ought to be subordinated, should find the Communist ideology with the strong puritan twist the Russians have given it extremely alien and even repulsive. In fact the Soviet Union that the French Communists exalt is not of course for most of their following a real country at all; it is the utopian negation of all that they most dislike or resent at home. Its main advantage still lies in its distance.

Comfort for those who hate and fear Communism is often derived from the fact that just because Communism is to so great an extent merely a symbol of social protest, the efforts by the Communists to use their strength particularly in the trade-union movement for purely political aims has been unsuccessful. Despite Communist opposition of the most strenuous kind, the Marshall Plan, NATO and the Paris Pacts all went through.

But such consolations are altogether too easy. Defeats have not substantially weakened the Communist hold on their followers, nor have the much-advertised divisions among the leadership. The Soviet line is still accepted as a whole; and the Communists continue to be 'separatists' in de Gaulle's sense, patriots of another country.

Nevertheless the significant thing for France has not been the menace of absorption into Soviet Europe—to this there are other impediments. It has been the absolute distortion of the French political system owing to the presence within it of a party which, since 1947, has been unable to enter into a government combination. It is true that the Communists failed to get the complete rule by the Assembly that would have been the result of the first proposed constitution and which was calculated as with the 'People's Democracies' to smooth their path to power, but the actual Constitution has in fact made the Executive as dependent on parliamentary permutations as that of the Third Republic. And it is here that the presence of the Communists has had its effect. In the first Assembly, it looked as though 'tripartism' was inevitable. With the 183 Communist votes removed, a government could not afford to sacrifice more than 125 of the others in order to avoid being put in a minority. After the 1951 elections, despite the fall in the number of Communist deputies, the position looked even worse, since the 120 RPF (Gaullist) members should, on their leader's principles, have been unavailable for any government combination. This meant that a government could not afford to lose more than 93 votes from the uncommitted. Only the gradual break-up of the Gaullist group eased the situation; and then not conclusively. Both the so-called 'left' coalition of Mendès-France and the so-called 'right' coalition of Edgar Faure were kept in being only by constant and ultimately stultifying manœuvres.

The difficulties have been even greater than this purely numerical analysis of the parliamentary scene would seem to indicate. In the first place, the Socialists, for obvious reasons, dislike being the exposed left-wing of a coalition depending on votes from the right. The same is to some extent true of at least part of the MRP. This means that in a country where the Left has been in a majority, whether you get this by adding the MRP votes to those of Socialists and Communists to get a 'social left' majority, or add the Radicals and their associates to get a traditional 'anti-clerical left' majority, the pendulum in the assembly has come to rest somewhere around the 'right-centre'. The Left also failed in 1948 to eliminate the Upper House from the Constitution; and even its very moderate powers of delay have still had to be taken into account in all political calculations. Since the new Council of the Republic is in composition and temper not unlike the old Senate, the 'right-centre' has derived a further element of strength from its survival; though the Radical element came out against Faure, and in favour of the second-ballot in November 1955.

Nor is this all. Because the divisions over 'Europe' have been added to the older ones over constitutional questions, over clericalism and anti-clericalism and over economic policy, the parties themselves are deeply divided; nor in the electoral or constitutional system has there been anything that can help them increase their internal discipline. The electoral system in the Fourth Republic, as in the Third, has been blamed for the multiplicity of parties. But the multiplicity has always expressed genuine divisions; indeed one can say that French parties are too few for the diversity of interests and opinions they are supposed to represent.

How true this is can be seen from the events of the late autumn of 1955 when the Prime Minister, Edgar Faure, tried to secure a bill dissolving the Assembly before the expiration of its term in order to appeal to the country on the British model. At once a struggle for the reform of the electoral law was set in motion—with the Upper House playing a leading rôle—and each party did its best to secure that system which would give it most seats. These efforts cancelled each other out. And by a final irony, Faure got his dissolution under the 1951 electoral law as the result of losing a vote of confidence by the 'constitutional' majority, and so being able to use the right of dissolving the Assembly conferred upon a Prime Minister, if the Assembly behave in this way twice within eighteen months.

Ministerial instability arising from a multi-party system did not, in the first decade of the Fourth Republic, appear to be a product either of the constitutional system which had been modified from that of the Third partly with a view to making the assembly more conscious of its responsibilities, or of the electoral system. The connexion in people's minds of the 'second-ballot' system with its opportunities for unsavoury local bargaining, and of the single-seat constituency with its alleged propensity to favour a parish-pump attitude on the part of the deputy and the electors—the two characteristic features of the method in force at the time of the Third Republic's decline and fall—had played into the hands of the larger parties of the immediately post-liberation period. They preferred proportional representation which they hoped would make the deputy the servant of his party rather than of his constituency, or of quite small pressure-groups within it. The electoral law of 1946 was modified in 1951 by a provision designed to facilitate local alliances and, by so doing, to weaken the Communists on the one wing and the Gaullists on the other. In this the law was successful, the Gaullists getting 26 fewer seats than they would otherwise have done and the Communists 71 fewer.[1] In the long-drawn-out dissolution crisis of 1955 efforts were made to get a change with the Radicals again trying to go back to the pre-1940 system, and other parties producing different modes calculated to suit their own particular situations. The dissolution cut these short; and the electoral law of 1951 survived to govern the election of January 1956.

These manœuvres provided conclusive evidence that the party system was the cause, not the result of, the electoral law, though in some respects it was bound in turn to be affected by it. And the party system itself continued, as in the past, to reflect the fact that France was divided not only into classes, and into rather well-defined geographical regions with distinct political attitudes of their own, but also into groupings around certain central ideas. These ideas were sometimes dismissed as abstractions by those who were depressed by the contrast between the chatter of the politicians and the real needs of the country, and who pointed to

[1] I am using the figures given by P. M. Williams in his *Politics in Post-war France* (1954), pp. 324–5.

the fact that many of France's real achievements in the post-war period, the modernization of transport and power and of important sections of industry under the 'Monnet Plan' and its successors, had gone on, as it were, on the margin of politics, in regions where the expert and the bureaucrat could work unhampered by party cries. But abstraction was hardly the right word. It was not the domination of reason but the domination of history that was at the root of the matter—the inability to find any political means of transcending divisions based on past controversies.

That this was so was partly due to the conservatism of French society; in few countries did traditional social institutions and patterns of behaviour more doggedly resist changes urged in the name of progress, or of such modern idols as productivity. Much of the anti-Americanism that disfigured French intellectual life and occasionally threatened dangerously to distort French foreign policy was due no doubt to jealousy, and to resentment at the presence on French soil of so many representatives of a more powerful and above all much richer ally. But behind all this was the stark fact that French civilization and American civilization were not based upon identical values in the mid-twentieth century, and even though the difference may have been exaggerated by the fact that most Frenchmen were almost as ignorant of the true face of America, as many of them were of the true face of Communist Russia, it was not a difference that anyone was entitled to ignore.

The result of such social conservatism—which the giving of votes to women, some not very far-reaching reforms of the educational system, an important elaboration of the system of social security, and some increase in attention to sport and other open-air activities as a consequence of the further extension of the principle of 'holidays with pay' did not profoundly disturb—was to make it certain that the new wine would have to go into the old bottles; there were no other bottles for it to go into; and the artificial plastic containers offered by de Gaulle or by Mendès-France revealed the fragility of their kind.

Indeed in some respects, the older divisions proved more important than the newer; possibly because the Vichy experiment with its conscious antiquarianism had deliberately revived the conflict between the Revolution and the *ancien régime* which, next to the Wars of Religion, or if one prefers it, the Albigensian

Crusade, was the oldest of them all. Since the republican idea itself was not seriously under fire—the fascist overtones of M. Poujade's 'small man' movement which made some headway in 1954–5 were not so far really menacing—this meant giving to political controversy an essentially religious twist. It was the decision, in 1951, to give a small subsidy to Catholic schools that caused the final split between the Socialists and the other possible parties of a government coalition. It provided a platform—if an irrelevant one—for Pierre Mendès-France to use in opposition to create a new *bloc* on the left and enabled him and his Socialist allies to enter the lists for the December 1955 election campaign on a 'republican' i.e. anti-clerical platform. The victims of the development were, on the other hand, of course, the MRP.

One undoubted result of the fall of France and of the Vichy interlude had been to give to elements among French Catholics a new impetus to find a bridge between their faith and the needs of contemporary society—particularly that urban industrial society, for the most part long-estranged from the Church. This impetus took varied forms. At one extreme there were those who at the time of the liberation cherished the utopian notion that the Communists were possible allies for Catholics in a movement to better working-class conditions. This tendency was linked with the attempt to go direct into the work of rechristianizing the factory-worker through the missionary activities of the so-called 'worker priests'—a movement which the Vatican cut short as incompatible with the worker-priests' spiritual functions. But much more immediately important, if it could be done, was the idea of replacing the small Catholic-democrat groups of the Third Republic with a new major party devoted to the Church, but definitely on the left in its social and economic programme. The artificiality of the circumstances in which the experiment was made has already been noted in connexion with the MRP's 'European' proclivities. But the revival of the clerical issue was the final and conclusive obstacle to its functioning along the lines originally intended for it. This issue was bound to bring into the foreground the fact that however progressive the sentiments of its active leaders, its electoral strength was in the strongly Catholic and conservative *départements* of eastern and western France, and that outside these it was suspect, as a party approved by the Church. If anti-clericalism was among the tests of being on the 'left', then the

MRP could not pass it, and in the election campaign of December 1955, the only alliances available to it were on the Right.

The geographical diversity of French politics and its roots in economic, social and religious factors have long preoccupied French students of politics, and their inquiries were actively pursued in the period of political introspection inaugurated by the liberation. Attention was drawn to the areas of unchanging allegiance under different labels to the same fundamental positions since the early years of the Third Republic, contrasted with others which had shown a marked instability. But the direct correlation of social and economic conditions with voting behaviour has its pitfalls and the coming of the Communists into the picture has increased the element of paradox. Their strength in the 'red belt' of the industrial suburbs of Paris does not need much explanation; but the same was hardly true of their even better showing in many rural *départements* of the South. Here the commentator could point alternatively to the tendency of peasant voters to vote on the extreme left for the historical reasons already alluded to, or to the fact that the tactical freedom of the Communists, and the narrowly self-regarding attitudes of some elements in the rural population, have enabled the Communists to profit by propaganda which in view of their basic beliefs is, to say the least of it, disingenuous.

More original was the attempt made by a leading student of this 'electoral geography' to draw a distinction on the basis of the 1951 figures between 'progressive France' and 'stagnant France'—that is to say between the behaviour of those *départements* where productivity was above the national average and those where it was below it. It was claimed that in the former the modern dynamic parties, the Communists and Gaullists, were strong while both the Radicals and the traditional Right—nowadays mainly passing as 'Independents' and 'Peasants'—were exceptionally weak. The latter's strength was found to lie in rural *départements* where economic advance was particularly slow. It was difficult to know on the basis of a single election how far these conclusions could be regarded as significant; or indeed how far a *département* which may include both urban and rural sections of very different types can be treated as a useful unit for an inquiry of this kind. Nor does the history of the Gaullists after the 1951 election give one much ground for classing them as representing any peculiarly dynamic element in French life. The disintegration of the Gaullists took place by degrees, and involved principally a move rightwards into positions almost indistinguishable from those of the traditional 'Right'. By the time of the 1955 dissolution, except for a relatively small number of former Gaullists who had hitched their fortunes to the star of Mendès-France, they were for the most part to be found not too unhappily linked with the other parties of Edgar Faure's 'right-centre' governmental coalition.

On the other hand, the Radical party which was considered, not unnaturally, to be synonymous with the most old-fashioned and least dynamic aspects of French society and government under the Third Republic had, during 1955, largely fallen under the sway of Mendès-France, who was trying to use it as the spearhead of a new left-wing grouping based on the idea of accelerating the economic and social transformation of France according to the most recent and approved dictates of economic and social science. It was therefore difficult to see how the figures of votes cast in January 1956, whatever they might turn out to be, could lend themselves to the verification of a thesis of this kind.

One thing was clear as the result of the two first assemblies of the Fourth Republic; political parties had not developed into the homogeneous and disciplined formations which some had hoped and some had feared would be the fruit of the adoption of proportional representation. Whether a more radical form of this, eliminating even the departmental division in favour of a nationalist system, could have obtained such a result is another question. The supposition must be that the whole tendency of the country's politics, fortified by the opportunities which the procedure of the legislative body gave to the private member as against the ministry, worked in the contrary direction. The Communists provided the exception by exercising their familiar procedures for the elimination of internal dissidence. But in this, as in so much, they stood outside the ordinary functioning of political life. The other parties could not act in this way; and to attempt to do so meant incurring the risk of a split. Given the strength of the local roots of political personalities, party excommunication was not the political death that it is in the Communist party, or in all parties under a more rigorous system, like the British.

But it is not only the peculiar features of French parliamentary life and in particular ministerial instability, that found an explanation in those terms. There was also something of at least equal importance to an understanding of the relations between government and society. Because the parties were weak, local strength was what mattered to the politician. Because administration was centralized, what interested the electors was to a large extent the nature of decisions made at the centre. Even when the *département* rather than the single-member constituency became the unit, the elector continued to regard his deputy very much as an ambassador to the government on behalf of local interests. The parallel to the deputy was not to be found among the whip-fodder of the British House of Commons, but rather in the American Senate; except for the fact that the deputy often had the prospect of ministerial office at the next turn of the wheel as a possible brake on a too overt self-identification with a single sectional interest.

If, in these circumstances, a certain cynicism had entered into the relations between Frenchmen and their governments it would not have been altogether surprising; what mandates for action could be claimed by governments based on shifting and partly fortuitous coalitions, dependent perhaps for majorities on the votes of the overseas deputies—83 (including Algerians) out of 627 deputies in the 1951 Assembly—whose primary concern was hardly likely to be a well-thought-out programme for the general good of metropolitan France? Curiously enough—and perhaps because Vichy had discredited the anti-parliamentarianism of the Right at least for a time—such cynicism did not appear to be reflected in the political behaviour of Frenchmen in the first decade of the Fourth Republic; the line taken by the humorous press and the music-halls is another matter. In the election for the Assembly in November 1946 (a year of two elections and two referenda) 78·5 per cent of the electorate went to the polls, and in 1951 81·2 per cent. (In the British General Election of that year 82·5 per cent of the electorate voted, and in 1955 only 76·8 per cent.) A proposal to institute compulsory voting in France was one of the casualties of the 1955 dissolution; but there was no indication that this was necessary in order to keep up a declining political interest.

Nevertheless many Frenchmen would argue that France was a victim of its political system during the first two Assemblies of the Fourth Republic, and that with a more stable governmental combination more could have been done in the way of finding solutions to the country's problems. It is natural that language of this kind should (apart from de Gaulle and his associates) come mainly from the Left. On the whole there has not been much the Right wanted to do or has had much prospect of doing; it has been driven most reluctantly along the path of remodelling France's relations with Indo-China, North Africa or the colonies; it has been opposed to further government encroachment in the economic field except by way of protectionism and subsidies. What the argument then comes to, is a view that France should have had a longer spell of rule by the Left—more or less equivalent to the period of Labour rule in post-war Britain—instead of the uneasy tripartism of the 1945-7 period.

But the failure to produce a government of this kind has principally been due not to the weaknesses of the parliamentary or electoral systems as such, but to the fundamental fact that the French Communist party has contracted out of French politics, and has by its conduct so widened the gulf between itself and the remainder of the Left that even in the post-Stalin period when it began to look once more for alliances it could not find them. Since the urban working-class is predominantly Communist this has meant that it has been, since 1947, subjected to a virtual disenfranchisement. A party incapable of entering into governmental combinations might from the parliamentary point of view just as well not exist. It is well of course to remember that this is treating the subject on the parliamentary plane only; and one must not exaggerate the figures. A recent study suggests that of the 19 per cent of the French electorate which public-opinion studies list as working-class, 47·8 per cent voted Communist in 1951, compared with 15·9 per cent who voted Gaullist and 14·8 per cent who voted Socialist. The Communist figure may be contrasted with its national percentage in that election, 26·4 per cent and with its showing of 39·9 per cent in the Creuse, the most rural of all French *départements*. (The most communist *département* was the rural Corrèze with 40·4 per cent.) Alternatively one could estimate the Communists' hold on the working-class by saying that of Communist voters, 38 per cent were probably working-class in 1951; of Socialist voters, 21 per cent.[1]

This does not necessarily mean that the French working-class has not improved its position as a result of the changes (other than

[1] See M. Duverger, ed., *Partis politiques et classes sociales en France.*

the nationalization of sectors of the economy) that have taken place in France since the liberation. Certainly classes traditionally more exposed to the blasts of currency devaluation and chronic inflation—public servants for instance—must have done worse. Strikes of state employees have been a feature of the social history of the period. In some sectors of social policy, notably family allowances, it may have done well compared with the position in other western countries; but it has been argued that, given the structure of French taxation, this largely amounts to a redistribution of income within the working-class itself. And in some other fields—the provision of low-cost housing—the French record is not impressive. What it does mean is that the working-class can quite easily add to its feeling of alienation from the French State—which is no product of the Fourth Republic—a sense that its interests still weigh less with the state than those of other classes.

It may be going too far to suggest, as has been done, that modern industry itself is still an anomaly on the French scene, a sort of interior emigration as it has been described, relying partly on aliens for its manpower, and governed by technocrats whose outlook is untypical of the French.[1] But labour is certainly and for the reasons given, unhappily placed politically. Nor does trade-unionism provide an answer. The post-liberation period found the Communists solidly entrenched in a trade-union movement unified (apart from the Catholic Unions) in the Popular Front period, and purged of some of its Socialist leaders because of their links with Vichy. The political rift between the Communists and their partners in the post-liberation governments had its reflection in the trade-union world. But the *Force Ouvrière* grouping of non-Communist trade-unionists set up in 1947 never attained the strength of the main movement. About three-quarters of the organized workers have remained in the Communist-controlled unions and the remainder are divided between the *Force Ouvrière* (more or less Socialist in sympathy), the Catholic Unions, and even smaller groupings. If the Communists had been able to use this strength for political purposes it is doubtful if the French State could have survived at all. As we have seen, they have not been able to do so. Nevertheless, even if often hidden from view by the antics of politicians who were eligible for office, the

[1] See Lüthy, op. cit., pp. 46–8.

Communists and the problem they represent remained in 1955 still at the very heart of the French political problem.

Much more difficult for a contemporary to assess than the different elements in the parliamentary and electoral scene, in the case of any country, is the rôle of the administration; and in a country with transient cabinets (even if the actual departmental ministers often show a much greater aptitude for survival) the rôle of the administrator must be of very special importance. Some students of the French scene believe that despite the post-Vichy purge, the reputed democratization of the methods of civil-service recruitment and the new methods adopted for its training, the French administration has not seriously been affected by the events of the past fifteen years. Indeed as one reads some accounts of its powerful and orderly functioning through all the changes of government, one hears echoes of Bodley's celebrated passages about the France of the end of the nineteenth century being still held together by the solid framework of its essentially Napoleonic institutions.

It has been argued that so strong are the powers inherent in the administrators, that in some spheres they have simply failed to apply legislation of which they have disapproved.[1] Other observers have taken the view that even a self-recruiting *élite* cannot for ever remain unaffected by the general intellectual currents of the time, and believe that there has been in process a notable move away from the traditional *laissez-faire* attitude on economic matters so evident in France's long reliance on deflationary methods to treat the great depression of the 1930's, towards a more modern 'Keynesian' outlook. Certainly there has been no apparent lack of vigour in pushing forward the industrial plan. It could indeed be said that what has depended largely on technical or administrative skill at the centre has been done well; particularly if the field is one from which private vested interests are by its nature excluded—railways and electrification for instance; the failures have been in matters like reforming the fiscal system, the tariff system or the colonial régime, where pressure-groups could get busy. Mendès-France was pursued by the implacable vendetta of the 'good Europeans'; he was overthrown by the producers of alcohol and the North African settlers' lobby.

The word usually used in France for such a placing of private

[1] See ibid., p. 37.

before public interests is *incivisme*; and the student of French history is bound to ask why it should flourish so dangerously in a country which was for so long an exemplar of patriotism and national feeling. Even such a disquieting symptom as the attempt by some members of the armed forces in 1955 to resist being sent to deal with terrorism in North Africa, does not necessarily suggest that national loyalty in the classic sense has ceased to function in French society; it is rather that the State's more everyday demand on the individual and the group meet with resistance. During the early years of the Fourth Republic it was widely held that this indifference to the State was a prolongation of the feelings of an occupied country, where the State was identical with the invader, and any deceit towards it laudable. But this would seem an inadequate explanation of the survival of this state of mind.

One line of inquiry does suggest itself. Is there not something to be said for the view that the whole of modern French history has conduced to an exaltation of the Nation embodied in the State at the expense of society? Certainly the Republic completed the work of the *ancien régime* in destroying intermediary bodies, and has not shown creativeness in replacing them except where the direct service of interest groups is concerned. The doctrine of the Republic has been hostile to any mediation between the State and the individual, even where society has been recalcitrant to its control.

It is argued in some quarters that one can exaggerate the extent of French administrative centralization; and it is true that such centralization is characteristic of all modern states whatever their constitutional structure. Indeed a recent work on French local government argues that local government is more active and important in France than in England and that administrative centralization has gone farther in the latter. The peculiarities of French local government, and in particular the concentration of powers in the Prefects and the Mayors, is seen as due to the close and necessary connexion in France between administration and politics. But the force of this argument is somewhat weakened by the admission that because of the ultimate responsibility of the ministries, and because of the weaknesses of local government finance, local councils tend towards irresponsibility where their own proposals are concerned. The importance of the departmental Councils seems to be connected primarily with their influence in national politics.[1] Whatever may be the upshot of a comparative study of France and other countries, the historian can only observe that one thing the Fourth Republic has not done is to make any basic change in the administrative structure. And what new elements have been introduced into the system—the IGAME or Super-Prefects for instance—have been designed to strengthen not to weaken central control.

There still seems to be a case for saying that the lack of intermediate elements of cohesion in society—whatever form they may take, and strong local institutions are only one possibility among many—will tend to make the State either too strong or too weak. The French clearly prefer the latter—tempering a nominal impersonal centralization by the impact of countless selfish and partisan pressures. In a period when the alternative has often been one form of totalitarianism or another, the choice has been neither unintelligent nor dishonourable. Nor so far has it been fatal.

As one looks at the first decade in the history of the Fourth Republic in the light of the general theme of government and society in France, it is clear that it is not a period in which much that is either novel or exciting can be claimed for government. Is this equally true of society? May not even a modern society have many mirrors other than the political or the administrative which may present a truer likeness of it? We have touched upon some aspects of post-war France in which the *élan* of the recovery from the depths of war and occupation continued unchecked even after more normal conditions of life had been restored. One index which is generally held relevant to the health of any society has shown a quite startling improvement. France, in the later years of the Third Republic, presented a classic case of a population in decay making up for the losses of wars and the declining birth rate only by extensive immigration. According to the prognostics based on the statistics of that period, by 1965 France would have had an active population of only $17\frac{1}{2}$ millions with 9 million old people to support. Since the liberation there has been a net addition of 300,000 a year to the population. It is true that the immediate problem is still grave; there will not only be great numbers of old people to support in 1965; there will also be far more children than was expected.[2] But in the long run the upturn should react

[1] See Brian Chapman, *Introduction to French Local Government* (1953).
[2] See Lüthy, op. cit., p. 225.

favourably on every aspect of the nation's life. It could be argued by the cynical that this change is not due to any recovery of confidence in the future of France, but to the simpler fact that so much of France's allocation of social benefits has taken the form of family allowances. Even if this were partly true, the results would be no less important.

Nor is it clear that this demographic upsurge stands by itself. If one considers the tremendous toll taken of France by the two wars, the shock to the nation's pride of the defeat and occupation, and the blow to her unity of the 'collaboration', and the often ugly way in which it was avenged, the creativeness of the country in many fields in the relatively short space of ten years is not without its remarkable side. In science and in scholarship, in literature and the arts, France remains among the unquestioned leaders of the world. And if the French language, which has been both the creation *par excellence* of the French nation, and one of the main instruments by which that nation has been created, is in retreat on the international front before the greater physical power represented by Russian or 'basic Anglo-Saxon', or the greater purchasing power represented by Spanish, its inward vitality seems unimpaired. Not since the Middle Ages has French government mattered less; some would answer that not since the Middle Ages has the essence of France mattered more.

BIBLIOGRAPHICAL NOTE

Works in English

English interest in the affairs of France has never been keener than in recent years and a number of important and illuminating works at different levels have been produced. Of general studies the outstanding one is P. M. Williams, *Crisis and Compromise: Politics in the Fourth Republic,* (1964). The valuable appendices include a translation of the Constitution of 1946. An ambitious attempt to elucidate the politics of the period through the American behavioural approach is Duncan MacRae, Jnr., *Parliament, Parties and Society in France, 1946–1958* (1967). Very useful are three books by Dorothy Pickles, *France between the Republics* (1946), *French Politics* (1953) and *France, the Fourth Republic* (1955). On more specialized topics there are two works by Brian Chapman, *Introduction to French Local Government* (1953) and *The Prefects and Provincial France* (1955), and F. de Tarr, *The French Radical Party from Herriot to Mendès-France* (1961); covering a wider field is P. Campbell, *French Electoral Systems* (1958). D. W. S. Lidderdale, *The Parliament of France,* 1951, is a unique treatment of the subject of French parliamentary procedure and has had the deserved honour of being translated into French.

Various journalists have given a narrative account of the early years of the Fourth Republic; the most illuminating is perhaps that by Ronald Matthews, *The Death of the Fourth Republic* (1954). A detailed account of both the Vichy period and of the first decade of the Fourth Republic from a strongly Left-wing viewpoint is A. Werth, *France, 1940–1955* (1956). Three other American works deserve mention: the collection of essays entitled *Modern France* edited by E. M. Earle (Princeton, 1951), the work (also published in England) by Gordon Wright, *The Reshaping of French Democracy* (1950)—the best account of how the Fourth Republic got its constitution; and Val. R. Lorwin, *The French Labor Movement* (Harvard U.P. 1954).

The work by the Swiss journalist Herbert Lüthy referred to in the notes in its French edition originally appeared in German, and has also been published in England as *The State of France* (1955). Although written from a very particular point of view, and often highly irritating, this is perhaps the most stimulating attempt at an interpretation of the entire French scene during the decade under consideration.

Works in French

The output of material on contemporary French affairs whether in newspapers, journals or book form is incessant, and to select the permanent contributions to understanding out of the mass of contentious writing would be a task in itself. The academic study of French politics in France is a relatively recent development. Its achievements can best be followed in the *'Cahiers'* of the *Fondation Nationale des Sciences Politiques*, a large proportion of which deal with French subjects. The writings of François Goguel and Charles Morazé on electoral geography and sociology, notably the latter's *Les Français et la République* (1956), and of Maurice Duverger on political parties, are particularly valuable. Available in English is his *The French Political System* (1958). The leading non-academic student of the French political scene is Jacques Fauvet of the newspaper *Le Monde*. His book *Les Forces politiques en France* (1951) gives a valuable picture of the political scene at a point half-way through the period covered in this lecture. A continuation is *La France Déchirée* (1957), translated as *The Cockpit of France France* (1960). Vol. III of E. Dolléans, *Histoire du movement ouvrier* (1953), while it is a general work, is useful for the background of the labour movement in France. Among writings by French 'intellectuals', the works of Raymond Aron shed a highly individual light upon the perplexities of the modern world as seen by a strong anti-Communist; those of Jean-Paul Sartre and Albert Camus reveal the ways in which a fundamentally 'left' attitude at the time of the Liberation could lead either towards or away from Communism.

Outstanding for the insights of a veteran observer of the French scene are the two books by André Siegfried, *De la IIIe à la IVe République* (1956) and *De la IVe à Ve Republique* (1958). See also *Les Elections françaises de 1956* (1957) and *The French Election of 1956* reprinted for Nuffield College from *Political Studies,* vol. iv.